101 WAYS TO MAKE MONEY IN HAITI

Lucrative Business Ideas, Insightful Success Stories, and Interesting Business Opportunities for Visionary Entrepreneurs

By

Christherson Jeanty (SeeJeanty)

Dedication

This book is dedicated to Haiti's incredibly resilient people. I'm proud to be part of a generational change which will bring forth Haiti's potential. Haiti is overdue for an era of economic prosperity. And so, this book's readers will take action, gaining knowledge from what was written. He or she will hold a portion of that credit when that time arrives.

Table of Contents

3

A Note to the Reader

Haiti occupies one-third (about 27,560 km) of the western part of the island of Ayiti, located between Puerto Rico and Cuba. Though most people know this island as Hispaniola or "little Spain," Ayiti is its indigenous name. It once was occupied by the original Taino Native American residents. Meanwhile, the Dominican Republic occupies the other portion of Ayiti. Hispaniola is the second-largest Caribbean island and the most mountainous. Around seventy-five percent of the island is rough mountainous terrain. Many mountains, in fact, exceed 5,000 feet. The highest mountain in Haiti, Pic La Selle, stands over 8,500 feet. Though mostly inaccessible due to rough terrain, the road network is poor. This often leads to burdensome travel since large stretches of the coast are inaccessible by road.

But this book is not here to discuss what Haiti lacks or does not have or shall it regurgitate its economic ranking in the western hemisphere that so many feel obligated to recite when referencing Haiti in any way. Instead, this book focuses on what can raise that low economic ranking and bring sustainable multi-generational change for the nation and its people: Entrepreneurship. While we respect charity for its capacity to reprieve immediate pain during times of crisis and be a solution for the few blind spots of misaligned iterations of capitalism, the only thing that has ever in history improved the lives of nation-states and their citizens is economic progress through commerce.

So this book explores what is possible in Haiti and provides our readers with suggestions of possible courses of action.

This book is an exhaustive aggregation, offering many suggestions for courses of **action**. We emphasize the word action. After all, the idea implies entrepreneurship. How many incredible life-changing ventures never see the light of day due to inaction? Too Many.

This book was written to ensure that, in the future, there'll be few to none. But the real reason is deeply personal. As a Haitian national born in Haiti, I was forced to relocate to the United States. I've lived here throughout my adolescence and adult life since I was denied a direct upbringing in my country. While I appreciated the opportunities of my adopted nation, many of which I took advantage, I will never forget from where I came. One opportunity involved achieving undergraduate and graduate degrees in economics at one of the nation's top public universities. It led a lucrative career. I had opportunities to work within banking, data analytics, and data science. Along the way, there were many trips to Haiti. And I felt the conditions that are ascribed to by other Haitian nationals. I felt obligated to figure out how to contribute to a world where Haiti is livable for all Haitians. At the center of this contribution became my focus on job creation. I further focused on activities that would increase work opportunities for those without formal work.

With this perspective in mind, I moved back to Haiti many years ago. I started several ventures. These included a staffing company an outsourcing company, a real estate development firm, an export-based distribution company, and an investment group. Additionally, I started a media company called SeeJeanty Media. I began this company not only to share my experiences living and being a Haitian entrepreneur, but also to visually show others who've done the same throughout different industries. Meanwhile, I was showing the county's beauty and sites. The latter's inspiring. The reality is entrepreneurship isn't for everyone. On some stressful days, I wonder if it's even for me. Still, the appreciation of one's country and visiting as a tourist can be as impactful as starting a business. Likewise, the expenditure of foreign currency is a direct means to job creation. Essentially, it supports other entrepreneurship activity.

Haiti's politicians have failed Haiti. But I believe that we can't wait for a better government to arise through re-immaculate conception before we decide to act. Therefore, Haiti's progress is our responsibility collectively. This book's not a get-rich-quick scheme. It presents studied and amazing stories of Haitian entrepreneurs who've already engaged in action; entrepreneurs who've built businesses. Overall, they employ hundreds and dozens of employees. These businesses are focused on individualistic fortune, which is the ultimate reward for their hard work and perseverance. Since they did not wait for the right conditions, neither should you.

It's not hyperbolic when you hear Haiti is a virgin country for business. In many of the ideas expressed in this book, you'll be the one of the first. Sometimes, if you move forward, you'll be the first to execute the idea or open an industry's segment. Not only will you enjoy a first-mover advantage, but also a lower level of competition throughout given the uncommon nature of pulling the trigger and doing business in Haiti. This isn't a haphazard list of business ideas. This book is the culmination of years living in Haiti. I've personally researched possible ventures and spoken with hundreds of entrepreneurs. The expressed opportunities aren't written lightly. Thus, we avoid "hustles" and "quick-hit" buy and resale ventures. Instead, the focus is on genuine and exploitable multi-million-dollar ideas. If these are correctly executed, and pursued with the utmost resilience, then they'll be successful. And if these opportunities are pursued by multiple successful people, it drives real national economic progress.

A non-academic reader could easily read this book. There may be a tendency to fall into habits associated with more formal discussions related to economic issues. These dive deep into the facts, figures, and statistics of such topics; however, any such figures will be only cursory and add general comparative context to an issue. As previously stated, the goal is to drive understanding and action. Those desiring a deeper prior understanding of underlying issues concerning ways of making money may later refer to the references section, located later in the book. Or visit the website: SeeJeanty.Ht. Many resources are available online that supplement the book's material, particularly in the section where the research is cited.

Each section will present an idea in a structured, predictable format. That process is discussed below:

Industry context

We begin with an overview of the industry. Each business idea will be categorized and separated. We briefly discuss the industry, discussing why the industry shouldn't be overlooked. Where statistics and larger metrics are appropriate, we list out those figures as well. We set the tableau in which we paint the possibilities.

Market Context

We've summarized what's possible for each business idea, exploring the potential market for it. We likewise explore the rationality as to why we believe there's potential in this space. Relevant dynamics are also considered, along relevant market factors to this opportunity outlook.

Business Concept

We aim to move into the realm of tangible and practicality regarding ideas. Possible concrete executions are given, in which one can try to exploit. Take a mango, for example. It can be cultivated and packaged for export wholesale or processed into juice. While it can be sold directly to consumers, it instead can be manufactured as part of another processed item. Examples include ice cream or candy. There're multiple potential concepts, even though the product was unchanged.

Niche Ideas:

Finding spaces or iterations of an uncommon concept leads to the least competition and space. Thus, one gains traction while taking advantage of the consumer or market demand already existing within that larger domain. Give yourself that advantage. Become the largest player in that version of the game. We focus on listing these iterative ideas for you. So, consider exploring them further.

Top Department & Policy Guidance

Haiti is divided into ten departments (analogous somewhat to states in America, albeit significantly less governing autonomy within the constitution). This section explores where any business/market concept is best realized within the main metro departments. This includes the Ouest Department, or more provincial departments like Artibonite and Grand'Anse.

Action & Tips

Here we provide real tangible steps and considerations. All these allow you to execute this idea with minimal resources or setup as soon as possible. Additionally, included elements will significantly improve one's venture's chances of success.

Success Stories

Wherever possible, we include ideas accompanied by referenceable actors. The entities in that space provide an iterative example of that market concept, along with what they've been able to accomplish. The idea involves providing real-world proof of concepts. Moreover, we must validate the truth behind the lucrative and social impact.

The Truth Behind It All

An extraordinary unicorn idea isn't required in Haiti. But also, there isn't much to gain by following 'entrepreneurial' ventures that overpopulate Haiti's economic space. What we need is a generation of Haitian entrepreneurs. These entrepreneurs provide a range of products, which make exceptional and day-to-day practice easier. While Haiti today is still experiencing stagnation in its socio-economic condition, its large population is mostly an undeveloped landmass. Its central geographic location within the Western Hemisphere means that, when it does start to grow, it's the economic elements to grow exponentially.

It's possible to become successful in Haiti with limited resources. Our countless success stories are evidence of that assertion. Even when the world sees it in turmoil, those familiar with Haiti understand its progress. It's by this understanding that they know commerce is always possible. And so, demand springs back at the first sign of calm. The nation lacks a community of business visionaries that act in the country's sustainable long term. The purpose of doing business in Haiti should simply supersede any desire of making money. In fact, it should be connected to your customers' and employees' humanity.

Haiti's lifestyle is one that's substantially less strained for those whose ventures have awarded them a stable source of income. Most can afford home help, drivers, and assistance. This affords leaders the time to stay focused on winning business. Personal family time is spent living in lodgings much grander than what they would have resided in beforehand.

Yes - corruption, infrastructure, personal security, national disaster, and political instability are factors that can't be ignored. Throughout this book, we tackle these issues head-on. We discuss these issues in our final section, "Concerning...". We provide strategies to insulate one from these factors as one reasonably can. The point is that none of these things are factors. Rather, they've held back those of non-Haitian descent from coming to Haiti and successfully embedding themselves within the fabric of Haiti's commercial sector. But this shouldn't hold you back.

Yes, doing business in specific parts of Haiti isn't recommended. Sadly, dense areas in downtown Port-Au-Prince, such as Martissant, Cite Soleil, Village de Dieu, and La Saline, have largely been abandoned by the government. Within that void, elements that contribute to deep insecurity have become permanently established. But don't forget that Haiti is much more than these pockets. Most of the country is quiet, stable, and accommodating to people looking to bring jobs and economic opportunities.

No matter where you do your business, entrepreneurship is fraught with risks. This is factual whether one is in Haiti or outside of Haiti. One can fail in Manhattan as spectacular of a fashion as one can fail in Petionville. But the reality is, that because of the volatility and risk, there's a consistent guaranteed opportunity. This is what it means to be in a developing and emerging market. Take the road less traveled.

See where Haiti will take you. In a life that's lived for only a handful of decades as an adult, don't live crippled in fear. Instead, bc steered by what's possible.

Haiti's ready for you. This book was written to inspire you. It's designed to help you envision and act on the opportunities that are before you. Don't merely scroll. Pick and choose sections to read based on perceived relevance. Fastidiously read the entire book. Each industry and market speak to a particularly dynamic and aspect of Haiti's reality. These will be crucial in your understanding and implementation of your business.

Once you get to the final page, you'll be in a position where those who've tried to do business in Haiti have been. You have the culmination knowledge of countless who've gone to Haiti and found their tranche of success. You'll not follow the path of those who came to Haiti with hope, only to fail when reality intersected with their idealism and nativity. They blame Haiti's environment, when it is their strategy that is the culprit.

This book will leave you with a grander perspective and distinct clarity for better decisions. Your moves will be faster and more confident. Milestones will surpass quicker than you'd believed achievable. Allow this to fuel you until you have the life you deserve in the country of your origins.

An Nou Kòmanse

Don't allow anyone to deter you from your ambition, not your parents, not your friends, and not the media. Take the leap and start with what you have. But do it with strategy and research at the core. When it comes to doing business in Haiti, you first must figure out how to have the business begin paying you right away. Amazon, Facebook, and Tesla were able to run deficits for as long as a decade until they became profitable. You'll not have that sort of luxury in Haiti. Your business must begin to make a return for you and your investors as early as it takes off.

More than anything, what you'll need to drive your business forward throughout the good times and periods of uncertainty. This commitment must be met, along with a schedule that doesn't have an end date. Major success in Haitian businesses can't occur from a distance. Thinking it will happen within a specific frame of time will not make it occurs. Patience and perseverance are the fundamental foundation of all those who've achieved recognized market victory.

Taking advantage of this book and the 101 business ideas doesn't require someone to be endowed with resources, intelligence, or luck. Come as you are. You already have the unique culture, perspectives, personality, and life experiences that make up who you are. So, modify each opportunity accordingly. Only, don't negotiate with consistency or commitment. Offer value to your customers and offer fantastic service. You'll rise appropriately.

An nou kòmanse! Let's begin!

Entertainment

"I would rather entertain and hope that people learned something than educate people and hope they were entertained."

— Walt Disney

Entertainment remains one of the world's most important industries, and this is equally true in Haiti. The quality of entertainment depends mostly on disposable income. The explosion of technology, mobile devices, and ad-based models, however, impacts the free content when revenue generates from ads. Haitian consumers now have a broader selection. Established entertainment entities and venues tend to evolve resilient models, thereby insulating themselves from competitive pressures. Reasons for this include customer habits, brand loyalty/prestige, and steady revenue which occurs through the unstable of times. Low ease of entry produces higher upfront costs associated with establishing a business.

Section one discusses the primary promise areas within Haiti's entertainment sector.

1. Aid in Controlling the Narrative by Becoming an Influencer in Haiti's Film Industry

Haiti has a long tradition of independent artists, both in film and music. All have contributed to an independent local ecosystem of performance venues. In fact, Haiti has flirted with the film industry off and on throughout its history. Their experience with film started in the 70s. It was within a portion of Caribbean countries already producing film in addition to Guadalupe and Jamaica.

As competition amongst internationally filming heated up, Haiti's industry got lost in the noise. It became mixed in with other Caribbean nation film industry entries. Still, certain events continue to put the spotlight on local productions. The Jacmel Film Festival and CineAyiti International Film Festival have successfully developed positivity in fostering a community of film talent, bringing attention to meaningful work. In its most recent year, The Jacmel Film Festival recorded 50,000 people in attendance.

Across the world, the film industry produces over $100B annually. Over 700,000 jobs are produced as a result, which in turn adds economic activity and real jobs. It's a similar capacity in Haiti. Still, it needs the help of enterprising artistic visionaries to bring the art to maturity and commercial success.

Business Concept

The value chain of the film includes production houses, cinematographers, movie editors, animation specialists, costume designers, makeup artists, sound producers, choreographers, and food catering crews. The film and movie distribution business provides another entryway into this industry. Through local cinema and consumer media (such as streaming apps and website streaming services), the entrepreneur will be handsomely rewarded for discovering this digital distribution. What must be watched out for is the penetration of internet access. As more Haitians gain affordable access to quality internet speeds, the potential market and its success grow much larger.

Businesses resulting from creative industry is boundless. It simply takes providing quality and persistence. Then, you only must work and grow that market.

Department Target and Policy Guidance

As previously mentioned, both Jacmel and Cap Haitian have had a larger part of film history in Haiti. Both are set to return as principal seats for a revitalization. Jacmel's Cine Institute is still functioning and educating youth to this day. Moreover, it continues to partner with graduates in films and documentaries. A key in a winning Haitian strategy is leveraging Haiti's landscape and geography. Additionally, shooting in many places around the country neither requires fees nor other administrative hurdles typical elsewhere.

Action & Tips

Given mobile phone technology's advancement, the only barrier of entry into the film industry is owning a mobile phone. Social media platforms are an incredibly productive method of getting your work out there. You can also earn revenue through a percentage of ad payouts.

Sponsorships are critical but difficult to obtain. When starting out, these will be a big part of what finances your production. Partner with online streaming platforms that emphasize Caribbean productions. Then, acquire distribution deals.

Tell stories that haven't yet seen screen time. Be consistent in the process.

Success Story

Rev'Cine - Rolf Louis

In 2015, Rolf Louis launched Rev'Cine after noting there weren't any movie theaters available. In fact, these had been non-existent at least ten years. That was the last time any movie theater had been in the country. Rev'Cine's original complex, located at Lambert Street in Petionville, has comfortable seats. It's a single air-conditioned screen with surround sound. What's more is that it has fully functioning popcorn machines. But unlike many American movie theaters, beer was readily purchasable for consumption during the movie.

In 2019, they moved to a new facility - Rue Faubert at Tropical Complex. It's adjacent to Kinam Hotel in Petition-Ville, which increased their seating capacity to over sixty-eight seats. French and English movies are both played at the theater, so patrons can watch movies in whichever language they prefer. The incorporation of social media has been a big portion of their success. Movie showtimes and schedules, for example, can readily be found on their Facebook page a week in advance.

The movie theatre currently employs a dozen Haitians. Likewise, it's a beacon to the community on what filling the marketing void in the film can produce.

2. Become a Player in Haiti's Culturally Significant Music Industry

As Jamaica comes to mind, we think of Reggae. The Dominican Republic makes us consider Bachata. Cuba harkens Mambo. Puerto Rico instantly suggests reggaeton. Saint Kitts and Nevis make us think of Calypso. The lists continues. Caribbean nations are often identified by their music genres, and Haiti is no different. Haiti's "Konpa Direk," or "Konpa" for short, has been inspiring artists since its birth in the 1950s. Haitian Saxophonist Nemours Jean-Baptiste inspires Haitians with his cocktail of merengue. Cuban mambo, Danzon, and down/regressed tempo have all emphasized percussion drums and sonic horns. The music has since evolved into its own genre. What's more is that it's evolved into a category of music which is closely associated with Haiti and its musical capacity.

Business Concept

This evolution's economic result has brought with its successful artists, many of whom have made a career within the genre. Alongside those artists are countless jobs. These jobs are meant to support, promote, and compliment those artists. It includes composers, producers, songwriters, audio engineers, choreographers, promoters, tour coordinators, stage managers, publicists, concert organizers, bodyguards, and DJs. The creation of secondary professions helps develop talent. Likewise, it builds and sustains the physical instrument. This further includes music instructors, music store chains, performance schools, and instrument repairers.

Haiti's industrial challenges are real. Their legal system remains prioritized for other social and economic activities. Still, it's neither yet provided the necessary environment, nor legal framework necessary for artists to efficiently settle contract disputes or issues (such as copyright).

As such, the industry's revenue is structured around concerts. This offers significant success to "Bals" and "Pwograms," a big part of how Haitians seek enjoyment during a weekend. Sponsorships are another important driver of music industry revenue. Major contributors include liqueur fabricators, traditional media outlets, and retail operators.

Department Target and Policy Guidance

Port-Au-Prince holds an unparalleled hegemony in the Haitian music industry. As the most populous city-region, its mature and established media markets, have high-quantity performance venues. It's developed a reputation for the country's most vibrant nightlife, making it the more initiative choice for any foray into the industry. Haiti's city of Cap-Haitian is a popular second venue for comparable reasons to Port-Au-Prince, but less economic to scale. Denial of the Haitian citizens derives from traveling to larger metropolitan areas. But this is necessary to participate in these larger events. Opportunities elsewhere are uncommon, but not exactly rare.

Actions & Tips

- Leveraging digital media means to differentiate opportunities, thereby bringing upon influence on Haiti's new global music economy. It's invaluable when the domestic environment provides limited revenue-generating opportunities, which are positioned outside the concert scene. This includes utilizing stream services. Amazon, Apple, Spotify, SoundCloud, and YouTube Music all expose individuals to music, driving per-stream payment where applicable.

- Mix niche alongside specific Haitian folk and traditional music (such as rara and raboday). Additionally, combine more international fusion sounds.

Success Story

Baoli Records - Carl-Frédéric Berhmann

J Perry signed to Carl-Frédéric Berhmann's Baoli Record in 2005 which made waves in Haiti. Baoli record's beginnings were humble and grew from the realization that no Haitian music labels were suitable to be *his* music label. His label took care of things such as media and contract management. They would leverage the organization's capacity to scale, which would increase exposure, revenue-generating opportunities, and contractual bargaining power. A good music label is a driver of an artist's success and Baoli records would provide that assistance. Most importantly, their revenue is based on commission, which is earned from deals they bring to the artist. For example, they facilitate deals with major domestic and international sponsors. Then, they distribute their records to international markets. Furthermore, they produce the album. This includes securing license deals across any market, including those markets where licensing laws exist and are enforced. For example, they secured a deal with Zumba Fitness that uses J. Perry's songs in their workouts. This deal pays royalties to J. Perry each time his songs are played.

The key difference in their business model, as opposed to how other music entities have predominantly operated in the country, is that others simply purchase the master copy from the artist for a single lump sum amount. Once this is completed, there's neither additional support nor additional dealings. The music entity or person now owns the entire royalties which come from that artist's work in perpetuity. While it's a great deal for the purchasing entity or person, in essence, it's terrible for the artist in the long run.

Diskòb Music App

Having comprised a team of Haitian coders and music enthusiasts, Diskòb is aimed at being Haiti's primary streaming source for Haitian music. Haitian artists within the country are provided an environment unlike any other space. Starting with 800 songs in their title, Diskòb expects to branch out to 25,000 in a few years. Their goal is to assist artists no matter their specific location throughout Haiti. This method, over time, will expose their artistic capacity to the country and the world. The project has already won a media innovation award by Hackathon Haiti. And they're well on their way to revolutionizing Haitian music.

Their business model is like other streaming platforms. Ultimately, they expect ads to support free access to the platform. Users can elect to subscribe for a monthly fee for an ad-free service, in addition to other small improvements. Most importantly, they intend to comply with Haitian copyright requirements. Artists receive an appropriate royalty for each stream occurring on the platform, just as other international platforms provide to their domestic artists.

Their app is available on Android and iOS.

3. Travel & Tour Business Has Tremendous Upside Yet to Be Realized Upside.

Travel and tourism remain one of the world's most impactful economic sectors. In 2018, the sector accounted for 10.4% of the global GDP. One out of ten jobs totaled 319M jobs. This strong growth continued for decades to come. According to the World Trade Tourism Council (WTTC), the potential in Haiti is strong. Nearly 7.9% of the total Haitian economy is estimated at $784 million. Likewise, direct, and indirect jobs increased by 309,000 within the same year. Haiti's reputation as a travel destination greatly lacks other countries in the Caribbean, but these figures alone indicate a tremendous growth opportunity.

What's more is that Haiti's unique geography makes it stand out. After Cuba, Haiti is blessed with the second largest coastline in the entire Caribbean. Haiti has more coastline than both the next two titleholders, which are more reputationally known for its beaches. These are the Dominican Republic and Jamaica, respectively. Moreover, Haiti has three of the Caribbean's highest mountain ranges. In fact, it's the third-highest mountain point in the Caribbean, Pic La Selle, which resides at 8,793 ft. Haiti also contains the second largest lake, Lake Azuei (Etang Saumatre).

Nevertheless, that doesn't mention Haiti's annual historical and cultural events. The Independence Day festivities and carnival happen at the beginning of the year. The International Jazz Festival and Day of the Dead, meanwhile, occur later in the year. There's always something going on that draws tourists to the country. The country has over nineteen national holidays. So, this ensures that locally driven days of celebration will drive domestic tourism.

Business Concept

Despite all this potential, Haiti has only scratched the surface of tourism. Numerous opportunities are available to those who can organize affordable and hassle-free solutions to the market's tour and travel needs. This includes recommending excursions, local logistic management, educational tour guides, accommodation, and exceptional travel experiences. These are all things for which tourists will appreciatively compensate Haiti.

The key to being successful in tourism and travel is to fill a void in the market. Identify and capitalize on a current trend. Alternatively, be a part of the founding and evolution of a new rage. You are more likely to be successful if your service can differentiate itself in quality, offering, and use.

Niche Ideas:

- Investment and trade mission tours.
- Affordable student trips.
- Accommodating travelers with pets.
- Spiritual trips.
- Culinary trips.
- Honeymoon tours.

- Dare-devil and extreme adventure packages (skydiving, hiking, total off the grid, etc.).
- Hunting trips.
- Fishing trips.

Department Target and Policy Guidance

There's a good rule to follow when it comes to Haiti tourism: you'll experience a better-quality trip if you go further away from Port-Au-Prince. Haiti's nature, the people, and the food are remarkable. But arguably, the security is better in Haiti's provinces compared to Port-Au-Prince's metro areas. For this reason, I strongly consider incorporating an itinerary that features some locations in other departments outside of the capital city department of the Ouest.

Action & Tips

- Carefully consider the international market that you'll be targeting when you visit the country. It's better to target a market with which you have some familiarity, rather than branching out to others. For example, an American would have greater success attracting other Americans. Likewise, a Spanish traveler would have better experience attracting other Spanish speaking travelers.
- Consider possibility that a political situation may affect your itinerary and business. Though such events are hard to predict, it's important to consider these events. Therefore, you can formulate pre-emptive reactions and strategize solutions.

Success Stories

There're so many incredible entrepreneurs in this space. It was difficult to narrow down one or two success stories. So, below are brief presentations of Haiti's most renowned entrepreneurs. All work within the travel and tourism space.

Haitian Nomad - Richard Cantave

Established in 2016, Haitian Nomad has engaged in the travel guide business. Richard understands that presenting Haiti is a part of his patriotic duty. Thus, he makes it a point to provide experiences that show an authentic Haiti. Meanwhile, he keeps his tours fun and safe. Their business model involves group trips to Haiti and custom Itineraries. It further includes private trips. Haitian services include airport shuttling, photography, and concierge. He has further been able to branch out and hold trips across the world, including in many countries within Africa and Asia.

Discovery Haiti - David Cardozo

After purchasing a boat, David launched a tourism business. To this day, it continues to be the country's standard-bearer excursion experience. Guests are treated to secluded island getaways for an affordable single price or group price. The price includes picturesque picnics, with food and drinks included. They've since expanded to include scuba diving, fishing, jet skiing, and many other water-related tours. All these tours will take you across Haiti's coastlines and islands.

A big tactical advantage of Discovery Haiti has been its innovative use of social media. Not only do they share the guest experience, but it helps to promote the country. It also attracts new travelers who may not have originally considered Haiti as a travel destination. Ease of payment and exceptional customer service ensures that first-time guests become repeat customers.

4. Plug into Passion for Soccer

A common Haitian sight is a mass of men huddled around a single television screen on the side of the road. They stand shoulder-to-shoulder, some tippy-toeing while others are crouching while focused on a soccer match airing over television. When they aren't amassed by watching soccer, Haitians are on a street soccer pitch. Using makeshift goalposts, they play a passionate and lively game against each other. The enjoyment of soccer in Haiti is overwhelming.

The recent success of the Haitian National football team saw a wave of patriotic energy rarely associated with the country. It's obvious that soccer holds an untapped potential to inspire and connect Haitians unlike any other; however, the industry remains nascent. One could easily point at the amateurish development of Haiti's native leagues, noting its basic development of Sylvio Cator Stadium (Haiti's flagship stadium). But there's more low hanging fruit for those interested in being a part of Haiti's commercial soccer industry.

Business Concepts

Soccer Gear and Memorabilia

Fans love to dress the part. Items such as jerseys, hats, banners, accessories, and bags are sold at the stadium and elsewhere. Sports fashion can be a serious revenue maker, with margins making it worth it. By taking a step further, one might discover that, instead of setting up for seasonal merchandise sales, set up a storefront that specializes in selling these items annually. Thus, stores have an opportunity to sell a wide variety of international teams along with local football team merchandise.

Talent Development Schools and Agents/Scouts

Most players playing in major international leagues (including European leagues, MLS, and Latin American leagues) are on those teams because of the already existing talent development network. The first part of this network are the talent development schools. These educate, train, and sometimes feed the student, like a pseudo soccer boarding house. Parents pay annual school fees. In return, schools earn additional revenue through competitions and sponsorships. They also earn a part of the signing fee once the student successfully attracts a club. The network's latter part includes the scouts. These talent scouts and agents help identify, recruit, sign, and ensure that talent gets the best deals at signing. Along the way, the scouts get a percentage for each of the activities. Given the size of some deals, the commission can be quite impressive.

Sports League Organizer

Haiti doesn't have a formal domestic soccer league, such as those which exist in other countries. These are single entities tasked with directing, organizing, and regulating activities for individual domestic teams. La Commission d'Organisation du Championnat Haitian de Football Professional (COCHAFOP) only does administrative tasks for the current teams. They might coordinate and publish play schedules, keep stats, keep records, etc. Teams are founded, meaning that they individually seek out other teams to oppose. Therefore, there's no superseding organization that oversees promoting the matches, collective bargaining for distribution rights of the media, revenue sharing amongst teams, and other cost-sharing apparatuses. All these would be aided by a league's economy of scale properly functioning.

A league's creation has been hampered by a myriad of numerous issues. Generally, it's circled around collaboration and coordination of stakeholders. Since nothing legally prohibits the creation of a league, there remains a tremendous opportunity for the right entrepreneur team to win big.

Betting

Las Vegas, located in Nevada, USA, has shown that betting can be big business. Within Las Vegas alone, as much as $4.8B was wagered in 2018. Such betting is legalized in Haiti. In fact, there's already a mature culture around "Loto" and "Paryaj." Many of these bets are still made physically by placing the bet at a local gambling booth or storefront. And so, there remains a tremendous opportunity for betting that can conveniently be done through a digital platform. Integrating digital money sources (such as mon cash offered by Haitian telecom provider Digicel) is one of these methods.

Viewing Centers

Haitians gathering and bundling around a small screen during a football match earlier indicates that Haitians need somewhere to watch games. What's appreciated are spaces. Haitians need large enough seating, shade, and multiple screens. All these offers general comfort. Revenue can be generated through either an entry fee and refreshments, snacks, and/or quick meals. Any such business has a serious potential for a winning venture. Moreover, when the venue isn't showing a game, the allotted space could further function as a restaurant, bar, or event space.

Success Stories

Sports Max - Digicel

Digicel has taken advantage of the cultural demand for sports viewership. It's created an app that allows patrons to watch any soccer match involving European or Spanish leagues. The app utilizes a simple pay-as-you-go subscription fee, payable through their current telecom retail infrastructure.

Sports. The app is Haiti's most downloaded sports app. In fact, it holds the majority market share for mobile soccer viewership. Digicel has proven that digital streaming can work. But there must be convenience, intuitive design, and fullness of offerings.

5. Recreational Offerings Are Timeless and Consistent Necessities

Driving around Haiti - either in the larger Port-Au-Prince metro area or in the smaller provincial cities acting as the primary waypoints for travel and commerce for the exterior departments - you'll be confronted with a common sight: "Bar & Restos." These are restaurant/bar/lounge venues. These businesses, identifiable from a distance due to their multi-colored strobe lights, stream out loud modern kompa. The venues, too, function as centers of social life for many working laypeople, taxi drivers, or moto transporters. All are looking to enjoy a few drinks and socialize with comrades after a long day. Though often not as flamboyant, equally numerous are traditional evening lounges and clubs for the upper-middle class and visiting tourists to enjoy. Drinks, food, and music are a centerpiece of how time is spent at these places; no matter the patrons' social status. Thus, there're opportunities to monetize offering such an experience to anyone who comes to your business if these things are presented.

Business Concept

Arguably, the surest and best option is to open another Bar & Resto. You might even open an evening night club. But it's to one's advantage to provide something that doesn't exist in the market. One such idea would be an indoor laser tag, which is combined with a sports bar. Another idea could be painting courses that are provided in a private art gallery. Your unique concept may attract partnerships, sponsorships, and paid referral deals. As a result, these ensure profitability.

Niche Ideas

- Skateboard and rollerblade park
- Bowling
- Billiards
- Cigar lounge
- Golf course
- Children focused on entertainment venues
- Amusement and theme parks
- Water park

Department Target and Policy Guidance

Possibilities within this concept are numerous. It all depends on the location of these businesses. Still, a location near a metro area is significant, since this sort of business benefits from population density and commuter convenience. A successful implementation requires consideration regarding the price stratification. Overall, this is critical. It must be accessible to the Haitian populace as a whole. After all, some earn only a few hundred dollars a month, while others have incomes considerably more generous in the thousands. While it's usually advised to look for the middle- to upper-middle class, the reality of income distribution requires versatile pricing. This captures income from both ends of the spectrum. So, figure out how to price your services. This is critical and requires close experimentation. In addition, it needs to occur early within your venture's life cycle.

Action & Tips

- Haiti has an immature entertainment industry. Utilizing any of the creative entertainment options in developmental countries is a potent strategy - not only in terms of being able to model and adjust winning business models, but in regard to attracting investors. After all, it's easier to convince men about monetary concepts already in existence rather than persuade them into believing uncharted ideas.

Success Story

Petionville Club - Sylvain Cote

The Petionville Club, founded in 1928, is Haiti's only golf complex. Sitting on fifty-six acres, it has nine holes of golf. The Petionville Club is critical as a leisure and networking venue, as members pay an annual fee to access its facilities. The 2010 earthquake and the widespread devastation, however, resulted in a humanitarian crisis. Thus, the facility was transformed into a makeshift internal migration camp. It attracted over 55,000 homeless denizens from the surrounding area. Over the next three years, the tent city slowly shrunk. Soon, it was reduced to zero, thanks to the aid and assistance from the international community and non-governmental organizations NGOs. But still, the property is in utter disarray and ill-repair.

Enter Sylvain Cote, a long-time member. He wouldn't accept Haiti losing a community-focused historical and cultural venue. So over the next three years, he spent tens of thousands of dollars of his own money - and a couple of thousand dollars from badgered donors. He further spent his weekends alongside volunteers. Everyone cleaned, shoveled, backhoed with a wheelbarrow, and renovated all nine greens. Today, the Petionville Club is open. It welcomes all its guests for memberships. The facility additionally features tennis courts, an Olympic-length swimming pools, a fitness center, and an art museum.

Waste

"We don't inherit the Earth from our ancestors; we borrow it from our children."

— **Native American Proverb**

The amount of uncollected waste within Haiti is noticeable as travelers exit Haiti's airport to commute throughout the city. It's estimated that thirty percent of waste produced daily is collected throughout the Port-Au-Prince metro area. What's more is the Port-Au-Prince metro area is the largest city in the world without a central sewage system. These are big problems. But where big problems exist, there's big money for the right set of entrepreneurs who can successfully tackle these problems.

Waste production results when multiple humans congregant in any area longer than a few hours. Anything which doesn't have a future use is discarded into this category. Given that the volume of waste is expected to grow in a multiplicative manner as Haiti's population grows, persistent opportunities are on the rise.

An old idiom, what's trash to one is valued beyond repute to another, holds value and worth. Around the world, billionaires owe their fortune to the businesses they found. These helped tackle waste issues in their own countries. And so, Haiti shouldn't be any different. Perhaps the biggest misconception of Haiti's waste industry is that it lacks players. There're over thirty waste management companies, for example, that specialize in various aspects. Opportunities can be seized, evidenced by those already who are contributing. Below we'll explore what may be currently limiting further growth and how they may be overcome it.

6. Waste Collection and Disposal Collection Servicer

Waste is a normal occurrence and viewed as an inconvenient aspect of industrial businesses. It occurs, too, throughout urban, and rural households. In relation to the quantity of time and level of effort/cost related to the disposing of the waste, people most often choose maximal convenience relative to cost.

One example is human waste. There's a significant lack of public toilet facilities in many Haitian communes. This is true for Port-Au-Prince, where only a comparative handful of public restrooms exist for its millions of inhabitants. In fact, only crudely public facilities are available in the provinces. Furthermore, public merchants similarly don't have access to public facilitates. So, they turn to surrounding ravines, ditches, and green areas for relief.

Another example is general trash. With no state-provided bins, they often collapse on major throughways. Eventually, a state garbage truck may come and collect this trash once enough has compiled enough. But when this doesn't happen, residents will burn the trash pile right there. Alternatively, they wait until local rains wash them out to the ocean. Both are unstainable methods and ripe for opportunity, given the right-minded entrepreneur.

Business Concept

Many other international developing countries have countless case studies of businesses operating lucrative and successful ventures across the waste management space. Some are niched, such as handling vendors' waste collection in open markets or creating innovative waste solutions for entire townships. Structuring one's venture from such proven models should be considered. It's possible to seek out an opportunity to franchise or partner with such operators. This could allow you to purchase and distribute products already in use, saving insurmountable time and money in research & development.

There's an incentive of not paying for waste collection. In contrast, an entire block or area does produce waste. Thus, they benefit from a service because they contribute to a cause. Because of this, waste management is most effective when you can connect with institutions pricing the waste collection utilizers through a mechanism. Therefore, everyone must contribute. Residential communities that pay HOA like residential fees, which exist in Haiti, are one such example. Haiti doesn't currently privatize public waste management through open bid contracting. Though, this is the case in many other countries. Many fault this to Haiti's horrendous track record of their consistent and orderly trash collection. Be positioned to respond to open requirements the day Haiti finally modernizes its public collection processes.

Niche Ideas:

- Demolition and deconstruction business.
- Medical / hazardous waste management.
- E-Waste (disposal of used electronic equipment).

Department Target and Policy Guidance

Waste management is needed throughout Haiti. There're obvious advantages, ease, and economies of scale leverage in metro areas. This all depends on the venture. Still, alternative setups may be devised for more provincial areas, including the usage of fortified collection sites. Likewise, you can leverage a local network of providers compensated on the quantity or weight of material collected.

Action & Tips:

- Look across markets in Africa, India, and Brazil for inspiration. The most concrete path to success is identifying models. These can be most successfully imported, while minor modifications for local Haitian cultural and economic preference are reimplemented in Haiti.
- Be on the lookout for major construction projects. Once complete, new residential and commercial tenants, will require waste collection. Be among the first to offer them this service.

Success Story

4Ocean - Andrew Cooper & Alex Schulze

4Ocean is an ocean cleaning company headquartered in Boca Raton, Florida, that also has locations in Bali and Indonesia. It expanded to Haiti in February 2018. Within six months, it had a two-acre clean up facility. Moreover, it had a fleet of plastic and trash recovery watercraft. Since their inception, they've pulled over 1.1M pounds of plastic and trash from waters and oceans.

Initially conceived in 2015 during a trip to Bali, where they encountered garbage on the beaches and ocean, Florida natives Andrew Cooper and Alex Schulze embarked on a multi-million-dollar idea. They wanted to collect this trash and fund its operation. Executing this idea required them to build a for-profit business. It'd further create a secondary market for the recyclable items found, such as by transforming plastic into bracelets or selling to entities that can transform the plastic into other things. The key is working with (and directly hiring) the collectors, fishermen, and laypeople. After all, they happen to have a boat in their "areas of impact" to leverage collection amounts.

7. Focus on Transforming Waste into Profit

Some may see the waste industry as totally unappealing and lacking prestige, but those able to overcome such perceptions are apt to be rewarded with handsome monetary rewards.

The majority of the material is entirely recyclable. As an industry, it's the largest within the waste. A mature industry exists - the most common being plastic, rubber, glass, metal, and textiles. There aren't exact figures for Haiti's waste, but institutions like USAID estimated that roughly seventy-four percent of Haiti's collected waste is recyclable. Port-Au-Prince generates over 2,000 tons of waste per day. This amounts to 4M pounds of recyclable material available per day.

- Food and other organic material make up Haiti's largest component, which equates to fifty-four percent of total waste. This includes many of the unsold and unsellable fruit, and vegetables. These are found in the many open-air markets throughout Haiti. Both are party foods and leftover components of consumed meal prep. Meanwhile, they're unceremoniously tossed into trash piles in the street by the late evening. A potential conversion for these items is fertilizers.
- Paper is in the most recycled item in the industry, consisting of ten percent of Haiti's waste. This includes newspapers, magazines, cardboard, and old books. Though not all paper is recyclable, such as nylon, most are biodegradable.
- Textiles are the second lowest at seven percent. Much of this waste derives from the leftover cloth product. Clothing is

Haiti's largest export to the United States. Moreover, it comes from worn-out clothing or cloth materials found in home furnishings. For example, it may come from cloth used to construct doormats, window dressing, or mattresses.

- Plastic accounts for thirteen percent of Haiti's waste. It feels like much more, however, since plastic is non-biodegradable. Plastic is sourced from nature, but it's an ubiquitous use in street food. It's used to construct white Styrofoam food containers, beverages (such as water pouches), plastic bags, and plastic bottles. This is despite Haiti outlawing these items many years ago.

- Metal, Rubber, Wood, Glass, Electronics -- We've grouped these other items. Though they don't individually represent larger portions of Haiti's waste, they still have mature processes within the recyclable industry. And so, they're converted into new and reusable materials. Many items, in fact, share components of this waste list. These include vehicles (metal, rubber, electronics), foundries (metal and rubber), and medical applications/technologies (metal, glass, electronics). All these waste items produce useful recycled waste items.

Business Concept

When someone chooses to recycle, options are available. Each above-mentioned example holds different opportunities. Trash can be gathered and sorted. Usable items are funneled into a process, outputting a profitable and sellable item on the other end. Selecting an industry which will have the most impact is key, thus you know your interest will carry you through as things become difficult. Affordability is important, since it's a natural advantage of recycled products. When structured correctly, the costs to acquire them is significantly less than the original cost of harvesting the precursor material to produce the product originally. Essentially, being cost-competitive in Haiti is crucial.

A distribution network to capture the recyclable items will be vital. If your product utilizes organic food waste, it's sensible to structure a process where a bin is placed near produce merchant marketplaces. Many unsold or partial expired wears go directly to the trash! Plastics have a relatively mature distribution network in Haiti, consisting of independent gatherers collecting bottles. Then, they sell large quantities of pre-organized bottles. Introducing a new recycling model leverages this already understood behavior, thereby giving someone an advantage.

Department Target and Policy Guidance

Recyclable items don't have any restrictions within Haiti. Economics of scale exists in metro regions, of course, but many schemes can be devised. These utilize systems that use locals to collect recyclable items throughout more sparse areas. In this way, they become more involved in the process through a recyclable item's incentivized monetary exchange. Whereas metro areas may lend more readily to statically located bins and capture facilities, Experimentation is essential.

Action & Tips

- Allow other successful projects implemented around the world to drive your own venture. Africa can be such a place. Each country has entrepreneurs taking what may have been viewed as an absolute nuisance and transforming them into a useful product. Meanwhile, they structure a revenue around it. The reinvention of the wheel isn't necessary here.

- Leverage social media. International audiences (and potential backers!) empathize well with these trash-to-treasure stories for Haiti. Instead of lamenting this association, use it to your advantage. Grow with greater velocity.

Success Stories

ArrisDesrosiers: A BackPack Manufacturer - Obed Arris & James Derosiers

Starting in 2016, Obed Arris and James Derosiers saw an amount of small plastic water bags, and realized it was problematic. These are ubiquitous throughout Haiti, consuming sidewalk trash piles. Likewise, they contribute to canals jamming. Ultimately, these water bags end up floating in the oceans and surround Haiti in massive numbers. But because they're plastic, they knew the bags could be turned into something useful. In fact, the water bags could generate revenue and jobs. After conducting research and some varying product testing, they came up with blueprints. These blueprints were designed for backpacks, handbags, and satchels - all of which use plastic bags.

These were transformed into rugged leather-like material and sold them to children and adults alike.

They've seen success from this venture. Their clients have included Haitian private enterprises needing branded material to distribute to their employees. These enterprises have further needed marketing. In addition, now NGOs and charities could purchase bags directly in Haiti instead of having the bags imported. ArrisDesrosiers currently produces 5,000 bags. Each bag contains an average of 200 previously discarded plastic water bags. That's as much as 1M plastic water bags recyclable a day! While employing fifty-four employees in Carrefour, Haiti, it became an area with a stark imbalance between people and work opportunities.

EcoRenew Solutions - Vanessa Pierre

Based on Croix-des-bouquets, EcoRenew Solutions turns discarded plastic into small pellet cubes. These cubes are sold to companies around the world, which are then reused and redeployed into other plastic products. Vanessa Pierre founded the in 2017, as a first-generation Haitian American. She acted upon a desire to improve the waste situation that she saw in her visits. The firm has since been growing. Now, it employs dozens of employees who support the mission for a cleaner and environmentally sound Haiti of tomorrow.

EcoRenew Solutions' business model involves paying individuals for their recyclable waste to the facility to be weighted. They're paid per pound for the waste. This model incentivizes individuals to become independent operators. In turn, they become plastic collectors who specialize in finding, preparing, sorting, and coordinating pickup with EcoRenews. To date, they've collected more than 500,000 recyclable items. Eighty-three percent of these items are repurposed as new products. Overall, the company has paid out thousands of dollars to collectors. They're currently looking to expand operations and work with collectors further in different cities across the country.

8. Recyclable Material as a Potential Alternative Fuel & Energy Source

Energy empowerment is directly linked to poverty reduction, while quality of life is proportional to the per capita energy use of a nation. Haiti's underdeveloped infrastructure provides an opportunity to leverage new forms of energy, integrating them as part of the larger grid. It incorporates recent advances that make these technologies more efficient in output and costs than previously conceived as possible.

One such development is waste-to-energy plants. Waste in this context is defined as organic waste. It's like human sewage, animal manure, kitchen waste, animal manure, food scraps, and plant material. One example are facilities that take these waste products. They utilize natural gas they emit during decomposition, such as methane, and capture that energy. Then, they are using metallic portable containers, where it's possible through pipelines. Other options emphasize leveraging the gas pressure, either through thermochemical or biochemical conversion. This equates to power gas engines or turbines. The potential result is the same. The added capacity permits patrons to have additional options for their heating, lighting, and cooking needs. This may benefit their homes, farms, or offices. Furthermore, it benefits public facilities. Hospitals, prisons, and hotels likewise enjoy these living amenities.

Business Concept

While Biogas is best implemented as large capital investment products totaling millions of dollars, smaller micro biogas projects are accessible to everyday entrepreneurs. All of them are seeking ways of making a regional impact with rural communities. For example, they partner with livestock farmers to collect dung from goats, cows, horses, and pigs. In turn, this utilizes this waste. Gas can be produced and sold back to the communities, where these suppliers reside. Where the fermentation process takes place should only be a short distance from these communities. Hire locals and provide them compensation. Offer him or her a percentage of sales, or purchasing units of the usable portable produced energy wholesale. Then, they can resell on a margin. Both are common structures in Haiti.

In essence, since business structure and technology already exist, you don't need to reinvent it. Implement what you've researched, for it makes the most sense. Focus on the fundamentals. These include minimizing building cost, building a trade network, and pricing. All guarantee you earn profit.

Department Target and Policy Guidance

Locating your business in provincial areas with a great deal of livestock owners is advisable. Incredible opportunities exist for creating scalable waste-to-energy businesses, given the abundance of organic waste already in the city. Both trash and sewage occur in the cities. Placement would ideally happen on the city's outskirts, where land is cheap. The possible resistance of residents from having such a facility as a neighbor would lessen.

Actions & Tips

- Biogas has yet to be used in a fully vested commercial application. What's more is that considerable attention is needed for the training and educating. In some cases, it's necessary to convince locals to buy into as a supplier or purchase as a buyer.
- Set up street collection locations, particularly in places where there's dumping.

Success Story Needed

Chabon Ticadaie SA - Phillippe Villedrouin

Within a forty-three-employee facility in Delmas, Phillippe Viledroud has created a company which consists of a twelve-member sales team. These collectors specialize in alternative charcoal production that use claw, sawdust, starch, and charcoal powder collected from Haiti's public markets. Bricks burn longer and more efficiently than real charcoal. They also began creating bricks with the residual of the rice harvesting process in Artibonite. Rice straw became an even more efficient and ecological harmonizing solution.

What's most important is that these charcoal bricks are sold at price points comparable to the damaging ecological originals. They currently sell forty tons of this material monthly across the country, hoping to sell as much as 400 tons of this material each month. It's certainly possible. In fact, the World Bank Group estimates $182M were generated in the Port-Au-Prince area alone.

Apparel

"Your clothes should be as important as your skin."

— Amit Kalantri

Clothing is fundamental to the expression of human society. Those in the upper class work to break the lower echelons. It's a requirement on the same level of water and subsistence, to be dressed and to express one's beliefs. It neither matters whether it's religious, cultural, nor ethnic. Instead, what matters is the material which they wear. Each individual soul within Haiti's twelve million population has a similar requirement. The question is: how can an entrepreneur take advantage of it?

Apparel remains a tremendous opportunity. The size of the industry changes by how much variety there's in demand, tastes, and preferences from the local market. Though because of the Haitian Hemispheric Opportunity through Partnership Encouragement Act of 2006 (HOPE Act) - which was first established in 2006, strengthened in 2008 and again in 2010 - the HOPE Act allows preferential access to US Imports of Haitian apparel. The idea is that such legislation would foster investment in the apparel industry, thereby rippling into other segments of the economy. The HOPE Act serves as a unique and vital economic opportunity afforded to Haiti. Entrepreneurs looking to make an immediate impact shouldn't be taken for granted. The numbers related to the HOPE Act's impact doesn't lie. According to InvestHaiti.Ht, ninety percent of Haiti's exports are apparel products valued over one billion. And they've employed over 53,000 persons across the country as of 2017.

This section will discuss where the most significant opportunities in this market that reside in Haiti, providing examples of successful entrepreneurs who impacted this industry's landscape. It's essential to mention that pèpè, cheap second-hand clothes necessary from first world countries, have posed a severe problem to the domestic apparel industry. They differentiate one's product from these items. For this reason, they'll be a critical deciding factor in one's success.

9. Footwear Holds Serious Potential

Some have cited that, even before clothing, there was material created to protect early men's feet. This ultimately protected themselves from challenging environments. Since those days, footwear has evolved from mere material support. It provides an ease of movement to status symbols. All the while, it differentiates from purpose, function, and setting. Slippers, sandals, sneakers, boots, loafers, and dress shoes all express individualistic personality and societal status. This is true in Haiti and across the world.

Shoemaking has been a rare hold out. It's lasted since the onslaught of cheap second-hand clothes made in the USA during the early 90s. In fact, these have decimated other domestic apparel sectors. Many artisans make sandals and slippers, and continue to find a productive niche. A more diversified and formally structured stream of shoemakers have launched and fulfilled orders, not only in Haiti but internationally.

JL Fine Shoes SA aims to contribute to Haiti's domestic footwear industry. They've opened the first Haitian industrial shoemaking company in Haiti, where they manufacture and distribute shoes to stores. JL Fine Shoes SA has been in business since 2014. Their motto, "elegance and comfort on your feet," helps the business strive to improve national production through a bold venture. As a result, they'll be able to produce 1,000 pairs of quality shoes a day for school children. Adults, too, can get at affordable pair of shoes for twelve to eighteen dollars a pair. The plant provides 200 jobs from Cité Soleil, a desperate job starved Port-Au-Prince area. Additionally, their operation is flexible enough to accept shoe orders internationally, often in quantities only found in Asian countries. And so, they work with low-cost shoe designers and distributors from around the world.

Deux Mains, or translated to two hands, is an all-woman-owned factory. Located in the Port-Au-Prince area, Deux Mains creates sustainable jobs by manufacturing high-end footwear for companies. These include Kenneth Cole, Faithbox, and Norton Point. It was founded in 2013 with a small staff on shoestring budget. The company began after the devastating earthquake, in response to the massive employment. It helped foster native artisan talent found during the recovery. Its focused was simple, hand-crafted sandals manufactured from Haitian goat leather and recycled tires. All sandals were marketed internationally. It's since grown to feature dozens of other products. These have graced fashion runways. A growing global footprint includes the US, Canada, and Europe. In January 2019, they inaugurated a factory which would greatly increase their production capacity. Likewise, it significantly increased employees' working full-time.

As these entities show, the shoe business's potential exists. Now, it can be started at different levels. Haiti has access to raw materials. These include recycled leather, shoemaking skills, and a quantity of talent to make sure a venture is successful. Haiti further benefits from original designs. It uses its connection to the most African of Caribbean cultures, to tap into producing domestically viable companies and an international competitive firm.

Supplier opportunities will grow as the industry achieves success. For example, the shoes' soles and shoelaces are often imported from China. This could create support for the different manufacturers as time passes. Such a concept applies to most industries, especially Haiti's apparel industry.

10. Consider Apparel Retail

Clothing must be purchased before it's worn. Opening a retail store helps support demand. Thus, opening a high-demand store is a lucrative and pursuable concept. Understanding the market segment to which you would sell this material and from where this material comes are both important in the store. So, it's important to analyze some segments. After all, it's all about the perception of quality and style. Conversely, some of it only regards social status.

- Mass-Produced and Non-Designer Primary Market

A primary source for many of the clothes sold in Haiti, these are generally produced in mass and countries cheaply in Asia and marked up significantly through European and North American non-designer brands (or high-end brands). Many Haitian-produced clothes are primarily mass-produced inexpensively in Asian countries. European and North American brands (both non-designer brands and higher-end brands) see a significant markup in their cost.

This fashion's appeal is its affordability and its general trendiness. A serious opportunity lies within Haiti. Haitians are encouraged to produce their brands with designs and phrases. These should utilize local creole phrases, culture, and history. Additionally, plentiful opportunities exist for selling sports clothing. These include selling jerseys of popularly supported teams such as Brazil and Argentina. Business owners can also specifically sell merchandise for players such as Lionel Messi and Cristiano Messi.

- Second-Hand "Pèpè" Clothing

Pèpè refers to second-hand clothing brought to Haiti from international sources. This clothing is mainly sold by street merchants, is common amongst Haitians. These are commonly worn by the "Pèp" or the low-income masses in Haiti, which derive from the root of its name. Second-hand clothing has been banned in many countries internationally. In fact, some recommended that Haiti should ban this as well. And the reasoning is sensible. This cheap clothing directly competes with native textile and clothing makers. Since the 90s, they've gained popularity and reduced the country's number of tailors.

Realistically, second-hand clothing provides a hard-to-find variety which is hard to come by in mature countries with clothing industries. Bras are one such example. These are in demand by pèpè buyers. Contrary to its perception, Pèpè doesn't only consist of nearly thrown away material. It also contains high-quality second-hand clothing. This high-priced clothing, in fact, garners demand from Haiti's medium- to upper-class. Some clothing brands - including those from Ralph Lauren, Puma, Dolce Gabanna, Lacoste, and Gucci - would be unattainable without a robust second-hand market.

As such, until Pèpè is formally banned in Haiti, it's filling an important need. Moreover, it's something an entrepreneur can innovatively provide. One idea is to curate Pèpè, while allowing buyers to make online purchases and their packages delivered anywhere within Haiti. Still, another might include a monthly subscription box. Each month, buyers would get specific items delivered to them. The possibilities are endless.

- Designer Clothing

Haiti's wealthy and upper class are discerning, wearing only the most trendy clothing. Brands matter. And, where one buys their clothes are just as important as what the brand may be. A boutique specializing in selling this attire ensures their patrons experience a shopping experience on par with their overseas counterpart. Moreover, businesses can concentrate their marketing on products. Thus, they curate a successful and profitable image.

Major brands are non-existent in Haiti, despite fashion being an opportunity for the right fashion-centric entrepreneur. Although, several renowned artists of Haitian descent have clothing lines featured on international fashion runways. Still, none of these are sourced or housed from a Haitian brand. This is a niche waiting to award the right person. Then, they'll be able to execute a successful winning strategy.

Imitation designer clothing falls on the other side of the spectrum. It comes from mass-produced sellers in Asia, where there're imitations of top-selling international designer brands. These are similarly popular in Haiti. Often these are geared towards those with high designer sensibilities, though they're limited by a budget. They also experience an inability to acquire the designer items from contacts that they may have abroad.

- Native/Domestic Garments

Haitian-inspired garments are relatively lacking. The market's competitive nature has suppressed market forces. As a result, indigenous talents draft a uniquely afro-Haitian style. The practice of Vodon, which involves purposeful attire, further involves patterns and designs. These simple, monotone colors consist of white and red. Generally, there has yet to be a distinct style of clothing attributed to Haiti. And so, this is where opportunity lies.

Tisaksuk, a local brand, has niched clothing. Clothing can also be imitated by specializing in a unique, high-end Haitian-derived flavor of chic dressy wear. The primarily focus is on dresses sporting traditional Haitian paintings, all of which are inspired etchings on the front or back. The fabric's designs work off variants of quadrille / Karabela dresses. In retrospect, these are low-cut or shoulder-top dresses constructed of sturdier fabrics. They've embellished colorful ruffles laces or "ric races." These clothes have since expanded to pants, shorts, shirts, headwear, and accessories. Moreover, they've acquired a loyal following of buyers. Each return for a new season of attire. Meanwhile, others try similar artist infused stylizations which have different styles.

11. Textiles - The Components of Apparel Which Are Never Considered

Textiles doesn't refer to cloth making, but rather to the raw materials subset used to make clothes. Cotton, silk, linen, wool, nylon, polyester, and leather are all examples. Haiti's textile industry participates in two major ways:

Imports:

China, India, Vietnam, and Bangladesh already have established a mature textile industry. In doing so, they've developed a supply chain that allows the sell in bulk, with an emphasize in foreign countries. Plugging into this distribution network is a matter of contacting these suppliers to ship and then resale to waiting local clothing producers in Haiti. Thus, specializing in such an operation is a relatively risk-free exercise. In Haiti, a primary consumers are local clothing manufacturers specialize in making clothing for school children. These garments are then exported to US and Canadian markets. As both segments grow, an increase in revenue can be expected since this industry has correlative flows.

Local production

Like domestic segments of various industries, local production is nascent and prime. It consists of the right factors for which entrepreneurs need to take advantage. The required investment, as well as the concurrence of prerequisite supply chain support that can be established at or near the same time, makes it challenging to realistically approach the country. Meanwhile, the crafting of local fabrics attunes with the particulars of Haitian's African roots. Unique textiles still exist and flourish. In fact, these may be an appropriate concept to pursue. Kanga in Tanzania, Chitenge in Zambia, Sweshwe in South Africa, as well as Aso oke and Adire in Nigeria are all textiles. These are all made from dyed animal hair, woven into intricate patterns that antedate centuries. For this reason, they could be replicated either in part or whole by Haitian companies.

Business Concept

International textile purchases and resales become the industry's entry point. This occurs as a result of local clothing manufacturers, tailors, and/or other clothing refurbishes selling their products to other nations. Niches can leverage these fabrics, making a financially sensible alternative for residential and commercial decor. Sellable items include tablecloth, curtains, sofa covers, as well as additional decorative ambiance-related materials. But other opportunities still exist as a business. These center around embroidery, a type of fabric store selling directly to their consumers. This rings true even for a fashion design institute, where the cloth is provided at a subsidized rate to tuition payers.

Department Target and Policy Guidance

Haiti has fluidity with the more established and mature apparel. So, this sort of business is either at or near one of these facilities, which are in industrial zones. Profitable operations within the textile industry prerequisites require a large bulk order of materials. Though, these don't last too long in inventory. The apparel industry has an insatiable need for textiles in which businesses could provide as an input. Importing textiles in large quantities further entails being near large ports. Moreover, all the infrastructure supports inbound activity. As a result, the Port-Au-Prince metro area and Cap-Haitien are both affected.

Action & Tips

- Opportunities abound through seasonal inspiration, different cultures, and varying times. All these opportunities drive product offerings and presentation.
- Because anyone with capital can source the fundamental material, it's necessary to create a brand under your enterprise. Thus, your product is differentiated from others within the marketplace.
- Since this is a vast area, network with current business owners within the domain. Also, stay on top with noticed trends and consumer purchasing patterns.

12. Clothing Accessories Are More Than Knicks and Knacks

Accessories are a very integrated aspect of the apparel industry. In fact, many of the highlighted businesses have forms of accessories up for sale. These items are sold as a part of their product line. There's a reason for this; it's lucrative. Lucrative enough not only to include as part of a portfolio, but these items could exclusively be built around. Accessories include jewelry, handbags, hats, belts, scarves, watches, bracelets, rings, sunglasses, stockings, ties, leggings, umbrellas, and bras.

In most cases, focus on one or two categories whenever starting with accessories. After establishing that niche, growing into other categories. Produce products related to an original product. Doing this leverages the customer's known brand, and it becomes a winning strategy. Partnering with local artisans is one route to success. Alternatively, create one's own facilities to produce viable solutions. In contrast, the former generally requires less capital. Meanwhile, the latter provides more control over quality and volume.

Papillion Marketplace is an online marketplace. It provides Haitian artisans an opportunity to sell clothing accessories to American buyers. It was founded in 2007 by Shelley Clay, after she realized the burdening number of orphans. Parents were unable to support their families and households. This happened not because they lacked living parents, but they weren't provided income opportunities or jobs. The marketplace allows Haitian women to sell their handmade bracelets, earrings, necklaces, bags, and purses. By doing this, they've encompassed every product made by Haitians.

Haiti Design Co. is another exciting company. It takes Haitian artisan-driven accessories and leverages it for transformation. It's a non-for-profit company founded in 2014 by Josh and Chandler Busby. Their primary mission has included providing artisans economic employment. They combine teams' talents. These talents may consist of leather workers, jewelers, and sewing professionals. They create original and luxurious products for sale, which are available to USA retailers through their online marketplace. These artisan teams are directly employed. Thus far, their producers have increased to over 150 people. And they return the profits to the participant artisans themselves. They further provide healthcare, entrepreneur training and mentorship programs to encourage them to start their businesses.

BelJoy has facilities outside of Limbe in northern Haiti. It follows a similar model, featuring Haitian artisan designed and inspired jewelry. The jewelry collection includes those constructed of clay, paper beads, and horns. In addition, there's gold and silver jewelry . The jewelry looks, feels, and is styled toward a positive reception regarding America. The Dallas market has seventy-five stores that stock their products, while there're another 150 stores in the Las Vegas market. These are two recent examples. They've even made their way to places like Coachella. Growth Prospects look strong.

Telecommunication

"There's no more important consumer product today than a cell phone."

— Mary Dillion

A few things have changed regarding how we've engaged and are connected with mobile phones. Mobile phones are as ubiquitous in rural areas as they're in urban communities. According to Safitek research, a Haitian-based research institute, three out of four fifteen-to-thirty-four-aged young adults in Port Au Prince report owning an internet-capable smartphone. They connect to social media just like their first world cohorts. Despite its prominence, mobile phones equate to sales. They're still expected to grow. Only, they'll become more centric to transformative changes throughout the developing world.

Opportunities of mobile phones includes encouraging digital technology. There're digital responses to transaction points, which lead to friction between not only businesses but also customers. Digital technology reduces access barriers. It allows parts of the socio-economic spectrum a better chance to participate. This includes marginalized communities, people, professions, and industries.

Most importantly, mobile phones serve as an accessible entry point. These aid budding entrepreneurs both within and outside of Haiti. There aren't any old guard economic actors in this domain. Yet to be able to impose influence and arbitrary limitations to activities, there must be an equal playing field. Next, we will discuss opportunities already existing in this space.

13. Mobile Hardware Market Is the Present and the Future

Mobile phones have consistently sold since their first debut in the 90s, dominating the market. In Haiti, the numbers have burgeoned to the millions. Eight-eighty percent of Port-Au-Prince's metro area owns a mobile phone. Popular brands across Haiti include ZTE, Samsung, Apple, LG, Alcatel, Huawei, and BLU. These hold the most market share.

Mobile phones are an attractive entrepreneurial pathway, arguably because the resale value of used phones is greater than that of new phones. Essentially, this opens the door for business models with diverse sourcing methods, such as businesses buying in bulk either from refurbishment redistributors or directly from customers. In the latter sense, businesses are buying phones to resale them in Haitian markets. The typical price of a mobile device hints at the resellers' advantage. Thus, the price ranges from thirty dollars to $130.

First-world countries have a persistent culture of upgrading to the newest model upon its release. And so, phones are consistently routing towards the second-hand market. Additionally, China-based brands (such as Huawei, Xiaomi, and OnePlus) have made headway. These brands provide new phones with very current specs but at second-hand prices. This trend is expected to continue.

Mobile phone accessories are a portion of the mobile hardware market and require attention. Each existing phone needs chargers, earphones, batteries, phone covers, USB connectors, and memory cards. Though some of these items come with a cellphone, many don't. Even when they do, these items have a much shorter shelf life. And they sell much better. Functional accessories, like screen protectors and protective cases, are incredibly popular. Decorative accessories, too, are commonly sold. Because of the consistent volume of the industry's accessory sales, these are as lucrative as the actual cell phones.

Finally, mobile phone service and repair other key segments. Phones break, either externally (such as through falls), or internally (such as through malware). Experts will always need to assist with poor drive space management and software troubleshooting. Given the gap between Haitians and technology, significant opportunities exist in contrite geographical areas. These can aid with mobile phone related. Capabilities are hard to find in Haiti due to a low entry point. For example, there may be a spare part inventory. There might also be certified technicians for each major phone brand. Likewise, as the phone market becomes crowded, multi-month warranties stand out.

Business Concept

No Caribbean countries specialize in technology manufacturing. And Haiti's no exception. Taking advantage of the market in the most straightforward manner involves importing the phones and accessories from abroad. It further involves selling them domestically. The most common way, of course, is doing this through a storefront. However, a more novel way is to leverage digital advertising. Present your wares and electronic means to provide payment.

At the time of writing this book, it's still commonplace to find someone with a mobile phone. As electricity improves in the country, faster mobile internet and public Wi-Fi options will become available. One's market will only increase as a result. Providing options to these realities thereby becomes a lucrative option. Mobile charge stations in public areas, where the customer pays a reasonable charge per session, is one option. Another solution is to place hotspots in dense areas for a moderate connection fee.

Other tactics include working with local artisans. Create custom accessories, such as leather- or fabric-based cases. Consult the artisans about designing small storage containers for one's home or office using the Haitian long tradition of metal workpieces. Moreover, consider spaces that are typically unconsidered, such as car and moto holders.

Department Target and Policy Guidance

Mobile phones are so ubiquitous Haiti. These ideas could work anywhere.

Action & Tips

- Poll people of a particular area, so that you grasp the demand for cell phones. This data provides how often (or how infrequent) a cell phone is purchased, serviced and repaired.
- Incorporating digital advertising is vital to being successful. Consider utilizing Facebook's marketplace, flash509, and other online spaces. These allow Haitians to find bargains and deals online.

14. Tap into the International App Development Ecosystem by Creating Apps Competitive Within Domestic Markets Around the World

A common question from those abroad wanting to enter Haiti's entrepreneurial market relates to apps and mobile software. In their minds, both will revolutionize Haiti. It seems to be straight forward logic. After all, mobile devices are quite common. But still, Wi-Fi costs, an imbalance in accessing electricity, and a culture still preferring face-to-face transactions over cell phones proves difficult. It'd take considerable resources to break that trend. Bear in mind that entities like Digicel is in much more of an advantageous position. For this reason, it can impose modified behavior given to a large market share. It had only limited success with mon cash, which is a proprietary mobile cash transaction platform. One day, Haiti will have many opportunities for a native domestic app ecosystem. But today, a greater opportunity exists. Businesses can tap into the young mobile developers' networks, connecting them with opportunities already existing elsewhere.

When one refers to the diaspora, they're referring to the descendants of second generation Haitians living abroad, First generation Haitians may have spent a decade or more in Canada, the United States, France, the Dominican Republic, Brazil, or Chile. These people have been using apps for a long time. But most importantly, they've become familiarized with the market in which they were raised, more so than the Haitian market. In fact, they're more capable of determining an app's popularity, as well as the app's structure for local markets. Thus, it's more logical to focus on that market. Doing this leverages the talent, capacity, and cost-competitive of Haitian developers. It allows them to execute and maintain apps.

Business Concept

The global mobile app market is in the hundreds of billions of dollars. An enterprise that built on providing thousands of coders, programmers and developers computer science programs, has an opportunity to create pathways. These wouldn't exist without international employers with important businesses already established. Simply put, digital property development outsourcing is an incredible business opportunity.

To acquire early clients, find young development companies and developers abroad. They should be working individually, to help increase the capacity. Therefore, the business can scale quickly. Position oneself as a service, providing qualified developer(s) time to dedicate to clients.

Top Department and Policy Guidance

An operation's success wholly depends upon steady growth. Businesses must have access to the internet and electricity. This is available in Haiti's larger cities. While talent will most likely be located within Port-Au-Prince, the remaining underserved cities across the country offer additional opportunities. Given the lack of competition for the smaller supply, these opportunities are still provided.

Follow close developments in Haiti that relate to internet connectivity, access, and electricity. Developments in these areas drive opportunities for domestic app production. Consequently, the market grows. These socio-economic factors restricting access and utilization rate of digital applications is a current limitation that focuses on the domestic market. So, there'll be a boom in the ecosystem as those conditions improve. The rapidly changing metro areas are due to population concentration and economies of scale.

Action & Tips

- Your global partners should all bring something different to the table. Consider slots such as a technical lead, a sales lead, and a marketing lead.

- Leverage freelance online resources. These already exist to capture leads. Work to find opportunities for your staff.

Success Story

Nou Kod - Ted and Rebecca Barlow

Ted and Rebecca moved to Haiti in response to the 2010 earthquake. After moving to Haiti, they began helping with the relief efforts wherever they could. This included a particular focus on families and vulnerable children. Within a short time, however, they realized that the majority of Haiti's sick was due to the lack of work opportunities and jobs. So, they decided to leverage their background and IT connections. They started an IT outsourcing company called Nou Kod, otherwise known as "we code" in English.

Ted and Rebecca Barlow operate a model that doesn't just train and move relief efforts. Instead, they qualify, train, and employ workers. The training process takes as long as six months. Upon its completion, junior programmers will have an opportunity waiting for them. With a pipeline of outsourced IT projects from firms in America, opportunities have been growing.

They view IT outsourcing as a legitimate industry. Outsourcing IT can drive growth, employment, and economic opportunities to India. And given Haiti's proximity to the United States, along with multi-languages spoken natively (English, Spanish, and French) due to its location in the Caribbean, it's a logical prediction. The company and foundation are still in its infancy. Although, they already staff more than a dozen programmers. Many have served satisfied clients. Along with its profits' reintegration in an effort to expand the quantity of youthful entry-level IT candidates, it's well-positioned for the digitally-focused economic age. Ultimately, this is certainly Haiti's future.

15. Opportunities to Service Haiti's Telecom Industry Abound

Millions of Haiti's population remain unserved by the telecom revolution, brought to Haiti by the current populace. It's tempting to advise someone to try telecom servicing, since it's brought developing countries fortune and success. On the contrary, this domain is highly regulated. It's further constrained by bureaucracy throughout most countries. This is especially true in Haiti. In fact, it's far more capital intensive to consider whether to support the existing telecom providers' operations.

Consider, for instance, accessories and equipment enhancements for the 4G LTE-based internet network on which the telecom infrastructure is based. The standard 4G LTE provides portable Wi-Fi boxes to telecom users. Generally, these are underperformed brand name Wi-Fi boxes that are sold over the counter. The LTE boxes are purchasable from manufacturers such as Motorola, Netgear, and Alcatel - to name a few. Additional router signal strength extenders can be placed throughout a home. This improve a home's Wi-Fi range, proving useful considering the concrete buildings that are standard for most Haitian homes. The concrete, in fact, often prevents 4G wave signals from passing through its walls.

Intuitively bound to providing telecom equipment is the reality that most Haitian homes and businesses require assistance setting up this equipment. In turn, a unique opportunity is created for a maintenance and service company. It focuses on providing consultation, permitting

73

men or women to install on-site Wi-Fi for residential and commercial properties.

Once established, growth into other supportive streams exists. This might include acquiring routine maintenance and repair of telecom infrastructure and facilities. Haiti's topography makes it inefficient for telecom providers to service their lines, however, particularly since many of Haiti's telecom fuel-based infrastructure is ran through diesel-based generators. Issuing contracts would be more suitable, for this allows entities to specialize and be able to outsource.

Food

"Civilization as it's known today could not have evolved, nor can it survive, without an adequate food supply."

— Norman Borlaug

A person's fundamental human need requires obtaining liquid and solid substances. Going a few days without food could lead to dire consequences, or perhaps death. And so, this segment is critical. Where there already exists an importance and need, there too exists opportunity and wealth.

The size of Haiti's population is notable. Haiti's population at almost 12 million strong. It's the most populous country in the Caribbean. In fact, its highly comparative growth rates ensure that it will continue to hold onto that distinction. The sad reality is, however, that Haiti's domestic agriculture supply has never kept up with its population increase. Instead, it's coupled with socio-economic strife. As a result, its food supply issues (such as famine) are an ever-present concern. But neither the advancement nor the growth of sustainability in Haiti's food supply is of a socio-humanitarian's concern. Entrepreneurs need to provide new energy into this category, because Haiti needs it now more than ever.

The amount of uncultivated land is significant. It's just not traditional agriculture where Haiti holds potential, but also food-processing, packaging, and trading. The potentiality for a well-run enterprise to earn millions in annual revenue is obvious. Success is more a factor dependent upon the robust and ingenuity of a business structure. It not only emphasizes the raw food process growing, but also the more lucrative processing. It further indicates the retail branding end of the agri-distribution supply chain.

The difficulty most related to this domain is acquiring the land, and that discussion we do intend to provide a deeper dive in later chapters (See: "On the topic of acquiring land"). But there're ways around this that we will discuss here, including working with associations or groups of farmers directly themselves.

16. Produce Haiti Must Import: Rice, Cereals, and Animal/Vegetable Oils

After Haiti produced enough sufficient for Haitians, it led to a lack of investment toward food production. Its further lead to an unbalanced trade policy, and unfettered illegal contraband from the Dominican Republic. This combination caused sixty percent of Haiti's food consumption, which derived from imports, to be lost - totaling almost a billion dollars in 2018. Below we'll look at a few of the most imported food products. These foods also have an opportunity to be produced domestically.

Rice has become the flagship food item. It was previously produced in self-sufficient quantities, though it's faced drastic turns in that capacity. Today, more than eighty percent of Haiti's rice is consumed from American-imported rice. This equates to a value of $238.5M, amounting to over 380,000 metric tons in 2018. Meanwhile, Haiti's agricultural region, specifically Haiti's Artibonite Valley, supports over 100,000 families. They're one of the largest rice-producing regions in the entire region. The Artibonite Valley is located on 28,000 hectares. While it's still languished, it's ignored by forward-thinking entrepreneurs. These individuals believe it to be a source of returns for possible investment. (Google: Haiti's rice-producing regions)

Cereal products (such as wheat, flour, maize, sorghum, and millet) are major constituents of routine Haitian meals. Despite this, there remains a significant deficiency in local mills and farms who keep up with this domestic demand. Maize and sorghum are grown in specific pockets, while whole wheat grains and flour are entirely sourced from imports. Still, Haiti recorded $253.12M in 2018 regarding American cereal imports.

Other food considerations

Other staples require important mentions in addition to the above-mentioned foods. Edible oil (vegetable oils), banana (banana plantains and banana figure), and other vegetable products are all imported. As a result, incredibly popular products are a cornerstone of Haitian diets. Yet, Haitians are still seeing a downward trend of domestic trends and simultaneous incredible opportunities. At this point, you should see that the opportunity in Haiti is wide open. Each of these sectors has seen a steady number of hundreds of metric tons of imported products. These have been unable to be fulfilled by the domestic market. If you believe it, there's an opportunity in that trench of the market. What's lacking, however, is engagement by interested players. These individuals need to combine capital, expertise, and motivation to push forward and create profitable ventures.

Business Concept

As the girth introduction to this sector indicates, the quantity of business ideas are numerous. Ultimately, it depends on personal preference. It further depends on how one's current assets and opportunities align. Understand that opportunities neither reside at the point of growing the crop nor raising the livestock. Instead, they exist in processing, packaging, marketing and branding. A venture can be placed anywhere within the value chain of Haitian food production.

Niche Ideas

1. Processing and milling food crops for specialized consumption, such as baby food or cattle feed.

2. Processing and packaging cereal products. The number of items which can be made run the gamut of those found in a grocery store. Thus, they can be sold as well. These include cereals, protein bars, chips, and malt beverages.

3. Opening a locally-owned bakery, in which you sell both to retail customers and wholesale groceries or to food stores.

Top Department and Policy Guidance

Policy guidance exists in every department. The ideal location is wholly dependent on the segment of Haiti's food production value. Intuitively, it makes sense to involve the larger metropolitan area. Provincial cities, particularly those with deep seaports like Miragoane and Goanaive, should receive preferential treatment. Instability Haiti generally takes longer to reach provincial towns. In any case, you still need to be cautious of instability. It's a harmful effect on time-critical food production processes.

Action & Tips

Opportunities don't exist simply by acting as a producer or investing in a distributive supply chain. Instead, they arise from attacking deficiencies that exist in Haiti's domestic food chain. These include:

- Consider providing rural access to supplies. By doing this, irrigation infrastructure can be built. It further reduces maintenance and material costs of transport, both of which are needed to maintain an existing infrastructure.

- Provide solutions that help farmers improve soil and water conservation. These solutions should provide a cost-effective yet profitable resolution.
- Support producers through the financial facilitations, providing them resources and access to information.
- Capitalize on a relatively open seed and fertilizer. Primary and secondary markets should be a facility's direct creation, since it provides regional assistance to farmers.

Success Story

Mana SA - Guelmana Rochelin

Mana SA is a Port Au Prince-based cereal production company. Despite its youth, it's only been in operation for a few years. But its products have already been featured on Conan O'Brien. Its products can be found in markets and merchants across Haiti, as well as many American cities. Mana SA's founder, Guelmana, is a first-generation Haitian immigrant. She took advantage of her parent's immigration to Haiti by attending Villanova University. Then, she went onto Harvard Business School before working at Goldman Sachs. But the desire of returning to Haiti and its impact never left her. Though on a trip to Haiti, she noted and acted on an opportunity. Many families could not buy a box of cereal, so instead, they purchased cereal by individual servings in street markets and madame Saras. Noting the ingeniousness of this option, she further noted the quality and safety issues of this repackaging. She then recognized an opportunity to step into the market. With the purchase of imported machines to transform wheat grain to cornflakes, she built a production facility. It focused on individual servings of cornflakes. Her facilities now employ dozens of Haitians and are eyeing exporting her product to the Latin American market.

17. Consider a Cassava-Focused Bakery

Cassava is a delicacy. Too few people outside of the Caribbean haven't been exposed to it, which is a shame. For many Haitians, it serves as an important carbohydrate. Cassava contains such nutrients as vitamin C, thiamine, riboflavin, and niacin. It's cultivated throughout Haiti as a tuber crop, though it's predominantly found in northern Haiti between Cap Haitien and Port-de-Paix.

Its composition is like a potato. When it's raw, a cassava is starchy and inedible; however, it can be substituted in many recipes. Mainly it's eaten in its hard, flat bread form or in soups. Additionally, it can be even prepared as a dessert whenever it's hardened and combined with sweet jams. It's a long shelf life after being transformed into its flat breaded form, serving additional potential applications. These include starch extracts, biodegradable plastics, ethanol, and animal feed except for its culinary use.

Business Concept

Cassava's most profitable aspect isn't necessarily cultivating and growing it. Instead, it's processing it. There're several methods of producing Cassava, all of which are relatively simple. These methods require water for soaking and boiling, a tool to help smash or mash food into a paste, and sometimes fire (which turns paste to flour). To make the most of Cassava, it requires leveraging marketing to foster a brand. Brand creation occurs in a very limited scope - not just in the sector but within the Haitian eco-system overall.

It's best to buy tuber crops from local farmers. Emphasize a unique processing element, while then branding the post-processed product into the domestic economy or abroad. Should this be correctly executed, then success is possible. But to be successful, you must keep your scale and the right marketing strategy in mind.

Niche Ideas

1. Production and distribution of starch extracts. Cassava-based flour, animal feed chips, and ethanol.
2. Mass consumable culinary items, such as bread and potato chips.

Top Department & Policy Guidance

Because the current agri-infrastructure predominantly existing in the north, setting up facilities in the northern department and leveraging the economies of scale of Haiti's second-largest city of Cap Haitien is logical. But since Cassava grows almost everywhere in Haiti, cassava-dependent production also occurs anywhere.

Action and Tips

1. China has imported over a million metric tons of Cassava over the recent years. Consider exporting to foreign markets already who are already attuned to this product.
2. Connect with farmer associations already producing Cassava.
3. Keep innovation at the forefront. Given Cassava's many potential applications, the possibilities are only limited by your imagination and work ethic.

Success Story

Manu Kasav - Deprivil Manoach

Manu Kasav have been in operation for more than three years, etching a niche space by working with southern Haitian farmers located in Léogâne. They produce a flat cassava bread available in different flavors, including peanut butter and sweet jam. Their product can be found in Haitian stores across the Port-Au-Prince metro area.

Their cassava product's texture is unlike those acquired from northern Haiti, which tend to be less brittle and significantly chewier. After purchasing the Cassava in bulk from Léogâne farmers, Manu Kasav immediately transforms the cassava's root into bread. Then, he takes them to his food prep facility. Once there, they're bagged and distributed across the city. The company heavily leverages social media and word of mouth. These drive growing sales, estimating how to begin exporting abroad.

18. Feed Haiti's Growing Need for Meat Consumption

The world has seen a significant increase in meat consumption. Haiti isn't an exception. Goats, pigs, and chickens are all predominant sources of protein. While Haiti has seen a nearly two-fold increase in meat consumption between 2010 and 2018, Haiti has seen a decrease of livestock availability. Nearly $99.03M was imported in 2018 from the Dominican Republic and the United States. This was despite a rich opportunity for domestic production after the Haitian government implemented a ban on Dominican poultry and egg products due to the Avian flu.

Haiti's creole pig eradication story is well-documented. It remains one of Haiti's domestic feed market's biggest and enduring shocks. Previous creole pigs served, not only as meat consumption, but as a Haitian subsistence farmer savings account. Generally, they were sold with the intent to provide unforeseen events such as marriages, medical emergencies, schooling, seeds, or voodoo ceremonies. An African swine fever outbreak in the Dominican Republic caused USAID to require the Haitian government to exterminate Haiti's pigs preemptively. Some pigs were replaced with pigs imported from the United States. These pigs, however, weren't adept at Haiti's climate. So, they had a much higher upkeep cost as a result. Many Haitians have since moved to other livestock, such as goats, and aligned with Haiti's climate. As a result, this livestock becomes more attuned to Haiti's mountainous terrain. Likewise, chickens can be housed in makeshift housing.

According to the USDA, chicken is another incredibly important staple. In actuality, it's Haiti's preferred meat. Since 2018, poultry production's domestic production has increased to around 5,000 metric tons per year. This production pales in comparison to the amount consumed. In actuality, it's estimated to be around 105,000 metric tons. A chicken import market mostly provides the difference in the multiple billions of dollars. This difference has resulted from a historically poor liberalization policy, which in turn hampered domestic production. However, these policies have been recognized and corrected by means of government action. This is an encouraging result. The recent banning of importing eggs from the Dominican Republic, as well as a large investment from Jamaica Broilers company into Haiti would've both affected food production.

Business Concept

Ultimately, the limitations of this opportunity for an entrepreneur is based on the amount of land each person can possess. It's further based on available capital supporting the animals' maturation until the earliest maturation and sale date. Supply chains already exist to leverage purchases of newborn livestock and their local distribution. So, your focus should concern using new technology to improve breeds, feed, and management practices.

One could also bypass the need to raise the livestock. Instead of serving as a butcher, one would sell different meat parts. Most meat consumed within the typical Haitian homes comes from open-air markets. Ultimately, this meat derives from slaughterhouses consisting of not-so-sanitary conditions. Conversely, there's a demand for alternative and sanitary options for restaurants, hotels, and groceries of professionalized butcheries. There's also significant demand from the middle- to upper-middle-income homes. These individuals have more discerning preferences and the ability to pay more.

Haitians have a particular infinity for burgers and hot dogs when they go out. So, focusing on burger patties and sausages is a recommended specialization. Other avenues may include a an untapped domestic market. A significant example is pet food, such as a cat food or dog food. Both cats and dogs are common in Haitian households. Though a typical home provides their pets whatever is left over from their meals, more discerning segments of society do purchase food for their pets. There may certainly be a market available by a domestic Haitian pet food producer, given the right marketing strategy. First consider market testing by utilizing the remnant meat parts of a larger butchery process operation.

Niche Ideas

1. High-quality burger and sausage production focused on grocery stores, restaurants, and hotels.
2. Chicken & goat farms requiring a moderate level of initial investment. These should be considered as an entry-level business.
3. Consider lesser known meats in Haiti. These include rabbit, quail, and turkey. These are of special interest to Haiti's higher-end restaurants and chefs.

4. Consider non-consumption uses of meat parts, like Glycerin from animal fat for soap. There're additional uses for beauty products, preservatives, and industrial lubricants.

5. Gelatin is another by-product that may be used for culinary products, beauty cosmetics, or medicine.

Top Department & Policy Guidance

Raising commercial livestock and meat processing can happen anywhere. However, certain challenges make the location more important than intuitively expected. Ideally, meat should be processed near the cattle. Then, it should be transported in cooled containers to its final packaging location and/or to retail sellers. Haiti's lack of infrastructure makes it necessary for meat processing to occur in the city or on its fringes. Therefore, the meat immediately goes to the end consumer buyer. Investments along any of the current baseline deficiencies within a business model makes way for considerable flexibility. This permits placement of a business's operations without reducing the quality. Ultimately, it could provide a critical product differentiator.

Action & Tips

1. Connect with the association of ranchers and farmers. Ensure that you understand the current production chain. It pays to utilize aspects of the chain. So, focus on specific parts through more modern processes. In retrospect, this to keeps costs down and productivity up.

2. Those most interested in domestic agriculture have had the most success. They're able to focus all their energy on reducing the cost of feed, which traditionally remains the sore point in this particular sector.

Success Story

Farmer John's - John Draxton

John Draxton, a North Dakota farmer, and rancher, has been in Haiti since 2012. He has been a part of the NGO sector, doing work with sustainable agricultural practices that focuses on improving farmers and their families' lives. After seeing the entrepreneurial opportunities which existed in Haiti, he sold his state-side business. Then, he focused his entire time and energy on building Farmer John's - a ranching estate that raises beef, goat, pork, and chicken products. These animals are butchered and processed into meats. Among the produced meats are ham, bacon, and other specialty meats. These are located in Fonds de Parison, on the outskirts of the metro-Port-Au-Prince area. They butcher and process countless varieties of cuts, jerks, smoked, and sausage options. At the time of writing this book, the ranch was expanding its butchery operations by constructing a modern slaughterhouse. It's on par with all international meat processing standards, packaging, storage, and distribution.

19. Fish Farming Can Be Started with a Pool in One's Backyard

Natural fish sources have been in the drastic decline as a result of increased global warming and overfishing. Planned fishing production facilities have been on the rise. Fishing and farming activities already account for thirty percent of fish production worldwide. Fish consumption is an integral part of Haitian food culture, with countless receipts that utilize fish as the core protein.

Haiti has seen various public and private investments in this domain, with current output well past 1,440 metric tons since 2017. In fact, it represents a many-fold increase since the start of commercial aquaculture a decade prior. The most common farmed fish in Haiti is principally tilapia. Meanwhile, catfish and carp are produced in smaller quantities. Once cultivated, these fish are sold whole to open markets. They may be otherwise packaged for sale in grocery stores. The fish are mostly used for sauces, or alternatively they may be fried. They're served for meals throughout the day.

Business Concept

A large misconception of fish farming concerns needing access to an expansive body of water. Small operations are occurring on Lake Azuei, Peligre Lake, and Miragoane Pond. Though, this business requires a fishing hole to already be established. Water must not stagnate as it moves through pumps. Thus, fish stay alive, procreate, and multiply. Ultimately, a fish farm can exist in provincial areas and the city. In other parts of the world, aspiring entrepreneurs have started fish farms. These entrepreneurs use discarded shipping containers. As the venture grows, relocating to a larger property and continuing to scale is vital.

Niche Ideas

1. Specialize in the fish's transport and storage. Keep the fish cold throughout transport. Fish farms can outsource this task.

2. Specialize in producing a final product. Allow your product to reach a significant distance. This might include various smoked, jerked, canned, or frozen fish nuggets, fillets, or sticks. This may even allow prepare the fish for eventual export.

3. It's possible to purchase fish farm kits from sellers abroad. Import them into Haiti. These kits usually include large near-portable pools, pumps, solar panels, ph-control, fish, and fingerlings. Moreover, the kits include things which help get your business started.

Success Story

Taino Aqua Ferme - Hans Wolley

Hans Wolley left Haiti in his late teens, at the end of the 1990s. He left his job to begin a successful tech career. However, a disastrous earthquake pulled him back. At that point, he desired a sustainable way to contribute to Haiti's struggling economic growth. By researching easy entry and potentially high-impact industries, Hans discovered fish farming. So, along with his brother and cousin, Hans piloted a tilapia farm in the Fond Parisien - a town on Lake Azuei's shore. They set up small aquaculture containers within the lake. Quickly they found that there was a demand with their fish. Now, they're Haiti's amongst largest fish farms and aquaculture distributors.

20. Powdered Milk Production Should Be Considered for Its Potential, Leading to Untapped Profits and Remains

Haitians aren't well-known for consuming milk, as opposed to those in developed countries. Because of the logistics of milk production, and Haiti's lack of infrastructure, to make milk in Haiti is a tricky process. However, condensed and evaporated milk, effectively named "laté kanasyon," is a cultural artifact. It's consumed by Haitians across the country and within the diaspora. Primarily it's used in cornflakes, as the core component of shakes, alcoholic drinks (such as cremas), and evening porridge. Still, much of this milk is imported.

An essential part of any national milk industry is the maturity of the dairy livestock. Cows are held and groomed by farmers. Extracting milk by hand is one way to start. When it comes to scaling, invest in modernized and mechanical dairy production facilities. As Haiti's socio-economic condition improves, entities already with baseline capital investments will be find it easier to capitalize on improved middle-class discretionary. Thus, they'll spend and improve infrastructure to enhance supply chain distribution.

Business Concept

Getting into the sector requires either direct and extensive landholdings, or the capacity to work with regional livestock farmers. Generally, livestock is something done by a secondary farmer. It may take more significant effort, since there's a broader range to acquire required milk input. But once it's collected, processed, evaporated, and condensed, then packaging can begin. It's a relatively automatic supply chain, of which early movers gain significant first-mover advantages.

Niche Ideas:

1. Production and distribution to school, NGO, and hospital networks.

2. Affiliate with ice-cream and yogurt vendors. They may purchase your milk directly.

3. Purpose milk for the creation of baby powder. When it's used in this way, it can be lucrative. In fact, when milk is fortified with additional nutrients, it impacts some segments of the population - especially those struggling to find daily nutrition.

Top Department & Policy Guidance

Milk should be processed near cattle. Then, it should be transported to cooled containers. Finalize its packaging to retail sellers as aligned with Haiti's lack of infrastructure. Once the milk is condensed, the product becomes markedly less perishable. The cost to maintain, transport, and store the milk significantly drops as a result.

Action & Tips

1. Though not as common as an agriculture association, livestock and breeder associations exist, And so, they should be contacted regarding the provisional department in which your venture will be located.

2. Upon approaching this sort of activity in this sector, consider leveraging bodies like IDB, World Bank, and USAID. Because of the large infrastructure support, it may be required to fortify farmers. Therefore, associations help them meet your orders as you grow operations. Such initiatives are generally favored. Likewise, considerable funding is set aside annually to encourage this activity.

21. Farming of Fruit - A Caribbean Island Capable of Growing Any and All Tropical Fruits

Fruit farming responds to Haiti's deforestation. It's been a source of great consternation and concern for conservationists, with estimates of about thirty percent in 2014. Many fruits are grown off the large trees' vines. Those that produce them off of vines or bushes require trees to be built around them, thereby providing the vines protection. Outside of the environmental benefits fruit farming en masse may produce, it's important to understand that most fruit sold globally is sourced from tropical regions. Haiti, in fact, resides in the tropical latitude with varied mountainous topography. It can be taken advantage of to produce a wide variety of fruits. There're twenty-six native fruit species of Haiti.

While a meager twenty percent of Haitian-grown mangoes are exported, Haiti still ranks as the sixth overall mango exporter as of 2015. This statistic can be interpreted in two ways. Fruit production has a strong domestic demand and supply chain. This is evident in that much of Haiti's fruit demand is still met by local production. Moreover, that there's room to grow in capacity for export, particularly when it's understood that, in 1990, Haiti was America's second largest source of mangoes. During the peak season in June, mango exporters are inundated with quality mangoes. They're unable to accept most mangoes brought to them for sale due to the lack of capacity.

Business Concept

The business model of fruit farming is pretty straight forward. One must produce a high-quality yield. They must either export or sell domestically, selling at a high enough price to return on the costs. Ideally, one should consider selling directly to grocery stores instead of wholesalers. By doing this, they can provide the best purchase prices.

Mangoes remain one of Haiti's most popular fruits. Other fruits - such as strawberries, watermelons, lemons, limes, grapefruit, oranges, and bananas - are also exported. Price points for these items can be unpredictable; though, they generally remain in high demand all year. One vital strategy driving more massive returns is investing in processing capacity for harvested fruit. It might be where a processing facility is centrically located, or a more mobile option. This allows fruit farmers the option to process fruit directly in a metro area. Alternatively, they can process fruit between farm areas, while either storing and shipping out the fruit from a distribution center.

Niche Ideas

1. Organic concentrates
2. Organic juices
3. Coconut milk
4. Dried fruit
5. Jams and marmalades (Made Haitian style aka "Confiture")
6. Yogurt

Top Department & Policy Guidance

Fruit farming requires water. As such, Haiti generally experiences less rain than other countries of its latitude. This is also accurate in most regions outside of pockets of Artibonite, the northeast, and the far southwest. Other places will require the founding of a well and a system of pumps to ensure one's entire lot receives the proper hydration amounts. Having these considerations in mind, it's possible to establish a fruit farm anywhere in Haiti.

Action & Tips

1. It's important to start a small operation on one's land, should one already have a business in their family or can purchase land for farming. Expedited growth can be achieved by working with local farmers. This growth can also come about through a formal relationship with an association.

2. It's advisable to start with domestic production. Once consistent profitability and scale are achieved, focus on exporting. International distributors usually require consistent and quantitative yields. Therefore, it will be easier to fulfill if an operation that's already at a moderate size and scale.

Success Story

Montcel Strawberries & Ecological Reserve - Philippe Villedrouin

Montcel Strawberries & Ecological Reserve is an ecological oasis in the Kenscoff Mountains, which sits on over sixteen acres of land. Its preserved nature is dotted with cottages and excursions visitors can experience. Originally, it was founded as a camp for students looking to stay in the country. They stayed in the mountains instead of being sent abroad for summer vacations. Although now it's grown into an eco-resort. More importantly, it comprises half a dozen greenhouses - all of which grow tons of delicate strawberries in a very innovative manner. They're grown in discarded Culligan water gallons that are cut in half. Then, they're stacked on top of each other, connected and separated by a single PVC pipe. Because they're in self-contained greenhouses with regulated climates, they can sell products year-round. Many of these strawberries find their way into Haiti's major grocery chains. At times, it might be the only "berry" product on shelves.

These multiple revenue models featuring lodging, eco-excursions, and cultivation operations. Not only are they innovative, but they help improve economic resilience and revenue diversification. Visitors can sample their strawberry products straight from the vine. Likewise, they're inclined to purchase the product upon seeing them in the stores. Montcel Strawberries & Ecological Reserve expects to continue to expand its operation. In the future, it intends to provide more national coverage of this sweet fruity delicacy.

22. Many Herbs and Spices of the Haitian Spice

Haitian food taste isn't a happy accident. Rather, it's a deliberate combination of spices and seasoning, which is affectionately named "Epis." Epis is effectively a cocktail of garlic, leeks, onions, peppers, scallions, celery, and parsley all mixed into a paste. Usually, it's used to either coat or infuse meat and fish overnight. Though it's not too common, Epi's can be spicy. It's at its mostly spice when it's used to make a particular sort of coleslaw, "Pikliz."

Other Caribbean cultures have had breakthroughs. They produce domestic seasoning styles to outside markets. The most notable example is Jamaica, where there're Jerk seasoning spices. It was first produced in scale to satisfy busy Jamaicans living abroad, who all sought to have an over-the-counter flavor. It's since been adopted by non-Jamaicans alike. There have been some attempts at producing Haitian seasonal items, but a company has not yet obtained it. What's more is that no company holds a significant market share.

Business Concept

1. Produce specialized seasoning. Purchase the ingredients from farmers or cooperatives, and produce the spices yourself. Export the spices to Haitian diaspora communities. Be receptive as other demographics show interest. Ensure your supply to those other communities can meet that demand.
2. Consider producing spices in Haiti that are common elsewhere. Vary your spices in availability. The cultivation of spices

depends on Haiti's region, as well as where they sell domestically. This should be taken into consideration for cinnamon, coriander, vanilla, nutmeg, sassafras, absinthe, annatto, and Comino. Most importantly, present & market them professionally. Therefore, the spices stand out from those spices and herbs being sold in bulk or indiscriminately in grocery stores.

3. Innovate seasoning offerings. For example, perhaps make a spice that fits BBQ-flavored epis or epis mixed with some fruit. This might be an orange or a sugary pikliz that uses a different chopped green. All these different spices can help drive market dominance of a brand, thereby giving consumers something they did not know they wanted.

Niche Ideas

1. Export specific nuisance species like Djon Djon ("Haitian Mushrooms").
2. Seasonally infused salad dressings.
3. Herbal tea products.
4. Haitian-seasoned spaghetti sauce and pesto.
5. Haitian spice delivered directly to the Diaspora. Mail custom-selected varieties and amounts monthly.

Top Countries & Policy Guidance

So much of Haiti imitates America's style of consumption and comfort. Yet, it still appreciates their own culture's distinction. And so, many of the ideas proposed in this section will port anywhere. Metro areas will in turn be successful, because of Haitians who are involved within domestic and international markets.

Action & Tips

1. Before investing too heavily, do small rollouts of the season's product. This ensures that there's an understandable and understanding and reasonable product demand.
2. Utilize any conference, festival, or pop-ups in grocery stores to test your market.
3. It's required to understand the Haitian Diaspora's consumption habits and preferences. Find out which products customers can't access. The herb, spices, and seasonings you provide should depend on this lack of access or convenience.

23. Edible Oils Is Another Booming Oil Industry Awaiting the Right Entrepreneur

Few things are as universally required for modern life as edible oils. Commonly referenced as vegetable oils, edible oils are used in a variety of ways. These are used to cook Haitian cuisine, which might include meats, vegetables, beans or rice. Edible oils, too, is an integral part of the sauces. Other than its culinary uses, edible oils are used for soaps, personal care, cosmetic products and biofuel. In short, few things are as versatile and useful in Haitian society as edible oil.

Gilbert Bigio, Haiti's only billionaire, is proof of this sector's viability. He's made a big chunk of his fortune importing edible oil. Despite the market's proven viability, Haiti produces zero percent of the edible oil in which it consumes. As such, it presents as one of the most lucrative nascent opportunities in the Haitian economy. The two most popular edible oils are soybean oil and palm oil. Still, there exists over twenty different types of edible oils. Many of these can utilize Haitian agricultural products. In turn, they've mature process supply chains. Products being produced include corn, coconut, peanut, avocado, rice bran, and grapeseed.

Business Concept

Partnering with an association of farmers is required, to help grow the edible oil crop you have chosen. The sector functions in large part by volume. Thus, price determines the Haitian domestic market's primary edible selections. Therefore, obtaining profitably by quantity of sales rather than margins is necessary. Upon first testing the idea's viability, start small. Put an emphasis on one brand and its differentiating qualities.

Niche Ideas

1. Given the popularity of peanut farming and a slow turnover of sales despite its popularity, peanut oil is the most obvious possibility. Asian cuisine is popular in Haiti. So, Thai restaurants may purchase peanut oil during an initial roll out.

2. Coconut oil is used both for cooking, and for health & beauty products. So, it should be specialized. Therefore, it'd provide immediate export potential.

Top Department & Policy Guidance

Edible oils can be produced anywhere Haiti. Its production consists of low-tech methods. These extract oil from its source. In the form of an oil, they're only required to be kept at room temperature.

Action & Tips

It's important to understand that the edible oil market is currently held by only two players. Buy oil by the shipload. Then, repackage and rebottle the oil with a supply chain. By doing this, you in turn supply Haiti with their demand. Smaller players exist as edible oils, but many sources their edible oils outside the formal import process. For this reason, they sell at an undercut price point. In essence, this sector is very competitive. There're formally through players with large market shares. Meanwhile, there're informally through players that use contraband.   So, it's important to have a clear strategy. Don't only differentiate your product or differ its utilization. But know how your operations and sales process will be resilient enough to fend off this competition and grow within one's niche.

24. Honey Can Be as Sweet to the Pocket Books as it Is to Taste

Few things are as distinctly enjoyed by Haitian natives and foreigners as Haitian honey. There's a referenceable flavor profile that the most casual consumer can enjoy. Additionally, a widespread custom consists of including not only the honey but also small portions of the chewy honeycomb. Because of Haiti's lack of pesticides, honeybee levels have stayed relatively stable for many years. This provides a unique market opportunity for interested agri-entrepreneurs.

The international honey market is one of the fastest growing markets. Major import markets are Australia, Japan, and China. The vast import is the $2.2B markets. If someone chooses to go that route, then Haiti's honey within the country is sufficiently in demand. And so, it could grow to a healthy-sized operation.

Business Concept

This opportunity doesn't take a particularly large swath of land. Bees are particularly capable of finding pollen across very large areas from their base. It's advantageous if one is looking to cultivate honey's particular flavors or textures. Consider exposure to certain flowers by planting those species near a hive.

A popular strategy for beehive entities is to lease out beehives, since these are exceptionally popular among various farms. After all, they're well-known for their pollination efficiency. Fees extracted from this service can be equally impactful to the bottom line because the honey sells itself. It's not exclusive to farms. In fact, urban areas and recreational parks occasionally request seasonal assistance from beehive firms to assist in floral bloom.

Niche Ideas:

1. Teaching beehive farming can be a big business.
2. Honeycombs make excellent wax. This can be used for a multiple applications which can be sold.
3. Honey can be processed into many different things, such as meads.
4. Wasp removal can be an incredibly intimidating act, particularly once a hive has grown to a critical mass. It can pay to become a hazardous bee removal expert.

Top Department and Policy Guidance

This concept is ideal for any provincial area in Haiti. Some provincial areas will have less competition than others. Thus, it will make your entry more ideal.

Action & Tips

1. Honey making is practiced informally. One can purchase a hive to get started from such a farmer at relatively affordable rates.
2. Despite Haiti's unique flavor properties, honey is still a relatively homogenous product. Marketing differentiates your product and is critical.

Success Stories

Miel D'Or - Daniella Bienaimé

Miel D'Or, a recent upstart company, incorporated in November 2016. It focuses on bottle marketing and sells Haitian honey, both across Haiti and around the world. For many years, Daniella was growing the brand part-time. Then, she decided to buckle down. She fully dedicated herself to the venture. Since then, she has seen significant growth in her business because of it. She sees an opportunity not in honey's consumption, but also in its potential. Honey can be used in for cosmetic applications, and she has recently announced those would arrive soon.

25. It Only Takes a Kitchen to Be a Leading Food Processing Business

Food processing combines two important national macroeconomic sectors. Both could potentially impact change. Agriculture and consumer products should both be considered. Processing food doesn't necessarily require large capital intensive. So, one can capitalize on cheap labor. Process foods boost capacity. When this is completed intently with export focus, a macro scale of growth can be impactful.

Food processing takes inputs from either Haiti or those foods being imported from abroad. Ultimately this restructure to a new output, distributing products domestically or abroad. Additives are added to the process. These prevent flavor loss, a loss of color, or ripeness by adding preservatives or a transformation to the food. This alone is added value. Due to the convenience, many foods consumed within communities may be presented to areas far away. How food processes is often as simple as seeing which foods are consumed within Haiti. All these foods benefit from at-scale production. Though it also effects unfamiliar foods to Haitians, many or all that could potentially transition to this market.

Packaging is a large portion of processed foods. Packaging preserves the food, while it also convinces the consumers to purchase the product. Appealing aspects of the packaging must differentiate between brands.

Business Concept

After an initial round of marketing tests, it's important to acquire capital. This assists with building an appropriate food processing manufacturing facility. Finding a niche is crucial. As such, more established food process operations exist in the country. These hold particularly strong market power as a result. Directly competing isn't possible. So, it's vital find products where you can be the first potential mover. Even when it's something that exists, innovating marketing and brand positioning can go the difference. Rather than simply stating that someone is selling "Confetti" Haitian Jam, position your production. Market it as an authentic organic french marmalade. Instead of oats, sell "All-Natural Muesli." Instead of sandwiches, sell "Italian-Direct Panni's."

The key is to get started, no matter the quantity of capital or financial resources which have been provided. If it means your food processing facility is your kitchen, so be it. Continue to reinvest revenue. Profit from this smaller operation's sales into better equipment. Finally, move to a proper facility.

Niche Ideas

1. High-end confetti's and syrups.
2. Peanut butter.
3. Hot & chili sauces
4. Ketchup (Haitian sweet Ketchup and 'Traditional' American style).

5. Traditional Haitian cookies (like 'bon-bon') with a unique twist.

6. Sausages (Very popular among the general population in Haiti)

7. Cornflakes.

8. Potato chips.

9. Traditional Haitian food that's shelved and cooked.

10. International food items which are popular amongst Haitians travelling/living abroad; however, be involved in making these foods available in Haiti. Given recent migration flows, consider Chilean foods as an example.

Top Department and Policy Guidance

Because this sector has plentiful opportunities for Haitians, building mature distribution networks becomes an advantage. Further, this sector is potentially lucrative by Haiti's middle- and upper-class during a growing economy. Because of products are being produced more frequently, they're much easier to preserve. Thus, in turn these products have longer shelf lives overall. These products will be suitable for Haitians who are short on time or income. Moreover, they're ideal for customers who take price and product convenience into consideration.

Action & Tips

1. Find examples of success stories from countries within the developing world. Implement these stories into your brand. Incorporate your own efforts into what other entrepreneurs have already shared about their journey.

2. As you research an appropriate move, ensure you have a small notepad and pen. Visit open-air markets, corner stores, groceries, and supermarkets. All these should have comparable price points for your chosen product. This additionally serves as a time review for what you'll find on the market. Ideally, this set's apart a product in terms of its quality, flavor, brand, etc. As a result, it clearly shows differentiation between one brand and another.

Success Story:

Myabel - Regine Theodat

Regine Theodat, a Haitian American attorney living an enviable life in the United States, responded to the January 12, 2010 earthquake. She put aside her US lifestyle to return to Haiti, where she contributed to Haiti's greatest need. Once the initial demands of humanitarian aid were met, an initiative to help foster job creation was launched. Myabel, a restaurant, began hiring locals and servicing local dishes. Awestruck patrons were moved by the innovative stylings of her drinks and main dish flavorings. All clamored for a better way of ordering them, either on-the-go or from home. So, she compiled a booming business. Mayabel sold prefabricated alcoholic cocktails. Haitian-inspired cooking and hot sauce lines were born.

She has seen consistent growth while selling across the United States and Haiti. Year-over-year customers have acclaimed her. Her products purchasable across many culinary boutiques in both countries. What differentiates her are her recipes. Her product names are evident. These include "Bwav," a hot coconut sauce using Haitian goat pepper; "Gede," a sweet, tangy sauce with a mango base; and "Nibo," an extremely hot sauce. It's an orange, cane, and lemongrass blend. Her products are uniquely branded and unified. Her export-oriented products are all winning strategies in the food processing industry.

26. Beverages: A Liquid Gold Opportunity

Beverages for this sector are divided into alcoholic and non-alcoholic beverages. This category's vastness includes juice, tea, soft drinks, coffee, chocolate, milk, and gaseous drinks. This might also include fruit and vegetable smoothies, blends, and cleanses. Alcoholic beverages include beer, wine and spirits, and cocktails.

Many alcoholic and non-alcoholic beverages can be made using popular native ingredients. These consist of Pitme, Blé, and Maize (in the form of Malts). It's possible to make beverages using cassava, plantains, and rice. Beverages can consist of a large variety of inputs, making this category vital for young entrepreneurs.

Business Concept

The path to success in beverages is knowing an abundance of people. Many past entrepreneurs have imported juice products or domestic distribution. Others explored the creation of newer brands, in which processing and distribution is domestically sourced. The second less traveled option is more difficult. Though it holds the long-term wealth, growth potential, and domestic impact. Distribution of wine and spirits is similar to a proven revenue-generating business. More potential resides in the growing, fermenting, processing, bottling, and distribution of Haitian-based alcohol.

Reduced capital likewise needs to include building a niche market, either through a specialty tea or coffee product. For example, there's a long tradition of mixing rum with coffee. Associating this mixture with other more modern flavors may be a winning combination. Selling to grocers, hotels, and specialty boutiques is a great way to get started. Then, transition to online sales after completing an initial on-the-ground testing period.

Street sugar cane sellers is a common site. These individuals will cut you a large sugar cane stock into hand-sized portions, that you can then eat. Some products can press the juice out of the cane into a bottle of apple juice. Crafting a business allowing these vendors access to a portable version of this juicing machine is beneficial.

Niche Ideas

1. Producing affordable, non-perishable fortified drinks for children and the elderly. This isn't just a marketing ploy but can yield tangible and economic market rents.
2. Given how culturally ubiquitous Cremas is, it's not a particularly novel idea. Still, it's not been dominated by a single firm. There's still a need for an entrepreneur to take this popular alcoholic eggnog drink to an international mainstream audience.

Top Department & Policy Guidance

The opportunities in beverage can be implemented anywhere in Haiti. Still, the best success will occur where there're higher populations. Higher densities of people often have an increased number of sales. As a result, there's a higher return on marketing.

Action & Tips

Getting your foothold into distribution is important whenever you're contacting current beverage companies. They've programs available that provide discounts to bulk orders. Thus, there's quick entry into this sector.

Success Story

Rhum Choucoune - Stéphan Lainé

Rhum Choucoune, founded by Stéphan Lainé, is an upstart company. It's a young company, focusing on Haitian rum. Slowly it's been making headway with its "Klerein" inspired spiced rum. All the rum is distilled, packaged, and distributed across Haiti. The rum is mixed with unique flavors such as tamarind, cinnamon, ginger, saffron, pineapple, and other rum flavors. The firm also creates cocktails which blends with its rum. Fresh ingredients are locally sourced from suppliers. "Choucoune," a Haitian rum produced by Rhum Choucoune, originated from many who consider Haiti's Shakespeare: Oswald Durant and one of his most beloved poems. This poem, known by the same name, celebrates the beauty of the Haitian black woman. It's a not-so-subtle reference to one of Haiti's beloved poems.

27. Restaurants & Fooderies Are Among the Most Proven Economic Revenue Generators

Even with Haiti's hamstrung GDP, restaurants remain a steady cash cow. This simplifies the process, should any entrepreneur desire to pursue it. "Bar & restos" defines these sorts of establishments. These places have a wealth of food variety. It's further an enjoyable place to converse with friends. Traditional Haitian meals include rice, spaghetti, Mais moulin, pitme, with some meat or legume on the side. When they go out to eat, Haitian staple foods might be wings, burgers, or pizza. Asian specialty cuisine has shown significant success on the island as well.

Outside of traditional brick-and-mortar sit down restaurants, casual bar & restos have become alternatives for Haitians. Food trucks are still relatively unexplored in Haiti. Although, these serve as a relatively low cost & low barrier of entry. Only limited restaurants deliver. Doing so can provide a meaningful way to differentiate from other restaurants, despite the food's specialty. Only providing delivery is another low-cost option. In this case, social media is used to broadcast daily offerings. Then, the food is delivered directly to consumers.

The most glaring opportunity relates to there being very few franchised restaurants in Haiti. In fact, there're neither domestic nor international franchised Haitian-based restaurants. Franchises aren't prohibited legally, as is evident in brands like Dominoes in Haiti. It only has two Port-Au-Prince locations. However, many potential franchises that could locate in the country - anything from

McDonald's, KFC, Subway, Starbucks, etc. - have still not expanded into the market. There remains a reputational elevation that the outside world brings with them in most countries. In this sense, Haiti is no different. Tapping into the instant name recognition of which these brands provide drives those unableness to travel abroad. Moreover, those who've traveled abroad can reconnect with past experiences to both patrons.

There also is a lack of domestic restaurant chains. Companies with more than a single location focusing on quick and inexpensive consumables, like Epi D'or & Point Chaud, are few and far between. Given the preferential popularity of Haitians from all economic sects wanting fast on-the-go food, there remains a growth opportunity. It makes room for those looking to implement this idea as well.

Business Concepts

The paths to entering this sector are numerous, with or without going the most expensive route and starting a brick-and-mortar restaurant.

1. Differentiation is key! Provide a specialty in high demand. Alternatively, it can be a high-demand but low quality product.
2. Start with a franchise in mind. Either build out a local domestic chain or successfully become the owner of an imported international brand. Provide Haitians access to brands without having to leave Haiti. This is a social and economic benefit.

3. Food truck and delivery only businesses provide the lowest entry barrier. Likewise, these are applicable anywhere within Haiti.

4. Standing out with exceptional customer service provides loyal, appreciative patronage, and high prices. These are more justifiable due an inconsistency of service that's comparable across Haiti.

Niche Ideas

1. As mentioned, Chinese and Asian food has established popularity. It still has room to grow further. Despite its popularity, sushi is underrepresented. Sushi restaurants are located within Petionville.

2. The vegan movement has yet to arrive in Haiti, since there aren't eateries focused strictly on non-meat meal options or its alternatives. A first-mover advantage awaits the first two options, providing the market with this additional option.

3. As in developed countries, healthy food options made available to consumers allows restaurateurs to extract higher rents through higher prices. Haiti is new and different. Haitians market around innovative, tasty, and hearty salads, sandwiches, and soup combos. All these win over searching for a discerning crowd.

Top Departments & Policy Guidance

Restaurants are ubiquitous. Success, therefore, can happen anywhere. When avant-garde restaurants are more specialized, they've a greater chance of success. Consequently, more customers will dine at Port-Au-Prince and Cap Haitian restaurants as a result.

Action & Tips

1. It's important to frequent Haiti's most populous eateries in Haiti. These extend from higher-end places often visited by tourists to traditional upper-class eateries in the country. Most eateries are pay-and-go, and depend upon volume places like Epi D'or. By understanding the design, interior, menu offering, and price points, you'll grasp how to provide substantial customer service experiences. This is a crucial part of the brand's differentiation and success.

2. The welcoming and modern interior shouldn't break the bank, especially if local talent and artisans are incorporated in its design.

3. Understand that this industry's competitive. Don't rest on your laurels, even during your early success. Continual innovation is key to longevity.

Success Story

Chicken Fiesta

After two Haitian American friends returned to Haiti, they founded Chicken Fiesta - a specialty Asian-fusion chicken restaurant. It's grown into a vital dining stop in the Petionville area. Locals and visiting foreigners both enjoy its cuisine. Chicken Fiesta stands out, not only because of their signature three-story yellow building but also because of its interesting modern twists. They add their own style to Asian dishes and recipes. You can't only get chicken fried rice, for example but chicken wing with uncommon combinations. The chicken wings may be flavored with sweet ginger zest, jerk, and/or spicy garlic. Moreover, they've focused on growing their farming operation to include local cooperatives. This ensures that they can provide customers food which has the locally-based ingredients from Haiti. Though there has been a recent uptick in Petionville's Asian restaurants, Chicken Fiesta continues to enjoy a loyal customer base. Many, if not all of their customers, have come to them for years. They routinely return to enjoy their favorite menu items and the new updated menu items appearing monthly. Their restaurant and its success model how a business can succeed.

Pot'Iwa Pizza - Rock Andre & Jude Valliant

Pot'lwa Pizza was founded by two childhood friends - one from southern Haiti and another from Northern Haiti. The pizzeria's name is a combination of both founders' regional areas in Haiti, specifically where they were born. Having been in business for over five years, they've built a resilient business. It's overcome rocky economic and political times. Pot'lwa Pizza prices their pizza pie offerings for locals more than their Petionville restaurant neighbors. In this sense, other local pizza restaurants price their menu items for tourists and ex-pats. Pot'lwa Pizza was the first pizza place to specialize in combining distinctly Haitian delicacies. These include Lambi and Aransol flavored pizzas. Pot'Iwa pizza plans to expand across Haiti. Additionally, they've signed a lease for a Miami, Florida location. Lastly, they feel as if there's a strong market for their unique Haitian style pies. So, you can soon expect a pizza shop in a local US town near you.

28. Produce and Sell Animal Feed to Fatten Your Wallet

A demand for meat causes the need to rise, bringing about an increase in how much meat in grown and consumed by customers. Each type of meat consists of cattle, goats, pork, chicken, or fish. All have their preferred type of feed, and each provides a unique type of revenue. Soybeans is a particular favorite for feed consumption; however, this isn't grown in bulk quantities in Haiti. Other alternatives include maize, cassava, and sorghum.

Sixty percent of the cost of meat production is spent on feed, which represents a tremendous opportunity for a feed seller. The domestic livestock and meat industry's growth is precisely correlated with its feed industry. It's possible to build a successful entity focused on a crop's export. That's if the case can be made that the crop is better in nutrients, quality, or cost. The destination's alternative must be positioned to replace the previous crop.

Business Concept

As with many of the proposed ideas here, it's viable to build in distribution around importing the animal feed. Greater long-term wealth exists by mastering the production process. In this way, it allow one to produce an equal or better-quality product at an equal or lower price.

The type of feed on which you focus depends on the land to which you have access. Those grown in the country's higher mountainous area differentiate from the fertile valleys of Artibonite, Aux Cayes, and

Grand'anse. It's advisable to utilize native crops. These have more accessible seeds. As a result, crops will be most attuned to that area's climate. Being aware of who the end client is essential. The needs, quantity, quality, and delivery processes will be different for a small cattle farmer, as opposed to a massive commercial meat processing operation. Additionally, this stage of an animal's life requires important considerations. Solvability, the density of certain nutrients, and daily serve quantity should all be taken into consideration. All the extra revenue extracting components and chances lead to extra profits.

Niche Ideas

As the market continues to expand in Haiti, consider animal feed for fish. Chicken farms, particularly those that aid with outputting eggs, is another option. Pet food is another considerable niche. Those with means in Haiti prefer to provide their pets and guard animals choice food options. And so, they pay premium prices for quality products.

Top Department and Policy Guidance

There's a large deficiency in animal feed for all in Haiti. Thus, production taking place anywhere will be successful. Nevertheless, stay attune to an area's cattle demand, and remain sensitive to prices.

Action & Tips

1. Speak with livestock owners and cooperatives. Interview them about their needs and how they currently obtain their feed. See

how you can improve their quality of life, because this will differentiate your product.

2. As always, start with what you have. Use equipment you can source locally. Find out where you can import machinery to drive large productivity gains. But still, be cognitive to cost.

3. Though it's advisable to use local crops, there may be crops from countries with similar climates to Haiti. Your particular farm area may be conducive within Haiti if the feed can be appropriately marketed and/or competitive in price.

4. Utilize Madame Saras that trade in meat for their contacts and sources. They'll lead you to opportunities for your product. They buy from meat sellers, who may not be landholders but do hold extensive holdings of roaming livestock. Even these traveling grazers purchase feed depending on the stage of some of their stock's lifecycle.

29. Food Making Products - Make the Stuff That Makes the Food!

It's hard to talk about food topics without discussing that which makes food consumption possible. Pots, pans, plates, cups, and silverware all are in demand. These items have a history or artisan craft within Haiti. Pots, in particular, have a rich Haitian history. Cast out of aluminum, these are absolute staples of any Haitian household. Pots are locally molded and refined, and are constructed with non-stick properties to even out heat while cooking.

Outside of crafting and trading these sorts of material, portable stoves and stovetops are essential item Haitians purchase with considerable demand. Stoves and stovetops are used either for home cooking or merchants cooking street food. These run mostly on cheap charcoal, and so the market for them is broad. More efficient versions are available. These can be purchased abroad. They can be imported and sold. Since these stoves require less charcoal and longer burns, there's an increased demand.

Business Concept

First and foremost are more professional-grade crafting of food-making products. Leverage the artisan sector and incorporate them into a process. Of course, the alternative is to purchase better pots from abroad, reselling them domestically. Even if the pots and pans are slightly more expensive than those on the market, they still add more functionality and provide better use of charcoal. There's even a cost alternative to charcoal that should be considered.

Haitian cast aluminum pots are so well-regarded throughout Haiti; however, this isn't the case in the Caribbean and other places. Haitians have gone to reside in these places. In turn, they've introduced a business. A business concerning the sale of cast aluminum pots could be formed around the pots' purchase, export, and resale. There's a real untapped opportunity in this niche when it's combined with other artisan food-making products, like mortar and pestle that's used for spice grinding.

Niche Ideas:

- Portable stoves for street vendors, with added functionality or usability.
- Retail or depot that specializes in kitchenware.
- Non-electric kitchen tools for staple recipes (i.e., food mill, wooden plantain smasher).

Top Department and Policy Guidance

Demand can be produced anywhere within Haiti, just as much as it can exist everywhere. Having this said, there're incredible opportunities to export artisan iterations across the world.

Action & Tips

1. Anywhere where there's a Haitian population. Food-making products will have a market.

2. Distribution of your products doesn't need to be difficult. Tap into the informal market. Provide your products at wholesale prices to quincaillerie (hardware) depots and Madame Saras.

30. Seed growing: The First Kink of the Agricultural Supply Chain

Seeds' cultivation and sale to farmers is often overlooked, but it's potentially a lucrative endeavor. Very often Haitian farmer seasons are put at risk, because of an inability to find purchasable, high-quality seeds that are affordable. Only recently has the state opened up seed operations to support agriculture. Still, they're unable to meet a fraction of the demand because they're vastly underfunded and have low productivity. Further, they're located too far from where farmers reside. Therefore, they haven't an easy way to provide delivery. View these deficiencies as opportunities. Their solutions can be incorporated into a business model.

One immediately thinks it's a requirement to have a large amount of land for seed production. Though, that may not necessarily be the case. Because the prize is the seed and not the end product, many plants begin seed germination very early in its growth. This allows for high plot turnover and seed harvesting. It requires very little acreage used. Furthermore, many industrial seed operations are able to use stacked agriculture growth practices, which overall require less land.

Business concept

Consider selling popular and established staple seedlings like maize, sorghum, millet, and blé. But also, give thought to variants that are enhanced to better adapted to some of Haiti's extreme climate. This is especially true of the climate exacerbated in recent times by climate change. While farmers are an obvious unignorable market, don't overlook retail gardeners or those planting smaller urban projects.

Other business opportunities can include providing agronomy courses and certifications at your facility. This not only provides additional income but helps increase your market. Each person who completes the course will purchase seeds from you. Moreover, partner with travel and/or NGOs. This may allow your facility to become an eco-tourist venue.

Niche Ideas

- Sell niched and uncommon varieties that may not be found in Haiti.
- Sell seeds to industrial/pharmaceuticals for their oils and other properties.
- Create specialty crops that merge different popular strands, thereby providing a unique and differentiated market.

Top Department and Policy Guidance

The state has only recently entered this market. What they call "forest propagation" facilities is focused on facilitating reforestation initiative. Also, it offers local farmers more affordable seed sources. These facilities can be found in Les Cayes, Fond-des-Negres, Malfranic (Grand'Anse) and Port-de-Paix. But these facilities only offer a small fraction of what the domestic market requires. Thus, more than possible. In short, setting up shop in similar provincial regions isn't out of the question.

Action & Tips

1. Consider providing a platform online, thereby allowing consumers to purchase from a distance. They can access your website from anywhere in Haiti. Arrangements can be made for them to either pick an item, or have it shipped to the nearest community center. That's, if direct drop off isn't possible.
2. Provide farmers sample packs for free or for a small cost. Therefore, they can validate the crop's potential.

31. What Goes into Agriculture as Inputs Needs to Come From Somewhere . Provide them.

An ever-growing agricultural sector in Haiti is agricultural inputs. Fertilizers and crop chemicals - such as pesticides, fungicides, and herbicides - are included within this. These inputs are important, because they improve a farmland's soil productivity. When significantly lacking ingredients are first obtained, nutrients that are still needed can grow if fertilizer if applied to the crops. Therefore, this can save years of rehabilitation time. Meanwhile, chemicals protect stock and reduce loss.

For reasons concerning a material's cost and availability, Haiti has been an organic farming environment. Non-composite Methods and materials are used in essence and are of natural origin. The developed world's preference for agriculture products consists of cultivating and utilizing eco-friendly fertilizers, pesticides, and herbicides. Ultimately, this puts Haiti at an advantage.

Because of historic poor soil management practices, along with a rainy and drought season adding considerable stress to vegetation even in the best of conditions, there's a large demand for agricultural inputs in the cultivation process. After seed purchases, fertilizer is farmers' largest significant expenditure in Haiti, both large and small.

Business Concept

Taking advantage of this opportunity means to find fertilizer sources. These may be sourced locally or imported, but then they can be processed and turned into fertilizer. Metro areas produce a lot of organic trash, and not all of it gets collected. One method, therefore, is an operation that builds out infrastructure of this organic waste collection, thereby souring its material. Additional ideas include partnering with any area manufacturer. They should produce organic, residual material. Alternatively, contact a cattle / livestock association to purchase manure from their properties.

Niche Idea

1. Human waste is a nitrogen-rich source of base compounds and bacteria. Organize a system of outhouses, placing it throughout public areas such as open-air markets and parks. Outhouses are useful anywhere that human waste is collected. Research efficient processes that quickly dehydrates the waste, making it easier and more sanitary for transport. A careful hygienic process that removes potential harmful pathogens is vital to turning this waste into manure, which then becomes profitable.

2. Ensure your process limits using commercial grade chemicalization of manufactured agricultural inputs. The world is rapidly moving towards organic products and processes. So, mastering production without artificial components will reap benefits over the long-run.

Top Department and Policy Guidance

The demand exists everywhere across Haiti; so, for this reason, it can exist and be produced anywhere as well.

Action & Tips

1. Work with farmers to understand their current practices. Grasp how their processes relate to fertilization and pest control. Not only can you tweak your product its realistic delivery for the most common processes, but they may teach you important alternatives which can be incorporated.

2. Agricultural inputs, as well as and their manufacturing and distribution processes used throughout developing countries, should be researched. Incorporated these into your efforts.

3. Work closely with agricultural associations. Sell your agricultural input in bulk and scale.

32. One Word Says It All: Coffee

Few in-demands tropical agricultural products have been sold so ubiquitously or universally as coffee. In Haiti, coffee has been an integral part of the economy since it was imported by the French for production. Haiti's coffee industry peaked in production and has been in fluctuation since its inception. Today, it remains one of the opportunities holding a vast production upside.

More than 200,000 families grow coffee in Haiti. Some families grow coffee individually, while others grow coffee through cooperatives. Haitian coffee sells to wayward international markets such as Ireland, Italy, and Japan with a mature export interface. The neighboring nation, Dominican Republic, remains Haiti's biggest coffee recipient. The truth is, Haitians themselves have an insatiable appetite for coffee. The greater majority of coffee that's produced within the country, the greater amount that gets consumed locally.

Further, value-added processes can be done to raw coffee beans. For instance, coffee beans can be roasted them in different ways. This adds as much as four to five times the sales price. When the coffee bean isn't being modified for wholesale, a coffee distributor can enter the retail space. Here they can and provide hip, trendy, and relaxing places to consume a cup of coffee with a variety of flavors and mixes.

Business Concept

Coffee genuinely sells itself. However, opportunities exist toward alleviating production constraints within Haiti. This includes providing technical assistance, whether it's to help farmers or cooperatives. Moreover, sell modern equipment that makes the collecting, sorting, and pre-processing of coffee beans easier. This further aids in pest and disease control, while improving soil resilience. A business can either focus on one of these difficulties or all of them.

One needs to also think innovatively. How can a cup of Haitian coffee be delivered to the Haitian retail market? "Coffee carts" have already been a part of Haiti's independent market ecosystem. In this way, small vendors push a cart that sells coffee in public areas. Customers purchase coffee at low prices. This can be scaled and franchised for wider use in Haiti.

Niche Idea

Haiti lacks a premium domestic and outward facing retail roast operation. So, be one of the first. The value-added pricing is substantial, for it provides a quick differentiation to one's brand. Reinvest in supply chain control, to drive long-term growth.

Top Department & Policy Guidance

Coffee farming, processing, and sales of coffee (whether it's wholesale or retail) can occur anywhere within Haiti.

Action & Tips

1. Many small coffee brands already exist in Haiti. Before entering the market with your offering, see what's being offered. Interview producers. Create an exact and precise niche early on.

2. You don't need to enter this market as a competitor. Instead, consider how you can complement the industry. Aid segments across the value chain, producing more. Also, manufacture a higher-grade coffee product.

Success Story

HaitiCoffee.Com

Mathias Medina, Dr. Myriam Kaplan-Pasternak, Yves Gourdet, and David Pierre-Louis founded HaitiCoffee.com. Together they collaborated to improving Haitian coffee producers' opportunities in two ways. The first avenue involved working closely in a farmer-to-farmer initiative. In essence, they would assess cooperatives, train members on enterprise strategies and offer financial planning. The goal of knowledge transfer was intended to improve the farmers' best practices and increase productivity. This had been a significant shortcoming of Haiti's smallest producer that had dominated the market.

The second involved capitalizing on this increased productivity. By directly facilitating these producers' access to the international market, they were able to purchase and resell their coffee in the global market as distributors themselves. Within their first year, they managed to etch out a small profit. Meanwhile, they imported 11,000 pounds of coffee. Since then, they've annually impacted 3,000 Haitian farm families. Now, that's a success story.

Singing Rooster - Molly Nicaise & Christophe Nicaise

Though registered as a not-for-profit, Singing Rooster is an important success story. As a business, they've infused commercial sustainability with their mission. Since 2009, they've provided Haitian families a way to support themselves. Essentially, Singing Rooster taught Haitians to earn steady and increasing income. By doing this, they work with local farmers to improve coffee bean production practices. They purchase their yields, and resale them internationally. They were one of the first producers that offered Haitian readily available coffee on Amazon. Likewise, they've streamlined their model and have added products to their brand. In the recent years, these include chocolate bars and artwork.

33. Cocoa - The Heart and Soul of Chocolate ... and the Multi-Billion-Dollar Market Consuming It

Haitian local consumables are Haitian-produced and distinguishable. They further match the quality expectations and an international demand. And so, don't look any further than Haitian 'Cacao,' aka coca. We know coca as its most common by-product: chocolate! Haiti has been producing coca for over 500 years. It's been infused with strains of connoisseurs worldwide. In fact, it produces over a couple of tons of chocolate each year. But this coca's production is equally unique. Haitian 'Chokola' is melded with cinnamon, vanilla, and nutmeg. Even in its most concentrated form, it tastes naturally sweet as opposed to a bitter taste that's commonplace elsewhere.

Nearly ninety percent of the world's cocoa is produced on small family farms. Haitian farms are no exception, with most cocoa being produced on less than an hectare. What's holding back a massive insurgency in this domain is actually the agriculture sector, which was discussed within this broader food segment. Immediate entrepreneurial opportunities, therefore, could alleviate those conditions.

Business Concept

The yields of some trees, otherwise known as "super trees," are better than others. Specializing in planting and selling these coca trees can be lucrative. These super trees produce more coca at quicker turnaround times, so, the demand for them is high. Conversely, at their early stages of growth, these trees take a specialized and nutrient-dense soil environment. But farmers may not provide this type of soil. So, become that farmer's supplier, or start a farm that specializes in producing coca from these trees.

There's a large market for providing solutions, that moves past getting into the supply chain concept through trees. Consider entering the value stream later. Instead, aid with the value-added process and produce chocolate. This means fermenting and processing cocoa beans. Transform them into chocolate, chocolate bars, and pralines. Having the capacity to do all this makes the most sense under your brand. It further denotes where a vertically integrates and better capitalizes on an economic scale.

Niche Idea

Secondary chocolate uses that may include proper domestic production. This includes:

1. Canned chocolate milk beverages, that're fortified with energy boosters and vitamins.
2. Chocolate ice cream.
3. Gourmet candies.
4. Protein bars.
5. Syrups.

Top Department & Policy Guidance

Coca farming and Haiti's limited processing of chocolate are concentrated across the northern and northeast areas. Specifically, this surrounds the township of Limonade near Cap Haitien.

Action & Tips

1. Success requires that you work closely with the farmers and associations. They'll source your coca. Moreover, understand their sore spots. Figure out how to alleviate them through training and capacity building.
2. Consider grafting as a low-cost strategy. Ultimately, this will be improving the output of older, less predictive trees.
3. Look into getting your operation certified. Three certifiers globally - UTZ, Rainforest Alliance and Fairtrade International - make this possible.

Success Story

Askanya Chocolates

Founded in 2015, this growing juggernaut of the Haitian chocolate industry was started by Corinne Joachim-Sanon. She's a young former graduate from the University of Michigan, as well as a Wharton alumna. Corrine Joachim-Sanon and her husband decided they wanted more than just an American salary and a good way of life. They wanted to make an impactful presence in Haiti. Since Corinne's family came from the cocoa-rich area of Ouanaminthe, which is in the most northeastern corner of Haiti, they began a small operation where they purchased coca from farmers. Then, they transformed it into chocolate bars and sold it to America. That small operation now sells to over thirty locations in the USA, Canada, and Haiti.

Their operation's impact is vital to share. Three thousand families who farm coca have a predictable and dependable buyer purchasing their products annually. In turn, these farmers transfer over $100,000USD to these providers. It helps that Corinne's company produces several flavors, all of which capture different international preferences. This includes milk chocolate, dark chocolate, extra dark chocolate, and Rapadou (a unique Haitian flavor that uses unrefined Haitian whole cane sugar). Also, she sells differently sized chocolate. She sells a regular two-ounce-bar, a-half-ounce-bar, and a bite-size bar. In addition, she sells gift sets that align with various seasons. Its multiple sizes and tastes well-position Askanya Chocolates to continue its international domination of Haiti's coca and chocolate market.

34. Leather: The Important Base Mass Input Considered by Too Few

Global demand for leather extends worldwide. Its demand is much greater than demands for meat, coffee, or rice. It's incredible that such an opportunity exists. Generally, it's overlooked in part of the local livestock industry, where the skin is too often discarded. Haiti's most common hide source might be a goat, cattle, horse, or swine.

Leather is appealing, because it's been traded for centuries. It's used to make shoes, belts, bags, gloves, jackets, and fashion accessories - to name a few. It's doubtful that there'll remain a strong and steady demand for animal hides. Haiti doesn't have a formal hide collection supply chain apparatus; however, an entrepreneur can still reap its riches.

Business Concept

Despite the high demand, leather material is often overlooked. In this case, an entrepreneur benefits at a source cost relatively lower than the hide's value. Furthermore, depending on how that leather is combined with textile-sourced material imported from the US, the combined post-produced item could qualify under the HOPE Act. This is the case for any reduced imports and procedural tariffs coming into the United States.

Start a leather harvesting process where transporters are paid a percentage for the quantity and quality of hiding that's being provided to your facility. Then, transform the hide into leather at your facility.

Another opportunity involves being contracted to deliver leather-produced dependents for larger manufactured products. Producing leather material directly or assembling them for immediate wholesale is another viable option.

A genuine competitive leather production company requires a sizable investment. This involves everything from the land, building, machinery, and staff. Don't let that discourage you. You can also start a shoe or attire accessory production with limited resources from a small workshop on your property with a shoestring budget.

Niche Ideas

1. Quality accessories such as belts, bags, wallets, and shoes.
2. Furniture: chairs or sofas.
3. Notebook leather covers.

Top Department & Policy Guidance

As non-centralized meat production occurs throughout Haiti, it's possible to set up a facility almost anywhere. Such an operation must occur at a reasonable distance. Scaling one's operation will require creating a network of transporters or delivery hubs where there're components.

Action & Tips

1. Wherever you find a meat seller, particularly those on the street, it's a good idea to speak with that individual. Discern their

source. They can provide a local source who can enhance your supply.

2. Don't be shy with grocery chains. Speak similarly with the grocery owner, while trying to obtain their supplier's location and contact information. It may take a few extra steps, however, because they sometimes acquire their food from meat distributors. Though given their usual increased volume, they may serve as valuable supplier contacts.

Success Story

Hawtan Leather LLC / Cuir Hawtan SA

Originally founded shortly after WWI in Massachusetts, Hawtan Leather LLC expanded their leather sourcing. Then, they migrated their tanning operation to the Caribbean, where Haiti became their hub in 1970. Their tannery is located in Carrefour, just outside of Port-Au-Prince. It's grown into the largest tannery in Haiti, but it's also the largest in all of the Caribbean. It's able to produce 700,000 square feed of custom and naked leather per month. Moreover, it employs over 150 people. Hawtan Leather LLC ships their leather to the United States, where it's distributed to leather manufacturers across North America, Europe, and Asia.

The firm acquires animal hides from all over Haiti and the Caribbean islands. It's distributed through its mature network of livestock owners and small family butcheries. Through this process, hides inclusive of goats, cows, calves, and sheep are all collected. Buyers appreciate this diverse sourcing of leather, since it differentiates Hawtan leather from their competitors. Because of this, they can provide a variety of colors and textures. They then transform their leather into gloves, shoe soles, handbags, wallets, shoes, sandals, and other leather accessories.

Personal Care

"Taking care of myself doesn't mean 'me first.' It means 'me too."

— I..R. Knost

A Haitian man or woman's hygiene largely constitutes proper cultural norms. Likewise, it's prioritized below someone's food and health. The personal care industry provides consumer products, which provide baseline hygiene. Meanwhile, men and women can personify their appearance and beauty.

Though this is true for rich and poor people alike, each economic segment has uses. These segments are disposable in this domain and can easily be extracted if they're taken advantage of by individuals. Hygiene includes body wash, skin cream, perfumes, and colognes, as well as teeth & whitening. The necessity of this sector's products assures lucrative returns for its items and gives it higher potentialities - not only in theory but also by citable examples.

In this section, we'll dive into popular personal care products & in-demand Haitian services. Then, we'll look into in-demand Haitian services from around the world in which Haitians have helped to produce.

35. Soaps and Detergents - Tap into In-Demand Products That're as Popular as Water and Oxygen

A day without soap is genuinely unimaginable. Maybe someone is washing their hands or their body; washing the dishes, the floor, or the car; or they're washing the laundry. In any case, it'll require a liquid solvent to aid the effort. A soap's properties are important. A customer's income class, doesn't matter; nor does the soap's purpose, concentration, smell, or the quality of its package.

Haitians are incredibly clean people culturally. In fact, they often shower two to three times per day. Likewise, they clean their household and office with water and soap daily. Haiti's population of eleven million all have different uses for soap. And so, there's a massive soap market throughout Haiti. As Haiti experiences economic growth, soap sales will be in high demand and yield high returns.

Business Concept

There're dozens of ways to create soap. Because of this, soap making and its adjustable components help formulate a business's niche. Once this is established, a business can get underway and eventually expand. This allows the flexibility to start an operation, even if it takes place at someone's home on a bootstrapped budget. However, this only limits a brand's trajectory, leaving their marketing creation capacity and imagination limitless. Integrate new media, packaging, and competitive pricing to additionally ensure your brand stands out.

Niche Idea

1. Consider various soap and detergent brands, specifically those focusing on sensitive skin. These might include products for babies or for the elderly.

2. Produce mini-sized and appropriately packaged soaps. Normally these soaps are sold to travel industry venues - hotels, BNBs, and restaurants. Unit quantities will be more concise, making it easier for entities to be purchased in larger orders. All in all, it makes it possible to reap massive profits by volume.

Success Story

Anacaona - Laure Bottnelli

Founder of Anacaona, Laure Bottinelli, became inspired by soap-recycling operations. So, she opened a Haitian-owned soap-recycling enterprise in 2016. Twenty-five hotels got aboard right away, both across Port-au-Prince and Jacmel. Her enterprise takes worn out soap and returns with reconditioned soaps, specifically for employees and staff wanting to purchase soap for home usages. These employees and staff can purchase the soaps at deeply discounted rates. The reconditioning process involves full sanitization. It's combined natural Haitian products and packaged in biodegradable paper altogether.

Now, Anacaona has partnerships with hotels across the country. They also ship internationally to France. Soap combinations include Haitian Citirius, Haitian Passion Fruit, and Haitian Aloe Vera &

Amyris. The enterprise remains a socially initiative-based business, while it keeps an eye on the coming years.

Huileries Haitiennes (HUHSA)

HUHSA owns the only powdered detergent plant in Haiti. It produces laundry products varying in sizes, shapes, fragrances, and purposes. All their products are shipped domestically across Haiti. From its humble production beginnings in 1981, they've grown to become Haiti's largest domestic bath soap manufacturer. In the process, they've produced tons of bars of soap for sale. These are available in Haitian retail stores. These brands include Kim, Puritex, and Branda.

36. The Tissue Issue: The Opportunity Existing with Toilet Paper and Toiletries

Toilet paper and toiletries are necessary products within the personal hygiene category. So, it's essential to discuss opportunities that exist within this category. Haitians have access to toilet paper and use it. This extends far beyond images of water, leaves, wastepaper, and earth being used in the Haitian provinces. In regard to population density, we see significant demand for toilet paper in small and large metro areas. This means that there's a market demand into the millions.

Other hygiene products that can be made within Haiti. Variants of traditionally sourced materials and processes include toothpaste, shampoos, face wash, lip balm, and deodorants. For example, a unique face wash bar uses carrot as a fundamental ingredient. Thus, it's popular in Haiti.

Business Concept

The startup cost for this industrial / manufacturing business ranges from $15,000 to millions of dollars. Then, there're the raw inputs which create the toiletry output. However, the production process, packaging, and distribution are relatively straightforward. One's ultimate potential depends on the ability to build a brand, as well as an effective marketing strategy.

Niche ideas

1. High-end Haitian hotels, spas, and resorts all use luxury toiletries. In fact, these are sold directly to upper-class Haitians.

2. Mini-sized toiletries are sold in smaller quantities, and consequently, they cost less per package. Although, the price per unit would be higher. As such, there would be more overall soap available. In turn, this becomes affordable to Haiti's lower-income buyers. Leverage Haiti's large network of Madame Sara's. They sold items in this exact batch quantity.

3. Consider specialized sanitized towelettes. These can disinfect hands, a person's face, and items that have been touched. The towelettes can be sold at an affordable cost.

4. Moisturizers infused with natural forms of mosquito repellent, like lime extract, may be popular - particularly for infants. Parents are always searching for safe skin products. These types of products protect their child's vulnerable immune system when they get a mosquito-based infection.

Top Department

The competition will most be felt in larger departments. Such items are already imported in large quantities. The best strategy is to focus on smaller towns, because options are limited where the population is smaller. Once your business is established and you've solidified your reputation, advance into the cities to a more effective strategy.

Action & Tips

Perform market research to discover what already exists. See how different demographics are getting access to what they need. Moreover, research what brands are the most popular. Why are they so well-known? Lastly, position your product as an improvement or wholly opposite.

Success Story

Glory Industries - Myrtha Vilbon

Myrtha Vilbon, a serial entrepreneur from a family of entrepreneurs, ran a boutique confectionery store. Then, she became a distributor of a Dutch milk brand. Her ability to spot opportunity made it easy to identify and jump into this Haitian market. Through a grant from USAID and substantially more from private donors, she was able to launch the venture with over a million in starting capital.

Her labels include' Joy,' 'Glory,' 'TouTou NI,' and five other branded products. All her products have different purposes and market segments in mind. This ensures that all Haitians' needs are met. She even leverages Madame Sara and their extensive informal network. By doing this, she's able to sell her smallest portion packs. These get some of the most desperate urban and remote communities in Haiti.

Myrtha's factory staff has over 100 employees. Seventy percent of the factory workers have since announced an expansion into new facilities. As a result, the future is looking up for Glory Industries.

37. Skin & Hair Products Leads to Fortunes - in Haiti & Abroad.

Given wealth in creatin within this niche, exploring how to create a similar success story in Haiti is only natural. Skin and hair products are consistent and voluminous expenditures, next after clothing for women. But customers aren't stereotyped in this segment. In particular, hair care is important for both males and females. The unique qualities of black hair, both its texture and nature, make it particularly useful for products to protect and nourish it. Common purchases include hair relaxers, conditioners, sprays, gels, shampoos, hair moisturizers, and oils.

Skincare products include shampoo, lotions, gels, creams, relaxers, moisturizers, exfoliates, cleansers, and more. Each has a unique purpose. The total inventory that someone purchases is only limited by their financial means. Haitian consumers are used to utilizing a large range of products. These helps alleviate things such as dryness, breakouts, skin sensitivity, and skin infections. It can be as simple as a desire to add a pleasant aroma to one's presence.

Business Concept

Develop and successfully market a Haitian hair and skin product. Utilize native in-country elements and ingredients. Though Haiti is inundated with skin and hair care products being imported from abroad, many are usually of poorer grade. They're additionally costly, and not particularly attuned for the realities of Haiti's black demographic. Further, it's possible to etch out a product niche, to sell the product abroad. So, use native Haitian products in foreign markets with an appropriate and attuned marketing strategy for that home market. In particular, organic, and farmed or cultivated material is fact-of-land in Haiti.

Niche Ideas

1. Pop-ups in-country and abroad. Develop treatments using your brand and products.
2. Organic products.
3. Baby products.
4. Mini portions for reports, spas, hotels.

Top Departments & Policy Guidance

When starting with a domestic audience in mind, look outside of the cities and the provinces. Here the competition for imports is slightly reduced. If the goal is to get into the international market, consider locating near large export hubs. These are located in Port-Au-Prince and Cap Haitien.

Success Story

Kreyol Essence - Yves Car Momperousse and Stéphane Jean-Baptiste

Haitian Americans Yves Car and Stéphane founded Kreyol Essence in 2013. Their company produces and sells natural hair, along with skin and aromatherapy products . They founded Kreyol Essence after having poor experiences with hair treatment processes and products in America. The goal was to provide more widespread access to hard-to-find black castor oil (more commonly known as "Lwil Maskriti," in native Haitian creole). The oil is a Haitian near-miracle product. For centuries, it's been used for Haitians' health, and maintenance of their hair and skin.

The company is based out of Fontamara, Haiti, a commune located on the very edge of Port Au Prince. It employs over 100 Haitians who work with thousands of farmers and cultivators. Their black castor oil product has been had countless unsolicited endorsements by cosmetic professionals and celebrities alike. Thanks to tactical distribution relationships with large well-known North American chains like Whole Foods and a large beauty supplier, in 2019 they're expecting $2M in revenue. That's a near double-digit percentage growth, compared to the year prior. They've even won the distinction of successfully acquiring investment from Shark Tank investor Mr. Wonderful.

Kreyol Essence is an example of what heights Haitian Americans can achieve after they return to Haiti. They're keen on creating internationally focused companies, which thereby leverage Haitian domestic products and foster economic opportunity.

38. Beauty & Cosmetic Products - A Tremendous Wealth Potential

The beauty and cosmetic section are vast, consisting of things that might not be made for the subject. Though, this can be converted into a substance which promotes someone's perceived attractiveness. The beauty industry includes makeup, fragrance, facial skin, hair care, and nails.

This category has led to voluminous cash, leading to lucrative revenue opportunities for those having beauty products. The market demand for beautification products is extensive in Haiti. This falls across all income categories, while growing at a rate proportionate to disposable income. A Haitian economy on the rise would see strong winners within this space.

Business Concept

Haiti uses a handful of inherent native products for cosmetics. Such is the case with vetiver, which is crucial for the international supply chain. It's both used and recognized by brands all around the world. Haiti is one of the world's top exporters. Outside of being an import & direct resale operator of an established brand, building a cosmetic and beauty network allows resellers to scale strategies more quickly. Often these are strategies that have worked elsewhere; and so, it'd work in Haiti.

Beauty centers, such as salons and makeup boutiques, are top-rated. As a result, these lend to an easy entry as initial capital requirement.

Consequently, they're dependent on the target demographic. A larger initial investment is required, which derives from a higher disposable income of that demographic. Like barber shops, some nail salons pay professionals to rent chairs. Overall, this is a core revenue line for such facilities.

Niche ideas

1. Makeup training and courses.
2. Pop-ups providing makeup and access to in-demand brands which are hard to obtain.
3. Nail salons.
4. Makeup products created with organic native materials commonplace to Haiti. These include Castrol oil-based lipsticks and mascara.

Top Department and Policy Guidelines

Necessities of city social and professional life within cities drive up demand. This is the most recommended strategy.

Action & Tips

1. Market query those who've already become involved in the industry. They can provide insight on what may sell domestically. Or they may advise a business on what could be domestically produced for international resale.
2. Query customers. Revenue can be generated from providing customer service toward difficulties that consumers are experiencing.

39. Sanitary Pads for Low-Income Women Becomes an Enterprise Having a Social and Economic Value

Women in many parts of Haiti's low-income majority don't have access to critical sanitary menstruation products. In lieu of proper pads, young women use newspapers, old rags, leaves, and other makeshift things to absorb blood. It's appalling that, in this day and age, so many young Haitian women are put in those sorts of positions. Still, it happens. The cost of proper pads is prohibitively expensive for many. And so, some girls choose to avoid the embarrassment by avoiding school and their education.

Though, there's a straightforward business idea here. Low-income Haitians need low-cost alternatives to sanitary pads. These consumers want a functional and affordable pad that allows them to live their lives. Meanwhile, the pad remains discreet while taking care of a woman's normal biological functions.

Business Concept

This ideal product that can either be proposed by a capitalistic entrepreneur or a social entrepreneur. You can profit from this venture, while also impacting society on a social scale. Moreover, having this in mind, you can potentially structure your resource's input and distribution. An ability to leverage non-for-profit style for fundraising opportunities, brings forth a significantly subsidized price designed to meet customers' needs.

Strategically, focusing on provincial towns, as well as lower-income or urban areas, is recommended. It's possible to focus on the population's sanitary needs if the proper marketing is set into place. It's also possible to also focus on the needs of the general and higher-income population. Perhaps this is completed through a different brand. While they sell at a higher price point, they offer additional benefits - extra absorptions and more expensive material, for example.

Niche Ideas

1. Production of tampons.
2. Urinary incontinence pads for older consumers.
3. Hospitals and clinics deal with those patients' temporary needs. Because he or she is receiving medical care, they might be incapable of caring for their own sanitary needs.
4. Dispensable sanitary products for women in jails.

Top Countries & Policy Guidance

As discussed, focus on marginalized communities and demographics. Compete on price & overall availability. This can occur anywhere throughout Haiti.

Action & Tips

1. Nothing beats market research by querying the in-need demographics directly
2. Keep up with current events that relate to your niche. Places affected by the recent natural or political crisis, for instance, will have the most demand afterwards.

40. Beauty Salons & Barber Shops -- Community Centers Become Consistent Cash Cows for Owners, Because Of the Value of Looking Good

In Haiti, grooming is normal rather than optional. Grooming affects more than making a person feel attractive. It's more so a way to differentiate a person's social standing, providing him or her various access and treatment from society. Men's haircuts are typically stylized or shortened. And they might use products to treat their facial hair. In contrast, women utilize a much greater variety of products and services. These include getting hairdressing, weaves, extensions, perms, hair restorations, manicures, and/or pedicures.

There're many barbershops and salons throughout Haiti. As expected, competition is fierce for new clients. However, once a salon wins over a customer's faith and trust, the client stays with the salon for years. Generally, these clients only stop visiting the salon when he or she moves out of a reasonable commute range. Further, all of Haiti's barbershops and salons target a different socio-economic demographic. Despite having such a well-designed system already in existence, there may be a handful explicitly geared towards you.

Business Concepts

Concentrate on being unique if you seek to move into barber shops or salons. Bringing stellar customer service, along with novel treatments. Spa massages or facials are amongst these.

Treatments that get attention in international salons may, in turn, generate a wealth of profits for a Haitian barber shop or salon. He or she has an opportunity to build up a client base, while staying on top of modern styles and beauty practices.

A salon's modern design or how its services are laid out, may further demand higher service prices from customers. Moreover, it attracts patrons willing to pay those prices. Consider how a service delivery might stand out, for example, such as allowing stylists to bring services to a client's home. Where this exists in other countries, patrons happily pay a considerable premium. Building a brand around a salon can further this cause. After all, it collaborates with a personality that builds the brand's credibility.

Niche Ideas

1. Spa and natural treatments.
2. Traditional massages from Asia and India.
3. Barber and salon training courses and/or certifications.
4. Home or on-location servicing.
5. Emphasize the community hub aspect. Offer drinks, Wi-Fi, music, and a genuine social atmosphere.

Top Countries & Policy Guidance

There is more feasibility in the metro areas, where higher disposable income leads to more sustainable demand for the service. The provinces can be incorporated into a success business model, by providing eco-excursions where the services such as massages are performed in nature.

Action & Tips

Visit Haiti's different barbershops and salons. There's street salons, tailoring their focus toward affordability for the higher-end boutiques located within city centers. Understand where the market opportunity points are. Then, provide a tray of service offerings complementing those opportunities.

Success Story

Fresh Up Barber Shop

The Fresh Up Barber Shop has been consistently voted Petionville's best barbershop for years. They've understood that to stand apart, you must offer what no other barbershop can consistently provide. Those waiting for a cut can enjoy an air-conditioned facility. The salon may additionally offer free Wi-Fi, a television with a ps4, free outdoor parking, and a cappuccino coffee maker. The haircut might come with a hot towel service, as well as optional manicures or pedicures, hot wax facials, and/or the ability to style any hair texture with which a customer might have. The attentive customer service experience has anchored the salon's position as the premier barbershop in the Petionville area.

41. Dry Clean & Laundry - A Steady and Sure Opportunity

Laundry across the world and throughout Haiti is a tedious and time-consuming process. It's one of the first household tasks that's outsourced using disposable income. As an economy becomes modernized and women gain better access to economic opportunities, manual services like laundry are unavailable. While waiting for this phenomenon to occur in Haiti, there important opportunities still exist in the laundry industry, and its more formalized cousin - dry cleaning.

Business Concept

At the time of this writing, a traditional Haitian laundry mat isn't particularly feasible. There's high electricity requirements, but there's an inconsistency of electricity in Haiti. Furthermore, there're subsequent high upfront and long-term maintenance costs from having large generators. It's important to keep an eye on these inputs for this reason. When it's clear that those issues have a national remedy, to take advantage of opening a traditional laundry mat.

Given these options, an alternative model leverages the current cheap and plentiful labor. Meanwhile, it collects dropped off laundry. A team of segmented laborers wash, rinse, dry, and fold clothes. A service could further be built that picks up laundry at specific places across the city or at a client's home. The client could either pick up their clean garments or have them dropped off for an additional convenience fee.

In particular, dry cleaners are popular in Haiti, and resemble those in operation elsewhere. You drop off garments for professional cleaning. Then, you return after a few days and pay a fee to pick up your clothes. By all accounts, dry cleaning is profitable in Haiti. Those with modest means try to keep enough money on hand. Therefore, they can clean their formal and delicate clothes which attribute to a typical Haitian's wardrobe. However, if you enter into either a laundry or a dry-cleaning business, keep your eye on more than just a little dry cleaner. Instead, a chain of branded stores or franchises offer great services at a competitive price.

Niche ideas

1. Haiti doesn't have a self-service commercial laundry service (i.e., laundromat). So, figure out a cost-effective way to start and maintain it. Over time, a large profit will result.
2. Home pick-up and delivery laundry service.

Top Countries & Policy Guidance

Your set location depends on what strategy you use. A labor-based laundry mat can be placed anywhere; however, a more mechanized laundry mat should be placed in metro areas, since the latter requires consist electricity.

Success Story

Ayiti Lingue Service (ALS) - Dominique Carvonis

Since it opened in 2012, ALS has remained Haiti's only industrial-grade commercial cleaner. They employ thirty-five staff, with many who've been with the company since its foundation. It's grown its service footprint, servicing mainly along the resort coastline between St. Marc and Arcahaie. Additionally, they are having many Port-Au-Prince clients. Its efficiency and pricing structure has been a godsend for its large resorts and hotel benefactors. Decameron Resort, Haiti's number one leisure destination with over 400 rooms, is one of ALS's clients. ALS decreases the cleaning costs of these sorts of businesses, cutting the cost in half by doing the services in-house. Since they've begun offering low prices, they've earned many quality customers and residential clients. Their business is well-positioned to continue to grow well into the future.

Child Care

"A child is a beam of sunlight from the infinite and eternal, with possibilities of virtue and vice, but as yet unstained."

—Lyman Abbott

In 2020, Haiti became the most populous country in the Caribbean, having an overestimated 11.5 million residents. Haiti is the most fertile country in the Caribbean with 2.56 births per women. Furthermore, the median age of Haitians are 23.3 years, which is amongst one of the youngest lifespans globally. So, most of its population falls within the childbearing age. That amounts to around five million new babies possibly being born during the upcoming decade. These metrics place child-bearing women much higher than more developed state counterparts throughout the region. Still, this is often viewed as an opportunity and a complicated path forward for Haiti.

The implications are clear: Some of Haiti's most marketable ventures may be within the servicing the youngest amongst the population, as well as their parents. Suggestable products and/or services include assisting parents with the rearing and physical and emotional growth of their babies and young children, along with people caring for them.

The advent of urbanization remains a recent phenomenon in Haiti. In fact, most people born outside of Haiti were born two to three decades ago. So, there's a need for products and/or services that enhance safety, convenience, and aid. These improve Haitian's time management across different income demographics. Since the economic rising, Haiti will push the need further. Women continuing to be a primary care-taker decreases. This coming section will detail the potential product and service categories, which benefit sharp entrepreneurs and businesses to take advantage of all it provides.

42. Baby Food and Formulas: Needed by All; Big Profits in Return

Baby formula is specifically produced to feed small children less than twelve months old. Often, it's used as a replacement or enhancement for breast milk. For this reason, there's a particular need for formula in Haiti. Baby food additionally includes soft food, either as a liquid paste or a chewable pureed vegetable mixture. Likewise, it may be an easily consumable mixture of fruits or grains that's eaten by children of an older age group. Low-income women often are the primary income earners. They earn money, either by selling products in the street or by working in the factory.

Gerber and Nestle, along with many other brands, import these items. While most imports are prohibitively expensive, purchases can also be costly. And so, entrepreneurs must figure out how to keep these essential items affordable. One such way is by using alternatives produced through locally sourced food items.

Business Concept

Start with simple-to-produce grain porridges, fruit purees, mashed vegetables, & dry snacks. These items don't require complex ingredients. These can be processed, bundled, packaged, and shipped as a result. Efficiencies can be gained right away by using more modern equipment; although, these will require sizable capital to invest. Of course, the goal is targeting the masses who can't readily afford these baby products. It's not viable to price products competitively when they're more traditional quantities. Instead, consider selling smaller quantities at more affordable prices. Meanwhile, minimize distribution cost points by tapping into Haiti's decentralized whole and street resellers (Madame Saras).

Niche Ideas

1. Natural / organic baby food.
2. Toddler-based drinks & smoothies.
3. Porridge (rice, fruit, grain).
4. Dry food snacks, specifically those on which children can nibble.
5. Squeezable plastic packs with baby formula.
6. Pre-processed bite-size meat sticks (fish, turkey, etc.).

Top Department & Policy Guidance

Baby food production is a flexible operation. It either occurs in the city or in the provinces. Then, it's distributed to other areas. Retail consumers are the ultimate selling point, for they'll gain from economies benefitting from large populations.

Action & Tips

Genuinely educating oneself on the baby food market and how to ensure what's produced will be sanitary and digestible by young children. Utilize the most stringent regulations available.

This market's demographics mean you'll be targeting parents, specifically mothers. However, other professionals should be considered - doctors, nurses, midwives, and other healthcare professionals. All these individuals can guide customers to your product. Lastly, ensure that your product is fortified with nutrients and minerals, because these lack in a Haitian's diet (such as iron and other key vitamins).

43. Diapers Are More Accessible to All Income Earners

As previously described, Haiti's a young nation. With a high birth rate amongst women, it's likely an estimated five million babies to be born in the upcoming decade. A typical infant must be changed five or more times a day. Reusable diapers are popular in Haiti, but still, there remains a strong preference for disposable diapers. Many Haitian women forget the convenience cloth diapers provide.

Business Concept

Regarding diapers, here are two avenues to pursue in Haiti. First, diapers may be imported and rebranded from countries like China. Alternatively, diapers may be manufactured from someone's own brand. The latter provides qualities unlikely to be found in alternatively imported brands (such as Pampers and Huggies). The market for disposable imports often outpaces availability in many cases. In fact, many parents encourage diaper remittances that were sent abroad from either friend or family.

Reusable cloth diapers are important to a child's waste disposal. Over time, these generate less cost; still, it may more expensive to purchase per unit. Haitians outsource their washing needs for this reason, often hiring domestic help or washing diapers themselves. And so, these sorts of diapers are more durable than disposable diapers.

Niche ideas

1. Diapers suitable for babies having different sizing needs. This is vitally important for prematurely babies or babies born larger-than-average.
2. Diapers made with special considerations for special needs or disabled children.
3. Diapers for the elderly or hospitalized adults.

Top Department & Policy Guidance

While this works throughout Haiti, mostly it benefits cities' residents or customers who've readied themselves.

Action & Tips

- Find and survey recent parents, asking about their current pain points. This data helps track the current market and product availability.

Success Story:

DriButts - Michael Wahl

Michael Wahl took a mission to Haiti while working as a pastor. During this trip, Michael recognized the difficulties of poor Haitian mothers. While visiting places his church supposed, he saw how challenging it was for the mothers to obtain reliable diapers for their children. So, he considered this concern, and offered a more sustainable solution. Soon after he returned to the US, he and his wife designed reusable cloth diapers. These diapers had an adjustable clasp, which allowed the diapers to fit more snuggly as the child grew. Additionally, the cloth was made with breathable athletic material. Moreover, a highly absorption wick-like material inside the diaper reduced rashes, irritation, and moisture.

Initially manufactured in China, they've since began manufacturing the diapers in Haiti. This providing jobs and opportunities to the same moms, all of whom want a more sanitary solution for their children. Now, these diapers are being sold at different retail places, both in America and online. Because this business is equally a social, profitable business, it's also supported through donations. Individuals can purchase reusable diapers to be given for free to Haitian mothers in need.

44. Clothing Brand Tailored Specifically to Children's Likes and Needs

The children's segment of the global apparel industry, valued at over $200B per year, is lucrative. It's to be expected that children must grow. And so, consequently, clothes must be replaced. The right entrepreneur can take advantage of this revolving expectation. Though, we won't yet consider the seasonal changes of fashion. These drive a large portion of the demand and are independent of a child's growth.

In Haiti, most clothing comes from the second hand 'Pepe' market (described earlier). But some stores are starting to sprinkle more novel clothing options – both luxurious and affordable - at different ends of the market. An opportunity exists in this space, both a chain and a series of independent stores already located in Haiti's metro areas. These may include stores selling predominantly Western-style clothes. Alternatively, it might also include those attuned to a more distinct Haitian style with Quadrille / Karabela style for young girls or Guayabera for young boys.

Business Concept

The most advantageous course of action is to develop one's own 'Made-in-Haiti' Haitian clothing line. Social media's advent provides an entrepreneur a relatively low cost. Yet, they still have a powerful marketing avenue to build a brand. Also, it allows industry-standard events. These include bringing awareness to fashion shows. In turn, the brand has a much larger audience to reach as opposed to the few individuals that may attend. The push here is to sell locally. Push out internationally, instead of trying to reach brand notoriety or eventual clientele.

Niche Ideas

1. Clothing for infants.
2. Uniforms for primary and secondary students.
3. Children's costumes for holidays and occasions.
4. Headwraps, socks, undergarment, and other accessories.

Top Department and Policy Guidance

Leveraging Haiti's already existing textile infrastructure makes it easy to source material, hire staff, and export products. This will most appropriately be done in the metro areas of Port-Au-Prince and Cap Haitien.

Success Story

Haiti Babi

A Seattle, Washington-based commercial real estate development advisor, Katlin Jackson, visited Haiti on a recent business trip. Her analytical mind couldn't help but immediately seek the root cause of the economy's stark difficulties. For example, she learned that eighty of children residing in an orphanage had parents. However, the children were there because the parents could not support them. The parents, after all, didn't have reliable work or jobs. So, she decided on creating a social venture that could help with that reality.

Leveraging her Seattle network, she connected with Cascade Yarns to purchase 100% Ultra Pima Cotton Yarn. By leveraging professionals' networks to consult on the best practices around creating high end knit and crochet, they began producing baby blankets, hats, and other baby apparel. The company now employs a cadre of Northern Haitian mothers, where they produce products to distribute and sell across the United States and Canada.

45. Nurseys, Daycares & Preschool - Caring for the Young Isn't a Fruitless Activity

Childcare facilities are in high demand in Haiti. Which type of early childcare that's requested ultimately depends on the parent's income. Low-income earners utilize family and friends, although they may also take their children to work. Above all else, those with children must acquire consistent and stable income. So, they use facilities such as nurseries, daycares, & preschool.

These sorts of early childcare facilities are beneficial, for may take place at any facility (like a person's converted home) or they may rent out a space that has limited rehab. This flexibility allows there to be operations near large corporate offices. Centers work with professionals, who appreciate the convenience of childcare. Alternatively, childcare centers are tactically placed in or near residential areas. A popular and valuable approach may be considering picking up and dropping children off for parents.

Business Concept

If the daycare is endowed with initial capital, they can start immediately. They're at an advantage with a more modern chain of private daycare centers. These are rented, leased, or owned and supported by families paying a monthly, quarterly, or annual fee. Otherwise, families provide childcare in your home. This seizes on immediate semi-passive income at a minimal cost or effort. The restriction of a family's home shouldn't be a limiting factor. After all, there's a potential of operating a home-based daycare network. Leverage and organize the connectivity between providers and clients for a fee.

As you move past supervision, focus on instruction and proper care to a child's nutrition and diet. Both be a differentiating factor which can draw higher fees to parents eager to give their children a leg up. In fact, it's shown that children receiving early education not only achieve well throughout their academic careers, but they're linked to fewer crime rates. Moreover, they become better professionals and achieve more as adults. Few businesses can impact another person for what can amount to a lifetime. As parents understand this, the demand for such services will only continue to rise.

Niche Ideas

- Daycare for special needs children and adults.
- Daycares with special philosophical and pedagogical practices. (Montessori, all back male, or women schools focused on African historical lineage and achievement, etc.).
- After-school care.
- Babysitting services.

Top Department and Policy Guidelines

Larger metropolitan areas are more likely to see be extra-large differentials between the client's willing-to-pay and operational costs.

Action & Tips

- To learn more about your market, research parents' current options. Find out what they don't do, what's already provided, and what they do well. Lastly, find out what can be done better.

- Couple your service with an online repository for guidance. Finding information on quality childcare options is often difficult. But at the same time, prospective clients usually appreciate a brand that's concentrated on parents' growth.

- Even though the French curriculum remains Haiti's norm, there's been a recent push for the "American style" academic curriculum. As such, early education isn't any different. So, capitalize on this.

46. Producing Baby Care Products That Give Parents Utility and Productivity

Products centric to baby care is endless, limited only by one's imagination. It's not restricted by one's initial funding since potentiality of home product can grow into manufacturing successful products.

A child's birth comes an endless array of items, all of which maintain a child's growth. Bottles, beds, baby seats, strollers, playpens, rattles, toys, are included. Moreover, the list further includes health products: bug repellent ointment, skin creams and lotions, and bathing products. While items in the first list may only be purchased, items in the latter list may be purchased often.

There is, of course, competition from imported brands. Though, it's possible to niche your products so they fit cultural or societal preferences. Likewise, rebrand imported products and create a new product altogether. Categories that provide a unique Haitian flavor include:

- **Sleep-Related Products:** Cots; bedding; bassinets; child monitors; sleeping bags; mattresses; and/or night lights.
- **Equipment Assisting Someone with Eating:** bottles and bottle-cleaning brushes; formula dispenser; bottle kettles; teething accessories; sterilizers; breast pads; feeding pillows; bibs; broken pumps; teats; breast milk cold packs; small bowls; plates; spoons; and/or sippy cups.

- **Other things:** Changing mats (for clothes or diapers); bathing equipment; strollers; highchairs; drawers; storage cabinets; development toys; bouncing chairs; and children's books.

Business Concept

Baby materials can either be produced domestically or through importation. If they're imported, however, the item must be rebranded. Create a niche product and leverage Haitian resources. In turn, this earns the producer a competitive wage. Having a storefront is further recommended. Don't forgo consistent and targeted branding, but instead spread the word to prospective parents. Get the word out that your store exists. Taking this measure validates any surplus of product expenses that may not have been considered as you made required purchases. In other words, focusing on the benefit justifies the cost.

If you don't desire to work in retail, consider being a wholesaler instead. Haiti's wholesaling is very competitive, and so, niched baby products may be a great entry point. In retrospect, it's limited comparative market providers.

Top Departments and Policy Guidance

There're still centralized locations across Haiti, specifically periphery cities, where baby products are unavailable. Even in the larger metro areas (such as Petionville), there's just one location. No locations are available in Cap Haitien. Consider the larger major cities when you sell your products. Eventually, branch out to periphery cities. These are tactically located close to families with a disposable income.

Action & Tips

1. Look to products already being produced in North America and Europe, Africa, and other parts of the Caribbean as inspiration. Being a product's first mover and bringing it into Haiti, not only reaps profits but brand loyalty.

2. Start with a handful of products that, despite being used abroad, these are considered to be of infrequent use by Haitians. Then, expand to more products.

3. Made-in-Haiti products are always recommended - not only to make an impact but to increase a brand's viability.

Education

"Knowledge is power. Information is liberating. Education is the premise of progress, in every society, in every family."

— Kofi Annan

The Haitian constitution requires public education to be available and offered to its residents. However, the government hasn't lived up their obligation.

The Haitian education environment has found a few points it could boast. As of 2019, literacy rates are sixty-one, as compared to the ninety percent average for the Caribbean region. Public schools are understaffed and under resourced. Often, teachers go months without pay. As a percentage of the national budget, the allocated amount is similarly one of the lowest in the Caribbean.

Despite these harrowing statistics, education is highly valued culturally. Students wearing uniforms are considered a mark of pride for parents and children alike. Parents are willing to devote a higher percentage of their income to their child's schooling, as opposed to their Caribbean neighbors. Generally, parents have high societal regard for those who've completed their "Philo." This means that students have completed their university diplomas and licensed examinations.

Haiti has an estimated 2.5 million school-aged children. Only sixty percent are estimated to be attending school, and so, they're in a desperate situation as a generation. Education is the lifeblood of prosperity, helping society as it emerges out of poverty's pains. As life continues for the youth, their knowledge provides the skillsets. Their experiences and perspectives will elevate both them and the economy.

The demand for schools is high. There're many fronts to education. Traditional paths include primary and secondary education, as well as university and vocational training. It further includes professional training and certifications. We'll be talking about these opportunities, its innovators and the change-makers who are taking advantage of it. Though the focus for the section focuses on the monetary opportunity in this sector, don't lose sight of the greater importance. This sector's role is to educate youth, thereby providing them with a quality scholastic experience.

47. Well-Established Opportunities Existing in Private Primary and Secondary Education

Haiti has well-established private education. Beginning in the 1970s, the practice was established under a Duvalerist policy. It required all religious missionaries to build an affiliated school with any new church. By the time of the economic liberation came about in 1986, eighty percent of Haiti's schools, both at primary and secondary levels of education, were already private. Since then, private education has grown. Currently, it's as high as ninety to ninety-five percent, which includes religious education and for-profit institutions. These statistics state that Haitians are accustomed to paying for education. And so, new private education-focused enterprises can nearly always expect demand.

The quality of even the Haiti's standard private school is held in greater esteem than its highest rated public school. However, it's vital not to open schools only for profit. Instead, provide exceptional and international standard education. This alone isn't just a moral obligation, but it leads schools can request higher monthly rents from parents. Simply put, it's beneficial to a school's long-term success. They can focus on quality over quantity.

Other primary and secondary opportunities exist, such as private tutors providing supplemental instruction. Extra at-home lessons are provided either done or located at specific centers. Students can perform better if they've individualized attention by a specialized tutor in an educational setting.

Business Concept

This pathway forward relates to education. There're many interdisciplinary steps involved. These include curriculum design, revenue forecasting, human resource operations, and marketing. It's possible to specialize, either in part or whole, on the construction or repurposing of a building for the specific purpose of education and school.

Instead, a less intensive venture could help you focusing on after-school care. You could provide academic workshops, programs aiding students with specific subjects or head a network of tutoring professionals. In essence, these tutors could offer their services at schools or within homes. A uniquely popular opportunity for Americans is to start is a private instructional practice teaching English. As in most parts of the world, it's seen as a language allowing professional opportunities in adulthood. And it's in high demand in Haiti.

Specific professional development and vocational workshops is another option. Haitian employers and Haitian professionals actively seek workshops. Usually, these provide skills relating to customer service, general computer literacy, specific software mastery, and client rapport soft skills.

Niche Ideas

1. American-styled schools.
2. Schools for individuals with learning disabilities.

3. Niche-specialized schools (art, music).

4. Athletic-based boarding schools.

5. Online schools with creole-based courses.

6. Skill development / Employment training centers.

Top Department & Policy Guidance

This business works anywhere in Haiti. Though if it becomes too large and leverages profit, consider targeting a specific audience. Focus specifically on where upper demographics live. Alternatively, focus on who would be willing to commute their children.

Action & Tips

- First and foremost, visit primary and secondary schools that you're taking under consideration. Understand the busines model they've adapted to suit their local patrons. Then, understand how one can differentiate. This can be by providing a more comprehensive course offering, or duplicative courses but at more affordable rates.

- Though many Haitian private schools operate without proper certification from the Ministry of Education, it's still morally appropriate to acquire and maintain certification. Your school's valued brand will pay off in the long run.

Success Story

La Petit Orchidée & Anseye Pou Ayiti

La Petit Orchidée is a primary and secondary school near the central, provincial city of Mirebalais, Haiti. Like many in-country schools, they face the socio-economic difficulties. They educate youth from diverse but mostly characteristically lacking communities. Their township is particularly representative of a majority in Haiti. Most students are primarily rural and taught on campus – an area not any larger than a handful of classrooms. Some classes consist of students of different grades, who all share the same room. They partnered with Anseye Pou Ayiti (APA) in an effort to maximize their for-profit school's value and impact. They've seen real results as a result. Eighty percent of students have successfully obtained a passing rate than regional rates that are closer to thirty percent.

APA is a socially focused organization. It uniquely positions itself as an organization focused on transforming Haiti's education through leadership, knowledge sharing, and the propagation of best practices. These drive critical thinking, improved communication capacity, and much improved changes that continue onto university. It trains educators to teach in provincial schools across the nation, keeping all participants in close contact. It further continues to share best practices and drive forward proven and tested academic innovation.

The partnership between private educational actors and more socio-public student welfare groups can yield results. APA and entities like it can leverage best practices by focusing on qualitative exercises that improve students' academic welfare. Schools having partnered with them have seen successful results. Absent a proper regulatory body to drive this sort of cohesion, independent actors are stepping in and producing real results. These can be either emulated or become associated.

48. Higher Education Can Be Profitable, so Build to Compete with Schools Abroad

The roughly 200,000 students enrolled annually in Haiti's higher education system make up a small percentage of Haiti's youth. They successively move onto university from the start of their academic journey, which began in adolescence. After passing Haiti's baccalaureate exam, some options consist of five public schools. These all have open enrollments together, but they only capture thirty to forty percent of the annual demand. Moreover, these public universities are poorly run. They lack the proper investment in infrastructure, resources, and capital to compete with higher education options abroad. University staff strikes are common and occur often during the academic calendar year. Usually, these are due to teachers' salaries being in many months' arrear.

Private university providers are in a unique position to fill in the gap in demand. In fact, it's one of the main things that make this an attractive opportunity for business investment. Parents and students are hungry for private university options, which keep them near their loved ones. Overall, there's less overall living expenses than having to support their young adults.

Some important considerations, though, include the set-up of a private university. However, this tends to require much more capital than primary & secondary schooling. The industry is competitive, because of national employers' predisposition for potential workers. Since they've been educated abroad, this means that the school's academic programs must produce alumni capable of handling those firm's needs.

Business Concept

Opening a private university from scratch is certainly a route to be taken. This is especially true if the goal is to fill a niche or service. Students will then get educated in a new and more modern way. The demand for schooling ensures a lower floor of consistent enrollment, no matter the location. Meanwhile, with the proper operational consideration, universities hold incredible potential They're able to draw excess revenue to founders, shareholders, and investors. An alternative path is to connect with foreign-based universities to set up a direct franchise or satellite campus. Not only could this offset cost, but leveraging the name and brand would grasp the attention of more students. And they would be willing to provide higher rents because of the affiliation.

The best students attend facilities that are wholly lacking in public universities. These include on-campus lodging, laboratories, libraries, and an access to a novel technology. Building a faculty may be easier than you think. There're countless within the Diaspora having had expressed a desire to return to Haiti. All of them contribute their qualifications, experience, and capacity to the next generation. They provide logistical and lodging arrangements to potential faculty who might not be familiar with Haiti when they relocate. So, this is an important part of helping the faculty attract attention while maintaining them.

The accreditation system existing through the Ministry of Education is wholly insufficient. It provides the sort of robust evaluation requirements that truly modern universities require. Obtaining the minimum Minister of Education certificate is a necessary and value-added pursuit. By doing this, it spearheads a higher education association. It emphasizes its own accreditation process, steps, and fees.

Nice Idea

- Online courses accessible to those outside an institution, available for a minimal fee.
- Specialization in a niche: law; business; vocation; technical; an agricultural school; computer science, or coding.

Top Department and Policy Guidance

Almost eighty percent of Haiti's options for higher education are found within Port-Au-Prince. Its population size, its percentage of higher-income residents, and legacy of centralization, make it exceptionable to have many of the nation's longest-serving and highest-rated schools there. And so, someone wouldn't be faulted if they leveraged that same infrastructure, thereby placing their institution there as well. However, possibilities exist when a university is located within any of the lesser-known metro areas. It not only taps into a population experiencing an underserved demand, but a high-functioning institution is often flocked by nationals anywhere from around Haiti.

Action & Tips

- Visit top universities across the Caribbean. They serve as the primary source for Haiti's students, who are unable or unwilling to attend Haitian universities. Understand what they're doing. Therefore, you can provide a competitive offer.

- Focusing on agribusiness is useful. While it focuses on agricultural needs, it further focuses on its legitimate potential for profit.

- New trends such as social media management and SEO. Both are crucial in the current technological era, because these merit a consideration for a specialization in curriculum.

Success Story

Azure College - Johnson Napoleon

Johnson Napoleon, a Haitian who migrated to the United States, established himself as a well-rounded business professional. He developed successful ventures in media, real estate; though, his largest success has been in higher education. In 2007, he founded Azure College. It quickly became one of the most successful and private health-focused universities in Florida. It's the first accredited Haitian-owned US college. Moreover, it's the first black-owned college to offer a nursing degree program in southern Florida.

In addition to having three southern Florida campuses, he's opened a campus in Port-Au-Prince. Not only can nursing students graduate with degrees holding the same level of accreditation as his US-based campuses, but his university offers courses that are non-existent anywhere else. Degree aeronautics is one example. Here, students complete their enrollment with commercial piloting and maintenance. Another is a course explicitly focusing on entrepreneurship. It's taught through an MBA program fielded by established entrepreneurs and economists.

Azure College is in a unique and well-differentiated position to win in Haiti's higher education market.

49. Exploring Individualized and Business Professional Training Because of Its High Demand

Curriculums taught in many universities, even in developed countries, struggle with keeping their programs connected with employers' immediate needs. This concern is exaggerated in Haiti, given the underfunded and deficient infrastructure of higher learning. Graduates enter the job market with serious competency requirements. So to get a leg up in Haiti's fierce job market, many Haitians seek professional training and certifications to complement their university and college degrees.

Professionals and employers actively seek certifications with affiliations to localized and internationally recognized professional institutions. The highest in-demand certifications are IT, financial accounting, management training, and specific software competency programs. Some professions require additional professional training in Haiti, specifically accounting. Consider establishing these programs along with centers, to provide standardized testing in addition to accredited programs.

Business Concept

A straightforward concept involves organizing and providing quality training in the segment of in-demand industries or professions. Don't be another place that provides workshops around Microsoft Excel. Instead, become an authority on computer software knowledge.

Entities can charge rates that function as part of the brand's reputation and are thereby expected to add professional value upon its completion.

Benefits of professional training are limited financial capital. The dependencies become the knowledge, skills, teaching aptitude, marketing, and social networks of you and your team.

Niche Ideas

- Employees with the necessary mid-level and senior management skills. Their competency is amongst Haitian companies' top complaints. Develop a curriculum addressing these issues alongside companies suitable for such professionals.
- Training and certification centers for international, technical, and professional qualifications. These include coursework for both international and domestic agencies.
- Courses may be offered specifically for online consumption. Consider translating well-established material.

Top Department & Policy Guidance

This can work anywhere in Haiti. In fact, your training doesn't need to be static. Hold training in different hotels and reception venues across Haiti. This not only provides you access to fresh paying participants, but it also enlarges your footprint and brands your business.

Action & Tips

As mentioned earlier, few competent mid-levels to senior management staff are a major problem. Thus, domestic firms seek professionals from the Philippines, Latin America, and North America. A solution must be providing to issues surrounding Haitian national professional progression. Preparedness means funding, networking, and sponsorship, so take advantage of it. Provide anyone direct connections to employers, after having completed a curated training program. These employees can help provide input to the university student's needs while diversifying revenue. By doing this, it earns a commission for each placement. Then, it generates chargeable benefits for trainees and private employers. It's a win-win for all involved.

Success Story

Ayiti Analytics - Casteline Tilus

Ayiti Analytics, a professional training group, is the brainchild of Casteline. After graduating from Stanford University, he became an analytics professional and began working with developmental outcomes. Morgan Mednis is an experienced data scientist in public health, economic development, and environmental sustainability. Together they noted that Haiti was significantly behind in their data management applications. This included falling behind on data analytics, business intelligence, system analysis, and data modeling. Their professional training program runs several weeks. It occurs in the same company in which Ayitic Analytics has aligned. Having embedded students in the enterprise's workplace within Haiti provides their students with direct, industry-applicable information. It further helps students practice and tailor their skills toward learning an employer's specific requirements.

Once the program ends, the completed participants are provided a paid internship. Likewise, they're given entry-level opportunities. Some participants can elect to stay aboard, working directly with Ayiti Analytics as an educator. This becomes part of their consultant group. It either aids in publishing research or becomes part of their outsource analyst staff. This staff performs temp / contractual services for North American companies.

Xponential Learning - Krystel Kanzi

Krystel, a distinguished professional, started her career with KPMG in Washington DC. She's spent years working with Compagnie d'Assurance d'Haiti SA (one of Haiti's largest insurance companies) as a vice president of finance. Over the years of hiring and training staff, she noted that many employees needed remediation in certain skills and competencies. Never allow anyone to sit idle while glaring problems exist. In essence, she could do something about it. She created a professional training entity, which leveraged all her experience and knowledge. It additionally distilled them into in-person seminars, online courses, and tailor corporate services.

Courses and competencies include varying levels of courses related to Microsoft Excel. and a mastery in QuickBooks. It likewise provides a customer service mastery. Also, she provides critical lessons in financial literacy, specifically focused on running a Haitian business.

Within the course she provides an overview of the Haitian labor code, the Haitian tax obligation, and an understanding the country's investment code. It's through innovative courses like these that she has ensured her in-person seminars. Since then, they've been packed affairs. And so, therefore Xponential Learning is expected to be a relevant source of empowerment for years to come.

50. Personal Development Has Proven Itself in the West. And It's in Serious Demand in Haiti

In today's modern world, we've the knowledge and skills to succeed; though, capacity isn't enough. In fact, it's only a small portion of the core essentials needed to be successful. A person's perspective of his or her world indicates how they view possibilities. It further indicates how he or she interacts with challenges, and prominent people with whom they're working. Some consider these the 'soft-skills,' since these are non-technical aspects of a person's development. Usually, the material is coupled into neglected aspects such as entrepreneurship, leadership, team building, communication, presentation, and selling skills, negotiation skills, career management, stress management, or time management.

While this niche is well-known throughout North America and other parts of the world, it's not as widely known throughout Haiti. The practice's core model involves the distribution of personal development concepts. Often these are learned at conferences, seminars, workshops, and retreats. The cost to attend a seminar or retreat depends on the size. It additionally depends on its speakers, and whether corporate versus the individual participants are expected.

Business Concept

To win here, it's vital to become an expert in a particular subject matter. This should be the niche in which you're elected to pursue. Engage your target audience through online social sites, and blog posts.

Create entry-level media, that drives interested and inspired participants. Guide the participants toward membership sites, e-books, and more comprehensive videos. Even if another Haitian company has already covered this content, it's essential to provide it in a differentiating way.

Passive income generated from online content and e-books covets into this domain. You only must create the material once. Then, it continues providing income in perpetuity, requiring only moderate updates and revisions. Consideration will have to be made for Haiti's multilingual audience. Whatever content you create, have a Creole version to English or French.

The big payout events are previously mentioned in multi-group sessions. So, provide more recognized value to the participants per the nominal cost of attendance. Participants should leave with copies of literature, copious notes, reference syllabi, and a network of contacts with which they can follow up. A true feeling of actionable information immediately translates, either to more productivity or more money.

Niche Ideas

- Entrepreneurship success coach and mindset mentor.
- Confidence-gaining curriculum.
- Relationship building.
- Mind, body, and soul classes.
- Interview and communication skills.
- Stress management.

- Female empowerment.
- Young adult and recent graduate employment skills and empowerment.

Top Department & Policy Guidance

This industry maximizes its returns. By leveraging platforms, it allows a brand to be anywhere. Distribute media wildly, holding regular in-person events around different places throughout Haiti.

Action and Tips

Review the models of top development coaches. Amongst these are Tony Robbins, Les Browns, Gary Vaynerchuk, and Iyanla Vanzant. Appropriate and tweak what has worked for them regarding Haiti's market. Became a model entrepreneur to which Haitians both in the country and abroad can aspire to become.

Success Story

PSB - Pierre Stanley Baptiste

"PSB" summarizes himself in four simple words: "empowering non-obvious winners." He's neither an expert nor a scientist. He also doesn't have a Ph.D. in poverty, hardships, humiliations, failures, or negative environments. Instead, he has taken his life story of adversity and desire and influenced a more prosperous generation of Haitians. In fact, he's made this into a career that can help enrich everyone. Outside of publishing for Huffington Post, he's been awarded the President's Service Award from President Barack Obama. PSB has an outstanding social and civic engagement and has received his higher education in the United States.

He's written three books, created podcasts, held conferences, led workshops, and established his brand. He's not only earned revenue, but his life, as well as his thinking, impacts the quality of testimonies of his followers. Currently, he runs Impact Hub - a social working space for young Haitian entrepreneurs. He and his team provide non-technical assistance. They also offer financing, accounting, and business plan support for all ventures housed there. PSB is a rare influencer in Haiti. He's actively demonstrating the effective power of personal development within Haiti.

51. E-Learning Is the Future, so Specialize for Big Profits

At the time of this writing, the world has completed a global pandemic. It's affected millions, while leaving hundreds of thousands of people dead. During that pandemic, the world shifted indoors. Traveling, except for essentials, became progressively more restricted. Distance living, including work and schooling, became increasingly important. Simultaneously, all this became equally possible because of technological advances. Even before COVID, there were demands related to distance schooling. In fact, e-learning has been rise. Due to an increasingly large number of global participants, there's been a greater demand and acceptance for it.

There're two prominent e-learning sources of for adults. First, an individual's must have a preference of wanting to take instructional lessons within their homes. Secondly, there's is an increasing number of companies looking to gain access to training resources for their staff. In doing this, they can utilize and improve their productivity. In the latter, computer-based training is an important component. Access through online portals will soon eliminate face-to-face classrooms in their totality in the coming decades.

Ultimately, flexibility is this domain's biggest feature. People can learn what they want and when they want it. Moreover, they can learn any subject in their language (Kreyol, English, or French). The opportunities for e-learning within Haiti's ecosystem are high. It's relatively low-cost to create qualitative courses utilizing proven instructional methods. These lessons come from experts in particular fields. All the instructors have high perpetual returns with minimal maintenance.

Business Concept

Create well-researched and professionally produced courses that have proven instructional methods. Then, make it available online. They can be produced by yourself altogether. In this method, a student depends on their direct experience in the field and their accumulated knowledge. Otherwise, they could draw from experts who are compensated for their information and/or recorded instructions. The key is finding your segment or niche. Specialize in a subject that's lacking either online or in traditional educational environments.

Where to make a course available is up to its creator. Options include a one-time fee or a monthly subscription. Both are common. Alternatively, utilize a freemium model. In this case, everything is free; though, the validation of course completion, such as a certificate, may require a fee. Additionally, host your content on your own site. Leverage established platforms and audiences, while generating additional exposure and revenue. Coursera, Udemy, and Linkedin Learning all have affiliate programs. These allow independent course producers to repost or create a specialized course that can be hosted on their platform.

Niche Ideas

- Preparation courses for exams.
- Courses for vocational opportunities.

- Courses targeted specifically for those wanting to educate themselves at home (working professionals, stay-at-home mothers, etc.).

Top Departments & Policy Guidance

An e-learning business is inherently able to capture users from all over the country, and so, consequently there could be Haitians abroad wanting to improve their education. Ensuring you produce multi-language episodes is a big part of driving general wider engagement. Of course, the primary restriction is access to the internet. As wider access improves, it drives opportunities for this market.

Action & Tips

- Leverage social media to grow exposure. Provide snippets of free courses. Therefore, people that're interested in the courses can grasp what the course offers.
- Start with one or two courses. Promote these courses and learn from the feedback. Then, expand your program while attuning it to your customer's preferences.
- Ensure that you're creating products compatible with both desktop and laptop computers, as well as mobile devices. These days, more people use the latter as their primary internet interfacing device.

Success Story

HaitiHub

Founded by Rafael Carlo Diy, this platform has grown into one of Haiti's primary e-learning programs. Their niche focuses on learning Kreyol. By leveraging many academic resources, it foundationally formulates strong and comprehensive course offerings. The first was forming a knowledge of its instructional professionals. They involved Dr. Jacques Pierre, a renowned Duke University professor of linguistics. Secondly, they collaborated with already existing offerings online to gain insight into the best practices regarding course creation. Finally, they partnered with tenured real-world language instructors. With their assistance, they formulated a foundationally strong and comprehensive online course offering.

HaitiHub initially focused on providing Haitians within Haiti a comprehensive course on Haiti's native language. This came about because they saw many education facilities lacking curriculums. Although, it's grown much further. It's now utilized by ex-pats, foreign nationals, dignitaries, and Haitians abroad. All seek to improve their mother tongue, both permanently and temporarily. Meanwhile, they want to improve their proficiency with Kreyol. Further major entities in Haiti, both private and NGO, offer their courses as part of in-house computer-based training. By doing this, their employees benefit.

Over 3,000 paid learners have utilized HaitiHub's services. In fact, they're number one in Google's search results, when someone searches for "learn Haitian creole." Likewise, they've had consistent annual year-over-year growth since its inception in 2011. HaitiHub proves there room for growth in Haiti's e-learning space.

52. The Production of Writing Materials & Writing Paper

Upon considering education, we must first consider the different levels of instruction—primary, secondary, and high education. Likewise, consider how these provide facilitation of the educational environment. A more important critical element includes considering the materials used by students and teachers. That's the stationery needed to share, capture, and register shared ideas and knowledge. This is paper, exercise books, notepads, textbooks, pencils, and ballpoint pens - to name a few example. Any item or tool used to impart education thereby improves a student's quality of learning. Therefore, it should be considered.

Each year, countless containers of these sorts of products are purchased by parents, teachers, students, schools, NGOs, and different government entities to support schools and universities across the nation. The demand for these items is high. Yet almost none of these materials are produced domestically.

Business Concept

Opportunities in education include publishing locally, as well as the manufacture of stationery items. The cost of production is initially capital intensive. Thus, makes sense to get started by rebranding items from places like China or India. This allows you to focus on your downstream retail and distribution chains. You can therefore brand reputation growth. As a result, credibility can be parlayed into leveraging resources more easily later.

The goal, whether it takes place immediately or down the road, lies in manufacturing stationery supplies locally. Pioneering recycled material, gathering the material from across the surrounding metro area, and producing the stationery from this material is a cost-effective yet quality enhancing manner. Don't think of just renewed paper. Instead, consider making writing material, instructional paraphernalia, and writing tools. All these are items that can used in-part or wholly from recycled material.

Niche Ideas

- Eco-friendly stationery produced with reused material sourced locally.
- Production of material that could culturally find a niche relative to the generic imports from abroad, either through historical significance or an island-themed presentation.

Top Department & Policy Guidance

Most schools are found within metro areas. So, your distribution - both wholesale and retail - should be first installed in these locations. But the provinces shouldn't be ignored. Strategize to quickly expand into these areas as the economy grows. Take advantage of the independent grassroots distribution network of provincial Madame Saras, which is a cost-effective way to expand.

Action & Tips

NGOs make up large contributors in this space. Thus, it sends potential clients to you. It's advantageous to make early overtures to those most active in the educational space. Find ways to satisfy their various programs' sourcing needs. If it's done right, they may serve as important and steady clients who're critical to your early startup success. They'll also add important credibility to your operation as it interfaces with other actors in the market.

Transportation

"Any businessman will tell you that transportation is fundamental to success."

— John Hicklenlooper

Even without diving into the statistics, a brief visit to Haiti quickly leaves you with an impression of Haiti's need for innovation in the transportation space. Haiti's become increasingly urban in the last few decades. More Haitians living in the city than the provinces. This in itself has put an increasing strain on the transportation. In fact, it's driven demand into the metro area's transportation infrastructure. Today, 56.2% of Haiti's 11.5M population lives in an urban environment, compared to just thirty percent of Haiti's population in 1990. This massive demographic change in demographics is felt more so in Haiti's transportation infrastructure than anywhere else. Likewise, it's is a huge factor in Haiti's quality of life for native citizens and visitors. With the trend nowhere near reversing, consideration of how innovation can be imported into this sector is essential. Ultimately, it could affect this island's future.

Higher population quality and quantity have one exact meaning for a budding transportation entrepreneur. More movement means more demand and more money. For most of the population in Haiti, work, school, business, pleasure, and other life activities are enabled by vehicles and transportation operators. But it's not just people that are facilitated. All matters of trade and commerce - including agricultural produce, food items, supplies, raw material industrial inputs, petroleum products, construction equipment, other vehicles, and consumer productions for consumption - are all moved by land, air, and sea. These items are moved into, over, and out of Haiti. In this sense, the veins and core of any functioning economy resides with the nation's transportation. This assertion has been backed up by recent studies, which show road installation or rehabilitation in communal sections can produce local GDP affects between 0.5% and 2.1%.

Yet, Haiti's transportation industry remains underdeveloped, even with this importance and ever insatiable demand. The few entities already having had established themselves have seen laudable successes. Perhaps the most recognizable symbols of Haiti's organic transportation sector are the colorful and industriously rehabbed tap-tap transport. Many more opportunities exist in this space, even beyond what has already been established. We're looking to explore all these details and more in the coming chapters.

53. Vehicles Are Needed & Someone Must Sell Them - Why Not You?

A vehicle is loosely defined as that which transports, although in comparison to Haiti's auto market, the auto market selling vehicles is relatively small. Recent statistics indicate that there're only 223.3 people for every registered vehicle, and seven vehicles for every 1,000 people. It's the highest and lowest percentages of any country throughout the Caribbean. Though over the years, Haiti has seen multiple years of auto sale growth. Even when more consumer segments may see volatility, commercial vehicle segment purchases stay relatively predictable, despite their larger macroeconomic conditions. This indication implies that the vehicle's type is closely related to the vehicle's usage and its user. Let's discuss those vehicle types, along with their potential Haitian user bases.

1. **Motorcycles** – Motorcycles are a relatively recent phenomenon in Haiti, exploding within the current decade. They've become the proliferation of cheap Chinese motorcycles imported into Haiti. Most of these motorcycles are used by young male entrepreneurs functioning as self-employed motor taxi drivers. These vehicles have been intricately connected to a bottom-up response, supplying an unmet demand for public transportation. Moreover, it's an answer to the lack of a formal governmental response. Relative to other popular transportation options, motorcycles provide a considerably inexpensive solution. Given the incredible congestion in the

major metro areas, motorcycles provide flexibility in circumventing the most painful traffic points. Motorcycles provide quick commuting options even outside in the provinces, as well as across sparse or under-maintained rural road networks. For these reasons, motorcycles are popular as personal or commercialized vehicles.

2. **Cars -** This vehicle is mostly eyed by metropolitan Haitians. Generally, car buyers are looking at entry-level options. These cars are cheap to purchase, have relatively minimal maintenance costs, and are economical on fuel. With a rising middle class, Haiti can be expected to have exponential growth in the auto market. That's, of course, until disposable income begins to catch up with demand. While motorbikes are mainly purchased directly from retailers, cars are generally purchased second hand. These are either purchased abroad from used markets or domestically from other Haitians. Japanese and Korean brands are well-regarded and sought after; although, Chinese brands have recently begun to capture market shares held by American brands.

3. **Buses -** Buses are used in a limited capacity. There're two primary types of buses in Haiti. Neither type of bus is used within metro commuting. First, minibuses comfortably fit around ten customers. Secondly, greyhound buses can fit up to around thirty passengers. The latter is large enough to haul extra weight. Both sorts of busses are used exclusively as intercity transportation. Both buses also haul agricultural and

other raw materials that their passengers have with them. Except for a handful of coaches, most of these busses are either driver-owned or leased out by the drivers. In the latter case, they independently operate the buses on intercity lines. So, there're strong opportunities related to providing these buses. Likewise, it's possible to carve out a niche for your intercity line on a less established route.

4. **Trucks** - These utility vehicles are the heart and soul of Haiti's transportation ecosystem. Commercial and personal drivers demand trucks, because of their versatility and response to Haiti's unpredictable road quality. Trucks are inherently versatile and usable for many different functions. Trucks are used every day to commute people after being converted to colorful makeshift hatchbacks, commonly referred to as "tap-taps." But they're also used to transfer agricultural goods, materials for construction, petrol products, and consumer goods. Diesel is the most in-demand type of truck, but gasoline-powered trucks still make up a large percentage of the Haitian roadways.

The market for buying or selling vehicles is far from centralized. Haitians often look for a vehicle and seek to acquire it from others from a secondary market. In this way, they're purchasing the vehicle from its owners. A small but sizable percentage are purchased vehicles, many which are new and from car dealerships. But and a smaller subset work formally as vehicle importers. These individuals sell the cars a la carte or at used car dealerships. While North America is a popular sourcing market, the cars are imported from across the Caribbean and Latin America.

Business Concept

An opportunity exists at multiple different points. An accessible entry point is becoming a retail car trader. One such possibility is purchasing, fixing, and selling cars domestically. Most commonly, this opportunity is expressed by purchasing vehicles abroad. Typically, cars are purchased through an auction or distress sellers. This minimizes the cost. Then, the cars are imported to be sold locally. The proliferation of older model vehicles seen throughout Haiti is partly due to import taxation rules. These apply a customs tax, based on the vehicle purchase price and/or bluebook value in the foreign market (whichever is more). Older vehicles go for less. Though, logically, it depends on which brought in more quantity into Haiti. One can plug into this process, just if one can find high-quality older vehicles for resale. It's possible to make a good profit from each transaction. An alternative to this model is to build out methods of purchasing new, affordable vehicles for the consumer. Therefore, the import custom costs are altogether avoidable. A profitable market innovator would include a method of financing a percentage of this high and unavoidable custom cost; but this usually takes places after the customer pays for the vehicle. Currently, dealerships that sell new cars, like Toyota, directly pass this price onto their consumer. This can exaggerate the price by tens of thousands of dollars. As a response, dealers generally keep a minimal inventory. They only pay customs after a client has already paid for the vehicle.

Furthermore, they only pay and the high, upfront customs fee. As one can imagine, this dramatically suppresses overall new vehicle sales.

These government-sourced constraints aren't withstanding. They are seeking out international vehicle brands, while work partnerships are an avenue that has proven worthwhile in Haiti. Great fortunes have been brought by current franchises holding representatives. If the brand exists elsewhere but is yet in Haiti, seek out the contractual and capital requirements. These will help toward acquiring such a relationship. Instead of a physical dealership, the Haitian online marketplace is mature. Facebook's marketplace is a particularly important destination for vehicle seekers. Capitalize off this, either with your own online marketplace or leveraging the many others in the country to post your vehicle inventory.

Niche Idea

Vehicle auctions aren't common in Haiti. Create a service that performs vehicle auctions, either in person, in different cities or online. It'd involve iterative bidding, like eBay, that may arise in popularity.

Top Departments & Policy

Vehicle purchases happen in Haiti's metro areas, both big and small. Because so many are already concentrated in Port-Au-Prince, starting in another important secondary city may yield more of a more massive market share gain. Note that Miragoane and St. Marc see a lot of vehicle importation occurring throughout their ports. So, these and nearby metro cities could be considered as options.

Action & Tips

- Use popular car purchase sites as examples. These will show a similar business's structure.

- Financing is the secret of auto purchases in other mature economies. Credit constraints today mean getting creative with that which is offered. It also means reaping big rewards by allowing previously unserviceable customers to access your vehicles.

54. Why Sell When Renting Vehicles Can Be More Profitable?

Private and public transportation options have limitations for domestic and international travelers. Locals making day trips to a well-regarded beach, as Cote de Arcadins, might prefer renting a vehicle as opposed to taking public transport. Cote de Arcadins is located just before St. Marc and along the coast, northwest of Haiti. Those coming to see family or friends, too, may prefer driving if they're coming from the provinces. Daily rental rates can be as high as $200 / day per vehicle. This alone solidifies this proposition.

Prospects for rentals aren't limited to passenger vehicles. Typically, businesses may need to lease a vehicle for a day. Think about retail stores with a common need to receive bulk orders. Often, it's these stores' responsibility to acquire their goods from the seller. In doing so, they use trucks, vans, or rigs. Construction companies are another commercial enterprise that needs the flexibility of vehicles. Though, it depends on the item needing transport and is related to their project.

Business Concept

A rental vehicle business works well in conjunction with vehicle trading. While you're waiting to sell your vehicle, traders often put their vehicles up to rent. This strategy allows car dealers to make revenue on their dormant vehicle inventory. Newer vehicles attract higher rental rates, while older vehicles provide locals and those on a budget an option. In any case, it improves your demand.

Though rather more ubiquitous in ownership, there's still a rental market for motorcycles. Many motor taxis are owned by someone else. Likewise, they're leased by the driver for a nominal daily rate. However, don't just consider consumer or passenger vehicles. There's an ever-growing leisure rental market. Quad, ATVs, and off-road mountain bikes are all great alternatives. These provide patrons the opportunity to rent motorbikes more often. In fact, these are more common than standard consumer vehicles.

As your business grows, perform survey research. More industrial and commercial firms have an ability to see which sort of truck, van, or type of rig obtains the most demand. Construction has been one of the most consistent sectors of growth in the Haitian economy. So, the purchase of relevant commercial vehicles for that domain can be recommended as a solid investment.

Niche Ideas

1. Rental of watercraft transportation (jet skis, small fisher boats, party vessels, etc.).
2. Moving trucks and transport bikes ('tuk-tuks').
3. High-end rentals for diplomats and visiting VIPs.

Top Department & Policy Guidance

Cities with international or trafficked regional airports are inherently better for these operations. They're exposed to local users' demand and the demand of out-of-area visitors.

Action & Tips

It's advisable to research online marketplaces. Get a good feel of what already exists in the market; likewise, get a sense of the potential turnaround time. Vehicles repeatedly showing up do so for a reason. Try to understand that reason, because it could either benefit or have an adversely affect your rental business. Therefore, make certain every vehicle coming near your business is accounted for or understood.

55. Transport by Air - Plane Not Required

Most economies have developed a transport method that's often overlooked by entrepreneurs until it's too late - air transportation. Transportation of people and cargo has increased at a multiplicative rate. As seen in these comparative cases, and it's very rational to assume that Haiti wouldn't be any different. Even with well-maintained road networks, the roads are neither straight nor wide. Haitian roads are tight corridors, prone to traffic jams and mountain climbers. With steep declines testing the robustness of vehicles" breaks, these roads have varying mileage ratings. Air transport, however, has considerable advantages over other avenues. This intra-travel has revenue opportunities. This integrates into a business's flow of trade, tourism, and cultural exchange.

Haiti has a total of fourteen airports, from the endowed international airports of Toussaint Louverture International Airport (located in PAP) and Cap Haitien International Airport (located in the north). It further has smaller, more domestic airports. These include Jacmel, Jeremie, and Les Cayes. Many provincial towns also have airports; though most are unpaved and have runways only capable of receiving a small aircraft. According to the most recent records, Haiti has had an annual count of one million passengers. It's also carried four million metric tons in cargo freight.

The air transportation opportunities discussed below concern service industries, that're connected to airports and air travel.

Business Concept

Taking full advantage of air transport would entail purchasing an aircraft and upkeeping its maintenance. Moreover, there're aviation licensing costs and regulation fees. It's a capital intensive sort of endeavor. However, other opportunities exist to build a successful business around aviation. All the same, you can either plug into it directly or indirectly. This includes airline food and beverage provisioning, cleaning services, shuttle services, cargo handling, airport shops, duty-free airport posters and signage marketing, in-flight entertainment, and much more. Anything you see or interact with at an airport has the potential to be monetized. Most of it's provided by a private firm.

While some of these ideas could start from scratch to purpose airport servicing, it's more doable to strategize how you can incorporate a business you already own. See what opportunities arise out of this business. For example, your restaurant could provide pre-made meals for domestic carriers. Alternatively, you could open a branch of your eatery within the airport terminal. If you're already in logistics or staffing, you can provide support to cargo or cleaning services.

Niche Idea

Domestic airline, flight, and cargo comparison sites don't yet exist. In fact, these are awaiting an entrepreneur to provide a service for them. Each company should be listed and linked. At the same time, they should be willing to provide an affiliate link for commission. Therefore, people can send this to others when they need a referral.

Top Department and Policy Guidance

Any of the large/medium metro or smaller provincial towns with an airport. At the time of this writing, Jeremie just completed major renovations. This consisted of lengthening the pavement of its runway. Airport Les Cayes is experiencing a major expansion. Additionally, Toussaint Louverture is in their late stages of approving a second runway.

Action and Tips

Acquiring these sorts of contracts isn't a straightforward process. One must network with representatives, speaking with prominent people working in domestic and regional airport administration. Be quick to take advantage of any expressed needs or deficiencies in which you overhear. These can lead to a cost-effective service, presenting itself as a solution with a minimal turnaround. Also look out for when small provincial airports expand operations or expand/pave their runways. These are usually signs of an increased demand of which you can take advantage. Begin such inquiries early.

56. Transport by Water - Boat Not Required

Water taxis are a form of transportation. These have popularized in countries where many residential metropolitan areas are connected by a coastline. Several metro areas across the country fit that bill. Carrefour located southeast of Port-au-Prince, has its entire border along the bay of Port-Au-Prince. As expected, the main national road passes very near its shores. It's a great venture location because of its geography, but also because of the traffic's intensity. On most days, daylight hours are plagued by bumper-to-bumper traffic. It effectively separates the Carrefour and the larger downtown metropolitan area, making distances even further. This is the case with drives to Petionville and Croix-des-bouquets, which are half-day commutes. The pain point is there, but, the serve alludes to the market.

Other international cities, such as in Canada's Montreal, have been successful with water taxis. They've integrated with other transportation services, transporting up to 60,000 residents a month. Montreal uses river shuttles to commute for work and leisure across the river surrounding the metro area, that connects to its suburbs. While these Canadian enterprises are public-private partnerships, Haitian transportation has thrived as a private-only industry. And so, a water taxi has a similar potential to be taken advantage of by a resilient-minded entrepreneur. He or she can build such a business.

Water transportation isn't new to Haiti. In fact, the primary way to get to the center island sitting in Haiti's bay is by taking large boats near St. Marc. These ferries transport residents and visitors between the mainland and Gonave Island.

Business Concept

A water taxi business would involve picking up pedestrian customers along the coastline in small to mid-size boats. Shuttle them along with the short, stopping at drop off and pick-up points. This is like a traditional land bus service. The shuttle path would be close enough to shore, thereby alleviating any fears of being stranded in the bay. Still, emergency life jackets are provided for those fearful of the water because they're unable to swim. Stability, speed range, and fuel consumption would be maximized with the right fleet of boats. This is a lucrative business venture that can weather most in-country economic turbulence.

It'd be possible to set up a logistics and transport service, while catering to passengers. Over-water transportation has always been a cheaper option. And so, it'd be sought out by mid-sized to large enterprises. This includes the capacity to potentially even allow car traffic to circumvent the roads. Essentially, those driving cars could shuttle their vehicles along with them in the ferry or water taxi.

Niche Ideas

- The purchase, sale and/or lease of appropriate size vessels. These can be commanded by individual operators instead building a single vertically integrated entity.

- Long-distance lines that can take one out to other cities in Haiti, rather than staying in a single commune.

Top Department & Policy Guidance

Nearly all of Haiti's major cities are located along the coast. This observation serves as additional opportunities scale through business lines. It further opens additional service branches to service different city communes. Water transport is a business that can work anywhere in Haiti.

Action & Tips:

Consider flex pricing; although, it depends on the time of day. Periods of higher usual road congestion should have a higher rate to compensate. A better value is provided relative to the increased demand.

57. Innovative Logistic Services Is an Opportunity Ripe Growth

Haiti's logistics market has incredible opportunities for entrepreneurs. In fact, it provides many avenues toward success and profits. This industry's direction and rate of growth are closely correlated to the economy's larger performance. Those making early investments in this space can expect to be exceptionally well-positioned as Haiti's economic tides change. Regardless of this tide occurring, this industry's integral commercial activities underlie its money-making consistency.

Proven lucrative services could flow inward through an import's facilitation when it's importing into Haiti. Alternatively, there may also be an intra-domestic process between provincial areas ad larger metro areas within the dominant norm. In this case, exporting is the big market that's being overlooked. In whatever direction logistic services establishes itself, transport infrastructure is still underdeveloped. At one time, there was a rail that connected Jacmel, PAP, and Cap-Haitien for transport and freight; but those networks have all ceased operation. The industry mainly consists of the port. It travels through the road, in route to the metro destination. Then, it travels back again. Along the way, it stops at the primary ports of entry and exit. Respectably, these are PAP, St. Marc, Port Lafito, and Cap-Haitien.

Transportation's entirety consists of large volumes of freight that includes industrial raw materials, refined petroleum, timber, construction materials, heavy & light equipment, factory goods, and consumer products. All this is completed by land transport, more specifically by trucks driving on the road. Thus, this segment is where someone must start upon considering their entry into this space.

Business Concept

Most of the commercial and industrial transport in Haiti either builds out their transportation completely, or it partially leverages the informal transportation market. The latter is operated by independent owners and renters of trucks. Their goal is to not outsource the service, but rather offer a reliable alternative. And so, this is where your firm can come into play.

Keeping a small fleet of firm trucks with on-call drivers is essential. It provides minimal service level agreements, especially for prominent clients. Still, this business entails connecting with the network or independent freight operators. It also helps to maintain relationships over the years. Whenever possible, obtain long-term contracts with domestic firms. By doing this, you provide a minimum of orders each month that ensures revenue predictability. The position and services offered by your firm should solve and reduce all logistics-related problems. Therefore, all the choke points for any business with which you interact will easily be resolved. If it's effective, word will naturally spread.

Building out a service allows for a painless distribution of goods to be produced in Haiti. Likewise, these are distributed to various regions of America, Canada, or the world. Ideally, it's distributed to wherever a logistic service is being requested. A streamline of such operations includes the pickup, temporary storage, and shipping. It further includes the foreign side of delivery, which is an intimidating operation for a startup and an established firm. If you can understand the Haitian rules and regulatory environment of exporting, then you'll find a market and firms or people willing to pay for that service.

Niche Idea

Courier and message services amongst businesses becomes a feasible entry point. For example, some businesses need invoices delivered directly to other businesses, as well as their orders picked up orders. A small amount of moto with moto drivers servicing this would neither require a tremendous amount of startup capital nor maintenance.

Top Departments & Policy Guidance

It'll be necessary to establish a core hub, perhaps locating it either in Port-Au-Prince or Cap-Haitien. However, branching out to as many provincial areas and towns as quickly as possible is crucial to success.

Action & Tips

It's essential to understand the in-depth pain points of current freight providers. Those dependent on freight providers are pivotal to providing novel responses to those expressing challenges or gaps.

Success Story

Shippex - JM Craan

JM Craan had a simple dilemma. He had amazon packages he needed to bring into Haiti. Although, he wasn't aware of reputable entity, who could provide service or customer service at the speed which he sought. So as a serial entrepreneur and problem solver, he went into action. He created a company focused on making the process of ordering products through international-based entities easier, by making their transport into Haiti seamless and effortless. This was how Shippex was founded. Folks set their delivery address to his Miami-based reception center. Once packages were delivered, the packages were loaded onto a plane or water transport in route to Haiti. Upon their arrival, customers were able to either pick up their packages within Metro Port-Au-Prince or have their packages delivered to a home address through TaxiPlus, their subcontracted entity. His service has already been endorsed by many well-known celebrities in Haiti. And it's well-positioned to cross into many other logistic branches. Consequently, opportunities will arise as a result, such as commercial servicing and export.

Electricity

"I believe that access to electricity and light can radically improve people, lives."

— Olafur Eliasson

Electricity is important, but modern-day conveniences too often taken for granted. Neither light bulbs, mobile phones, washing machines, televisions, industrial machines, nor transportation options would exist without electricity. People can neither develop nor achieve modernity without it.

For many Haitians, electricity remains too far out of reach. According to the United Nations, only twenty to forty percent of Haitian households have access to electricity. Nationwide, that's as many as eight million Haitians. This range varies distractedly, depending on the region of Haiti we're analyzing. In the PAP area, seventy-two percent of households receive some electricity. Conversely, rural households, which account for fifteen percent of the population, only have some electricity. This discrepancy is because there's many rural areas that're not part of the minimal national grid. For example, Fort Liberte (located in northeastern Haiti) and Jeremie (located in southwestern Haiti) haven't had a connection to the larger grid for over two decades.

What's frustrating, however, is that Haiti's Caribbean location lends itself to incredible opportunities. These renewable energy opportunities aren't yet exploited. Haiti has mostly sunny days, that account for its weather eighty to ninety percent of the year. Moreover, Haiti sits along very favorable trade wind paths. Much of its coast, in fact, produces ideal windy conditions suitable for producing year-long wind turbine electricity. Many rivers and tributaries could produce mini-hydro dam mini-grid systems. Further, it could produce waste-to-energy options. These could alleviate many sanitary issues that plague many parts of the country.

Haiti needs around 800 to 900 MW to meet its capacity needs, but now, it only produces around 250 to 300 MW. A considerable amount of investment is needed to make up the gap. We'll explore some of the structural issues that've restricted this investment from happening, but these will be discussed regarding possible entrepreneurial responses. Despite the huge challenges of the island nation's electricity supply, venture opportunities and ideas can provide affordable, effective, and convenient solutions.

58. Solar Power Is Already Making Important Inroads. Don't Delay in Joining the Prospects.

Solar is the future. If you had an opportunity to get into computers at its inception, would you have taken advantage of it? At that time, there were unknowns concerning its full possibilities and pathways. While there were a few advantages preaching the possibilities, it was still uncertain. We live in a world where the size of computer systems is unimaginable. Solar panels are precisely comparable. Its possibilities are being explored, with a potential to change the world. Countries like Haiti, that are unencumbered by prior electricity missteps, realize that it takes specific entrepreneurs to discover the true potential of solar energy.

Haiti averages over 300 bright, sunny days each year. Unlike the Dominican Republic, which captures more moist trade winds because of its position on the western end of the island, Haiti is dry outside of the few rainy seasons. Thus, more annual rainfall and subsequent cloud coverage falls in the Dominican Republic. Still, these consistent and predictable sunny conditions make for ideal solar energy conditions.

Increasingly international development partners, electricity industry players, and even the Haitian government are recognizing solar capacity. Most importantly, these influential actors all agree that large energy-producing plants should be shelved. After all, these provide strategies that exploit regional microgrid strategies. In time, these will inherently lend well to solar. It doesn't require extensive networks of power lines to migrate from one place to another, because the energy source can be placed very close to a cluster of residents. They utilize pay-as-you-go strategies. These require significantly less initial capital and less maintenance cost. Likewise, net profits are used to drive further investments while growing organically.

Business Concept

The most direct entry into this business is purchasing solar products, both to import into Haiti and to resale into the market. While the appreciation and understanding of the power's capacity and efficacy accompanies the Haitian public consciousness these days, many still require educating the public. Doing this provides direct proof of concept before making a purchase. So, be ready and willing to make that a part of your marketing and operational strategy.

The sort of products and appliances that can be traded will be explored below:

1. **Solar panels** - The core device that allows for the solar power system to function. These flat panels are usually installed on roofs made of glass. The roofs convert the sun's photon energy into usable electricity available for immediate use. Alternatively, it could be stored in batteries for use later in the day. Each year, more and more innovation are carried out in this technology. Since many countries have prioritized it, the prices have considerably fallen. The Haitian government having removed all its import tariffs for solar panels has helped.

2. **Solar water heaters** - These aren't as common in Haiti; although, they should be. They're increasingly being demanded and purchased. They're particularly in demand by hotels, hospitals, and consumer-facing commercial facilities. Solar water heaters collect heat from the sun, redistributing it through water for easy usage.

3. **Solar chargers** - Consistently use a portable battery attached to the device, either directly or by using an extension. These are useful for charging electronic devices: laptops, radios, and cell phones. Lighting is provided with much less initial expenditure.

4. **Solar fridges and freezers** - These solar appliances have tremendous potential. While they're high demand because of an increase in availability, they still aren't common in Haiti. Given Haiti's state of electricity, plug-in versions of these devices always have had limited uses. Usually, they function for just a few hours a day before losing all utility after a couple of hours of blackout. Being unable to preserve cooked food and/or ingredients without spoilage drives a considerable amount of waste. Haitians, therefore, are purchasing materials that takes up both materials and productivity time. Ultimately, this time could be used doing other activities. A solar fridge is a very attractive proposition to anyone with relatives. Moreover, it's useful for anyone having the disposable income to purchase it.

5. **Solar-powered home products** - Many products are battery versions of common home devices. These can be used without electricity; although, they also have a component where the battery accompanies solar panels when it's charged and maintained. The most common of these are light bulbs. Other items might include fans, ovens, water pumps, or laptops.

Don't forget. There's profit to be made. Profits are generated from wholesale imports of these products, as well as the value-added processing of new composites into Haiti. For example, consider backpacks that use Haitian textile workers to produce the bag and sew the solar panels into the bag's exterior. A small battery with USB ports is sewn into the bag's interior. The creation of new things is constructed with existing technology, while then infused with Haitian organic material. Its look and personality should always be considered as part of a winning strategy.

Niche Ideas

- Small electrified huts can serve as community electrical and charging stations, which are set up to charge for the service. Additionally, local establishments can serve as internet cafés if Wi-Fi is required. It's worth considering for rural areas!
- Small affordable panels, specifically for sale in rural areas.
- Specialized solar equipment to service small- to medium-sized commercial and industrial operations - e.g., butcheries & food processors.

Top Department & Policy Guidance

Solar based businesses can work ANYWHERE in Haiti. In fact, that's their biggest appeal.

Action & Tips

- Entry points for solar-based businesses are low. Situate yourself with a single location and spread organically, one household at a time.
- "Show-not-tell" is an important part of informing potential customers on a product's effectiveness. By doing this, you're improving their quality of life.
- Many of the products are imported, and thus attainable by current or future competitors. So, branding items or adding value personalizes the items. It further differentiates the product on the market and is critical to maintaining the long term goals of the business.

Success Story

DigitalKap - Patrick Eugene

Patrick Eugene, originally from Cerca-la-Source, had well-established himself as an American computer engineering professional. When he decided to return to Haiti, he assisted with improving electricity access to Haiti and its people. With $5,000 of his savings, he started and grew DigitalKap. Now, it's a company worth $20M. DigitalKap is a solar power company. It purchases custom made solar equipment from China, artifice with his company's brand. DigitalKap provides professional and centralized customer installation and maintenance of solar power systems to customers' homes. It further provides solar panel installation and maintenance to commercial and industrial businesses, non-for-profits, and rural homes or offices across Haiti.

His efforts are shown by their results. He's won Haiti's technology entrepreneur-of-the-year. He's created 30+ full-time jobs, while going on to employed hundreds of contract workers. Likewise, he's added new lines of businesses. These include solar-powered home products, that make differences in the lives of his customers.

GivePower

GivePower was launched by SolarCity, a company that made the news rounds after being acquired by Tesla. Its company launched GivePower (a non-profit) in 2013. At this time, they decided to bring their solar-based sophisticated initiatives that worked in places like Mombasa and Kenya to Haiti. Their first project, completed in February 2020 on the island of Ile la Gonave, is a 20,000-gallon-a-day desalination system. It's powered by a 50-kW solar system with 120 kW-hrs of Tesla batteries. It's seismic forfeited and centrally located within the downtown area of Anse-a-Galet. Thanks to underground pipes that can take water from the coastline, it's estimated that this one desalination plant can meet this city's 65,000+ water-starved denizens. Likewise, it can serve its neighboring villages and cities on the island.

What's special about this initiative is that, after the initial capital needed to fund the solar seawater osmosis station – along with maintenance, staff, and facility growth – it'll be driven by the sale of new five-gallon containers. This is in addition to the refilling of previously purchased five-gallon containers. The prices are competitive with current osmosis providers. So, they're prevalent in Haiti's retail market. However, they still couldn't operate on the island. Plans are already in the works for more facilities around Haiti.

59. Generators Are a Necessary Part of How Haitians Obtain Electricity and Shouldn't Be Ignored.

The two most recognizable sounds in Haiti: Kompa booming from a nearby bar resto and a nearby power generator's roaring. Haiti's electricity woes necessitate many households. It moves businesses to invest in their power generation capacity. Even with the recent technologically innovative progress of solar, the most common way has been small- to moderate-sized thermal generators. These specifically relate to gasoline- or diesel-powered generators. The range of generators doesn't include the large industrial variety; instead, it includes the "portable" variety that ranges from two kWh through twenty kWh electricity output. These generators are usually run for about four to six hours before switching to stored battery power for the rest of the day.

Portable generators are a two-billion-dollar industry worldwide as early as 2019, with expected growth to 2.5 billion USD by 2024. What's more is that it's expected to have 4.1% annual growth. The most popular Haitian brands are Honda, Generac, Yamaha, Atlas Copco, Siemens, Cumins, Kohler, and Caterpillar. Cheaper Asian brands have been making increasingly more inroads in Haiti, with cheaper costs expanding the market to buyers. The traditional brands priced out, while providing most of the sector's entrepreneurial entry points.

Business Concept

The business concept is as straightforward as one can get. Import generators, either new from manufacturers or second-hand generators from primary markets. Then, resell them throughout Haiti. Consider not just selling these devices but also leasing them. Instead of taking the high upfront purchase price, as well as the generator's installation and long-term maintenance, many companies would rather rent them for a short period.

Niche Ideas

- Consider small, handheld generators. Sell these to low-income patrons. These can hold up to two to three liters of petrol. They can also power small devices like a laptop, a light, or a cell phone.
- A detached maintenance servicing model allows you to charge for the generator's maintenance and repair.

Top Departments & Policy Guidance

These in-demand products are sellable throughout Haiti.

Action & Tips:

1. As always, implementing a personal branding approach when it concerns import and resale models. The material can be sold under your entity's name. This becomes a better strategy than selling as another generic brand.

2. If some assembling and repackaging can occur locally, ensure that additional value-added modifications can be made. This adapts the product to local conditions.

60. Battery-Fortified Appliances and Gadgets Are Increasingly In-Demand

Batteries are the most purchased item for an appliance in Haiti. There's now an ever-growing class of appliances & devices integrated with batteries. Even if a direct charge of electricity is unavailable, these can run for a specific period. They needn't be connected directly to solar panels; however, these can function on traditional electric sources. In return, it provides electricity to a device or appliance.

Whether this route analyzes a product's utility or functionality is still questionable. Battery-powered electric fans are a great example. These high utility products were used during Haiti's incredibly hot and humid summer months. Many of these have the capacity to operate for a full day; an incredible convenience. Radios are another battery-operated device popular amongst Haitians. Younger adults appreciate that radios play music loudly. In contrast, adults enjoy radios lasting well into the late evenings. They listen to radio and news programs throughout the day. The newest radio devices function as portable battery devices themselves, allowing people to plug and recharge other devices.

Battery-operated kitchen devices exist for every kitchen appliance, anything from toasters to blenders. It raises the importance of quality and quantity, regarding the demand for all products that are sold. It doesn't matter if they sell, but rather that they'll.

Business Concept

This is a similarly straightforward exercise, involving proper product-sourcing from cost-effective manufacturers, both abroad domestically. As always, considering the infusion of additional products through its local assembly and branding maximizes revenue and its long-term sustainability.

Alternative trends of energy in developing counties, which are formulated by institutional developers and consumers, potentially indicates that these investments are worthwhile. While the first can exploit opportunities, the latter focuses on the structural change electricity – effecting both its creation and consumption. Therefore, it's vital to combine sustainable components, such as solar and natural gas, when considering these options.

Top Department & Policy Guidance

Though battery-powered appliances are useful all throughout Haiti, they're most likely purchased with a discretionary income. This allows Haitians an opportunity to experiment on these qualities of life expenditures, that are comfortably often found in cities.

Action & Tips

Market testing is vital. Before committing ordering large quantities of these products, test with smaller batches. This will effectively gauge demand.

61. Revenue Can Be Generated by Becoming an Electricity-Generating Tycoon – It Needn't Be a Fantasy

Haiti has a large need for electric infrastructure. As previously discussed, generating energy neither needs to be capital intensive or scalable. Lower-cost options do exist, including solar and wind. And so, we want to spend some time to fully discuss these.

Before going any further, its important to understand that entrepreneurs' long-term viability within this domain depends heavily on a more modern legal and commercial accommodating framework for electricity in Haiti. Primarily, Haiti holds a state monopoly over EDH. And so, they'll have to change how their company operates. But the scope of this change's initiation is beyond this text. Still, EDH will have to give up its distribution and point of sale of its electricity consumption throughout Haiti. Otherwise, it could be empowered to take more action to alleviate endemic low collection rates.

It's notable to understand that some of these options will be priced out of an entrepreneur group. Still, it's necessary to present these ideas. Anything is possible with proper knowledge, imagination, and collaboration.

Hydro - Haiti has thirty-two named rivers and countless unnamed tributary streams. These flow from high mountain sources, which then flow into larger basins. Finally, they reach seas and oceans. Each one of these waterways acts as a potential electricity generator through hydropower. Hydropower is invaluable because it's renewable and doesn't pollute the water. Haiti already has one such dam, Peligre Dam. Completed in 1971, it was a joint project between the Haitian government and the US Corps of Engineers.

Peligre Dam produces hundreds of megawatts of power, whereas the current trend intends to create smaller micro hydropower dams. Consequently, these generate less than 500KW of potential output. Since they're less capital intensive, overall there's less ecological displacement in comparison to their larger behemoth predecessors. One such example: Smaller hydroelectric already exists on the Marion River located northeast of Haiti. While it's used to produce some power, it mostly controls irrigation.

Coal - The Dominican Republic has two large coal plants, which provide millions of its citizens electricity. Haiti could similarly capitalize on this inexpensive source of electricity. Coal remains an integral part of electricity generation in countries internationally. Although, it's been viewed as unfavorable in recent because of increasing environmental concerns. Building a country's electrical infrastructure centric to coal isn't recommended, though still coal's proven to be durable. It's mature supply chains, and per unit maintenance costs lower than other thermal generator power methods.

Natural gas - Increasingly, more of Haiti's macro energy generation has largely derived from natural gas options. Natural gas is cleaner and cheaper to build. Moreover, natural gas is inexpensive to maintain in comparison to hydro or coal. An absence of pollution further indicates these are much closer in proximity to the usage centers. Moreover, existing thermal plants can convert to natural gas for additional capital savings. The downside is that much like petrol and coal, natural gas must be imported. After all, Haiti hasn't any domestic natural gas reserves.

Gasoline & Diesel - Since PetroCaribe's agreement with Venezuela, the majority of Haiti's macro energy production draws from burning a high-density diesel grade oil. However, uncertain fuel prices have seen a per barrel rise. These have risen over a hundred dollars a barrel. Often there's a steep maintenance cost for facilities that requires motors to be completely overhauled every few years. And so, this results in less of an appeal for this manner of electricity generation. Despite this, gas and diesel generators play a crucial role toward homes and businesses acquiring stable energy sources. These primary sources of electricity connect many regions of Haiti are unconnected to the larger national grid. As a result, they shouldn't be written off.

Waste-to-Energy – Trash is Haiti's biggest nuisance. The vast majority remains uncollected. Worse, the number of landfills are neither insufficient for Haiti's needs nor efficient in their operations. Given Haiti's parallel energy needs, burning trash – as done in US, Sweden, Norway, and Denmark – a simultaneously attack both problems. A popular perception is that WTE produces considerable pollution. Still, it produces less harmful effects than coal plants. It's carbon-negative. In this way, it produces less harmful air particles than if the material were left in the landfills to decay naturally. Technology has advanced to where there's a way to extract the energy in waste material. Therefore, it emits pollutants air bound, such as fluidized gasification or pyrolysis.

Wind – Because of Haiti's position on the equator, it's often the recipient of strong and consistent trade winds. Wind energy has the earnest potential to provide a considerable amount of Haiti's energy needs. The wind is converted to electricity through large blades turning turbines. When these are bunched together, these multiple wind turbines are called wind farms. Recent advances in technology have improved yields per acre. Still, the output is around two megawatts requiring 1.5 acres of land. With the average farm producing around ten MWs of electricity, the land using it gets rather substantial. Haiti's ideal strategy for the mountainous terrain involves utilizing wind within microgrids. It's located in remote areas. Density might not justify the cost of other types of electricity production.

Nuclear - It's crucial to understand a long-time rumor states Haiti not only has Uranium; they also have its rarest form, Uranium 235. This radioactive rock has proven deposits found in countries along the perimeter of the ancient earth-shattering asteroid crater. It caused the dinosaurs' extinction in the Gulf of Mexico / Caribbean Basin. This includes countries such as Mexico and Honduras. If any of this Uranium could be found on the territory, it could be used to fuel a domestic nuclear power plant.

Nuclear remains the most cost-effective, efficient, and macro energy-producing method without controversy. As of April 2020, 440 nuclear plants are operating worldwide. This number is expected to grow. Many developing BRIC nationals seek to meet their dual mandate, that provides their population(s) energy and decreased Co2 emission resulting from nuclear power. Haiti should partake in modern-day energy-producing methods. But first, they must produce a nuclear energy policy. It's an active effort, benefiting this realistic energy source.

Health & Wellness

"It's health that's real wealth and not pieces of gold and silver."

— Mahatma Gandhi

Haiti's health & wellness is a deep subject, offering much nuisance. Perhaps it requires a book that provides the full perspective. We won't go deeply into Haiti's health stats because they're easily attainable elsewhere. Moreover, these lag considerably behind Haiti's the Caribbean and Latin American cohorts in many categories. We want this section to focus on tangible and profitable ways, which drive sustainable improvements to this sector.

Despite preconceived notions of Haiti's viability within the health sector, many sectors have found stable and consistent year-to-year revenue growth. Partnerships between donors, governments, and facility revenue sources are often a hybrid of social and for-profit operational structure. Most are priced within reach, including the nominal day worker or street merchant. Those requiring more advanced follow-up and service(s) can usually acquire these through diaspora support. This support is found from friends and family living abroad. Further, supply factors keep medical facilities' services low. This includes a large population of degreed and certified nursing professionals.

Drug manufacturing is pronounced on the island. Four major drug manufacturers sell various pills, syrups, and other generic remedies at affordable rates to the population. A growing middle class will necessitate more demand for drugs, medicines, and other pharmaceutical products. All this keeps the population healthy. Situating oneself early before this economic upturn ensures a facility's well-positioned to exploit that growth.

Within these next sections, our goal is to explore all of Haiti's business opportunities throughout the health and wellness market.

62. Gym Services, Fitness Training, and Boot Camps

Gyms are more popular than you would think. In fact, the amount of gyms per capita in Haiti leads considerably relative to their Caribbean cohort. Many of the gyms that are available, operate at above capacity, especially during peak hours before and after typical work hours. During peak hours, you'll mostly find educated, income secure professionals. They reside in the surrounding residential areas or around their place of employment. As time goes on, it's probable that Haiti will experience economic conditions improving because of an increased middle-class population. And so, these facilities are set to take off even more.

But it's not just gyms. There's been a growing count of health spas, massage parlors, and wellness houses in the past few years. But as these entities indicate, they're best situated for individuals who engage the and financial resources to participate. Culturally, Haitians value their leisure and self-care activities, just as their western counterparts. Alternatively, it may be because of their western counterparts. So, finding customers isn't a herculean activity.

Principal considerations include finding a location, an operating strategy, marketing uniqueness, staffing diversity, and area characteristics/competition. These are critical considerations upon considering entering this business.

Business Concept

This idealistic opportunity is for those who enjoy physical activities and a Sportif life. The extent at which one begins depends on available starting capital. Business owners on the minimal capital end can provide personal fitness coaching, training groups, or wellness seminars. These seminars can be either outdoors, or in free or paid meeting centers. Paid meeting centers might include renting out an empty church or a community hall for fitness sessions.

Moving into your own facility can be a staggering approach. As you gradually add equipment, focuses on specific niches. You might focus on a genre of group training, for example, that uses static and free weights or balls. Another step is building toward under-provided segments. For instance, these might include youngsters taking gymnastics or older adults taking CrossFit.

Once you can fill an entire facility with machinery that someone would expect to be included in a gym's membership, consider the trademark and the establishment's brand. Not only is it vital to stand out in a market where these gym services are readily provided, but provide a market aimed at providing long-term value to members. For example, African or Zumba dance, as well as far east disciplinary practices, are all uncommon differentiators. These would add value to your membership base. In turn, vary pricing. Revenue will reflect this added value.

Niche Ideas

- Yoga courses.
- Pregnancy wellness.
- Weight loss / dietary regimen programs.
- Self-defense instruction.
- Therapeutic services (physical therapy, chiropractor, and massage).
- Sports training.

Top Department & Policy Guidance

Health and wellness can work anywhere. It depends on the extent to which a person chooses to capitalize on the activities. More extensively, facilities require a base to pay the increased premium. This needs to offset those higher costs. Focus it upon metro areas where there's either residential affluence or white-collar employment.

Action & Tips

Be inspired by international fitness programs and facilities. If a franchise can be simplified into an existing international brand or program, such as Zumba, than leveraging the brand's recognition should be simple. There's no need to reinvent the wheel here. See something abroad? Emulate it and provide it within the local market.

Success Story:

Haiti Total Fitness - Gilbert Biamby

Haiti Total Fitness was founded by Gilbert and his brother who is a former Olympian competitor. They saw a need to improve the health access of Haitians in the Tabarre area of Haiti. They had learned about a girth of available warehouse space, which had originally been built to support Haiti's UN mission. But now, it sat underutilized because of recent deployment reductions. So, they put together their savings and opened Haiti Total Fitness. To boot, the facility was in a stone's throw of the U.S. embassy. The fitness facility earned professional residence of their staff and working-class of Tabarre, while overall benefiting from that patronage for predictable revenue. With their commitment to state-of-the-art equipment, they've a mission to keep their well-maintained and operable. Haiti Total Fitness has unique fitness offerings, that're not provided elsewhere amongst Haiti's current fitness environment. And so, they quickly garnered a reputation as a modern facility. They're able to plug into visitors from abroad or those residing in Haiti that need a modern fitness experience.

63. Drug Manufacturing Is an Oft Unconsidered Potent Cash Cow

Drug manufacturing in Haiti is self-evident. Because of a rash of preventable ailments that unfortunately inflict Haiti, there's an unmet demand in variability and quantity of drugs sourced domestically. As a result, the market is large. In turn, this contributes to many pharmaceutical imports both from India and the United States. Issues have arisen due to this high dependence of external drug providers. Most distinctly occurred throughout the recent COVID-19 crisis, where delays of critical medicine effected Haiti. More and more nations prohibited the export of medicine from their territories.

The natural, low-cost advantage of already economically scaled industries concerning current pharma exporting nations admittedly makes it difficult to rationalize a pharma operation in Haiti. But the reality is that, since the World Trade Organization ratified the Trade-Related Aspect of Intellectual Property Rights (Trips Agreement) in 1995, there's been given codified space for least-developed countries like Haiti. They've had an opportunity to manufacture and distribute generic drugs. A handful of drug manufacturers in Haiti, in fact, have taken advantage of this. Today, four pharma manufacturers in Haiti are proof that such an industry can be supported and sustained by domestic aggregate demand and expenditure.

Generic drugs are replicated versions of brand-name drugs. These also have the same properties and net result on one's ailment as an original drug. These generics are much cheaper to produce and are sold at prices reflecting their lower retail cost. Painkillers, antibiotics, and sexual dysfunction drugs are amongst popular types of generic drugs.

Business Concept

The upfront capital, machinery, technological investment, and skilled human talent to start a drug manufacturing company can be substantial. So, starting such a venture shouldn't be taken lightly. It's critical to size up the local market. Figure out how you can differentiate yourself against established incumbents. A detailed market analysis is key to establishing certain perspectives within your niche. However, when done correctly, the gains can be tremendous.

Niche Ideas

- Multi-vitamin and other supplements.
- Dermatological skincare.
- Contraceptive pills.
- Pregnancy test (with affordability in mind).
- Alternative / natural medicine.
- Drugs for livestock and animals.

Top Department & Policy Guidance

Drug manufacturing is successful anywhere in Haiti, particularly as you build out your distribution network. This allow your drugs to be sold across the country at greater distances from your specific production hub. Regulation of the drug manufacturing industry can cause initial registration to be onerous. Though once it's in operation, you can enjoy hassle-free relationships.

Action & Tips

Exporting your drugs from Haiti to other countries is a time consuming and resource-draining endeavor. Of the four pharma companies currently producing drugs in Haiti, only one exports to other countries. Further, Haiti only exports drugs to the Caribbean. It's important to consider the appropriateness of such an outward expansion, but only after your firm's domestic maturity.

Success Stories

Farmatrix Laboratories - Ralph Edmond & Alain Vincent

Faramatrix Laboratories, originally based in Carrefour, started during the turbulent era of post-Duvalier Haiti. It was founded in June 1989 by two young pharmacists, Ralph, and Alain. Ralph openly shared that he went almost five years without earning a profit, primarily due to that era's turbulence. However, they preserved. Their strategy consisted of providing an inventory of medicine closely in tune with local demand. Based on feedback, there was constant revelation of those product lines. They're now one of only four large and established pharmaceutical drug makers Haiti. They've produced over 134 pharmaceuticals products and have been in business over thirty years. Moreover, they're among the four major drug manufacturers in Haiti. They're most proud of their ISO standard operation certification and their continued community impact, as they support dozens of employees.

64. Retail Pharmacies / Drug Stores Are Crucial and Profitable to Communities

The first part of manufacturing medicinal prescriptions, while they then must be sold. Quality, convenience, and price are all a factor for Haitians when they're purchasing medicine. People want to be assured that their medicine will effectively treat their medical conditions. After all, most Haitians must purchase it within a reasonable distance from their home; and the medicine is formed at a reasonable price. Retail drug locations in metro areas is evidence that current demand provides sustainability.

Though retail pharmacies sell many locally produced drugs, there's a preference for domestic brands. There's an equally great demand for international branded medicine. Haitians willingly pay the higher prices because those brands provide them reassurance. Brand your pharmacy retail store, ensuring that you standing behind the pillars of quality, convenience, and price. Overtime, this will improve operational revenue. Ultimately, revenue will increase as a business owner opens more stores. Haitians prefer going out their way to purchase items in a recognizable place as opposed to a place in which they're not familiar; although, this only goes so far.

Online shopping is another untapped space in Haiti. Physical retail locations are restricted by the location's space, whereas this isn't the case with an online store. Through inventory control, a purchaser can get medicine delivered. It's either held by a retailer or a warehouse many miles away. In many cases, this medicine distribution channel may be tapped. For example, they may provide medical facilities and on-demand medicine delivery when a patient's prescription needs filled immediately. Or the delivery facility may not have a convenient pharmacy located near the purchaser. More Haitians utilize digital currency apps like Moncash and Natcom Cash, making schemes' viability more pronounced and viable.

Business Concept

Residential community placements serve as effective retail points. Demand for medicine stays constant, as it cuts across income brackets. One way to differentiate business, especially if there's already other pharmaceutical retail options, is by providing free basic medical consultation. Rudimentary guidance is available for drug options, as people give their symptoms. And so, having a staffed and on-call pharmacist and or general physician for advanced cases is another value-added proposition.

As discussed, an alternative is running an online drug store. This can service patrons across Haiti. Currently, there's not a drug provider within Haiti. Coupling this online retail with nutritional and health consultants provides additional traffic. As a result, it produces additional sales. Providing customers with invaluable information and guidance generates customer loyalty entrenchment. The site, as a result, becomes an important resource for medical and drug information. Creating trust provides an important psychological desire. It repays revenue, pushing growth higher.

Niche Ideas

- Preventive/curative remedies for tropical diseases. These include Malaria, Dengue, Zika, Swine Fever, etc.
- Family planning / contraceptive pills.
- Pregnancy tests.
- Veterinary medicine geared at livestock farmers.
- Lab testing.

Top Departmental & Policy Guidance

Pharmacies work well across Haiti. Since poorer areas are often neglected, often they visit a locally-placed pharmacy instead of a pharmacy's that's located further away. Because of their affluent incomes, higher-populated areas can support multiple pharmacies. Usually, these are placed in a nearby area. Thus, it allows businesses to focus and differentiate their services through products and services relatable to service delivery.

Action & Tips

- Because of Haiti's complex relations with international drug enforcement, seeking the counsel of a competent attorney is crucial. Incorporate your entity, ensuring that all proper regulatory rules have been followed. Therefore, you'll not must run afoul of authorities.
- An online pharmacy is particularly attractive since only a small amount of initial capital is required.

65. Join in the Effort of Filling Major Needs for Hospitals, Clinics, and Health Centers

Some people think that medical facilities, hospitals, clinics, and health centers fall under governmental regulations or are exclusively within NGOs. Although, this is incorrect. As it exists in developed countries, the most reputable hospitals are often private. These are either founded by either religious entities or by commercial foundations. In any case, however, initial starting capital comes from a sponsoring entity. Still, revenue contributing to solvency comes from fees for services rendered. Thus, the incentive provides quality health facilities and skilled staff. It further provides the convenience of access, and preferred outcomes. Both validate health center's reputation, justifying those service fees.

The target should be those with sustainable income. These individuals support services, which are given to insured patients. Though Haiti does offer health insurance to lawfully employed workers, others who're working may contribute individually. Both remain uncommon, however, before formal jobs are so rare. Those working in the open market don't produce enough disposable income. Therefore, they can't set aside for their uncertain or indeterminate needs. They're prioritizing more pressing daily needs instead. Thus, appropriate pricing is paramount toward maximizing the probability of operational longevity.

Business Concept

The first step is either building or renting out a facility. Second, purchasing medical machinery, devices, tools, and instruments is crucial. The final component is the vetting and hiring of competent medical professionals. These aren't minor tasks, but instead, they're combined as one project. Medical facilities become entrenched with members of their communities. As a result, patient demand supersedes capacity.

Upon starting a health care facility, a primary concern remains getting consistent revenue. Successful medical facilities seek out grants, while also hosting international donor drives. Both offset operational costs, keeping prices low. And so, medical centers can now accept Haitians of more diverse income levels.

Niche Ideas

1. Medical facilities being rented out to doctors or clinicians.
2. Ambulance and medical transport services.
3. Mobile clinics / home health services.
4. Specialized dental services.
5. Physical therapy.

Top Departmental & Policy Guidance

Medical services are required throughout the territory. Advanced and cost-dependent procedures economically support metropolitan areas. Rural areas, by contrast, support smaller clinics. These might be staffed with one or two full-time nurses, as well as and a doctor visiting the facility every few days. He or she visits to give patients advanced consultation. In this manner, the overall cost of supporting a full-time doctor spreads over a larger area. Consequently, there's less of a burden against a rural community.

Action & Tips

- Partnerships are crucial, and so, these should be used whenever possible. International donors, NGOs, local non-for-profits, and individuals focused on providing social or health services throughout Haiti should assist in the facility.

66. Private Medical Health Insurance Has Real Possibilities

Developed countries driving down costs, which provide access to medical services. And so, this has brought medical insurance into existence. A premium plan offers full access to medical facilities, diagnostic services, and emergency treatment for a single monthly payment. This monthly cost alleviates the sudden and significant cost that often causes a serious medical emergency.

Still, Haiti has some medical schemes. They're either badly run, non-functional, or inappropriately structured for the country's realities. Big returns exist for entrepreneurs, who can provide a unique offering. They can overcome the already existing difficulties which exist in the market. Then, they can provide a real solution.

Business Concept

Privately led initiatives can succeed in several ways. Targeting wealthy, middle-income, and corporate clients is an important tranche. These must not be ignored for those reasons. However, Haiti has lacked a critical mass of uninsured within those demographics, which traditional ventures within this domain have depended. And so, new innovative schemes are required.

One scheme requires engaging low-income groups. Medical services and monthly pre-imperative payments aren't lost on the poor. In retrospect, it's that they're not properly courted, educated, marketed, or prioritized. One strategy to engage these individuals is to seek out those who are paying untraditional medical insurance and paying premium costs. By having insurance through their employer, he or she is paying five to fifteen percent of their income monthly to insurance and sending it to collectors. Micro-insurance packages is another term for this hyper low-income scheme that focuses upon affordability.

Another scheme involves leveraging the Haitian diaspora. The Haitian diaspora defines those who've recently arrived in a foreign country. They've a purchasing power that's greater than those with middle-incomes Haiti. Accessing this earning power provides them emergency Haiti health insurance for themselves. It not only provides health insurance for themselves as they visit Haiti, but also in-country family members. This insurance covers everyone's healthcare needs. In this way, they're able to negate the disparity of not being able to pay in-country Haitians. This compensates and/or offsets the capacity by Haitians abroad.

Top Departmental & Policy Guidance

Health insurance opportunities are viable anywhere in Haiti. That's, of course, if an ingenious scheme can be successfully derived and executed.

Action & Tips

- Work closely with institutional healthcare providers. Ensure that insurance solutions are appropriately attuned with day-to-day realities.

- Imitation of firms, just as with insurance, manages the pool of collected premiums. A portion of this amount will be invested as an additional operational revenue support stream.

67. Traditional Medicine Has a Market too Strong to Ignore

Traditional medicine is formalized across the medical field internationally. Traditional medicine covers various practices, approaches, knowledge, and beliefs. These are used in pursing health treatments and conditions. Doctors use a variety of herbal, animal, and/or mineral medicines. They also use spiritual therapies, manual techniques, and exercises. All these treatments and/or medications are either applied individually or combined with a person's well-being. They're used toward treating, diagnosing, or preventing a disease. This is recognizable as acupuncture, oriental and African herbalism, homeopathy, and/or naturopathy. Also, it's widely used in chiropractic treatments, massage, yoga, and meditation.

According to a 2013 World Health Organization study, traditional medicine had seen double-digit growth in many of the places it reviewed. Included within the study were China and the US, which saw total sales volumes over $100BUSD across both countries. According to the Ministry of Public Health and Population (MSPP), more than eighty percent of Haiti's population uses traditional medicine. These practices potentially provide real positive outcomes. These are provided in a more universal and affordable way. And they're more accessible than modern medicine. Still, these are profitable in ways which we'll explore.

Business Concept

Business opportunities concerning traditional medicine are vast, but are categorized into two types. The first consists of its productization, concerning known and anecdotally substantiated traditional medical products. Harvest and packaged native herbs are used to preserve their efficacy. Material such as incenses, acupuncture needles, specialized boilers, and body oils are needed to perform traditional medical servicing. Those within the field recognize quality. In this way, prices of these products reflect the fact of hard-to-find material, as opposed to general market comparatives.

The second has to do with servicing traditional medical practices and paying participants for a premium. This means that doctors provide seminars on meditation. They offer appointments for massage therapy using therapeutic oils, have a facility for restorative acupuncture or home incense, or offer spiritual cleanses. Doctors genuinely engage in learning the best practices. Meanwhile, they are investing in the proper execution. This maximizes the procedures' effectiveness, going a long way toward building a reputable brand. It's further convenient for those already on the fence about this alternative medicine.

In both cases, Haitians living abroad are a sustainable target market. Haitians having grown up in Haiti are very aware of how effective traditional medicines can be. They've grown up taking many of these remedies and have positive associations. What prevents them from purchasing these products or services, however, is its availability or convenience. Traditional medicine's value has grown tremendously with the larger non-Haitian population. Therefore, it can simultaneously be target markets and be exploited.

Niche Ideas

- Online courses on the safe and effective use of traditional medicine.
- Books on traditional medicine's best practices.
- Therapies focused on mental health rather than physical health.
- Contracted home cooks focusing on natural eating recipes.
- Retreats that connect diaspora with restorative in-country alternative practices.

Top Departmental & Policy Guidance

Cities provide the clientele, whereas provinces provide inexperience. Connect both together. Many Haitian places have extraordinary spiritual significance. This intensifies the perceived benefits offered by traditional medicine services through association.

Action & Tips

- Work closely with Haitian elders and provincial herbalists.
- Acquire licenses and certifications to bolster credentials.

Finance

"Money is good for nothing unless you know the value of it by experience."

— P.T Barnum

A functioning and well-capitalized finance service market in Haiti – where all Haitians access credit, banking, and insurance – can't be understated. Financial services are an economy's grease and motor. Innovative entrepreneurs must elevate the industry to its potential, giving the stark realities of the population their services.

To be sure, the current financial actors have found enduring success. Despite Haiti's economic turbulence and challenge that befell their socio-economic condition more frequently than their neighbors, entrepreneurs have been successful. Haitian banks enjoy an affluent and profitable rate greater than their contemporaries. But this success occurs by the facilitation of the population's tranche. Millions in Haiti remain without access to any financial services outside of the occasional money transfer service.

In this section, we'll review the top areas of Haiti's financial services that hold the grandest opportunities. Then, we'll consider how it impacts entrepreneurs and investors.

68. Banking and Payment Services to the Pép At-Large

According to the world bank, sixty-five percent of Haitian businesses have access to conventional credit. Eighty percent of Haitians similarly don't have an account at a traditional financial institution. Ninety-one percent don't have a savings account, while ninety-five percent have never borrowed from any of the country's primary financial service entities. An upwards of at least 9.6M inhabitants in Haiti could benefit from banking services structured in a way they could use. In fact, real potential upside fiscal benefits exist here. These could be made by getting these individuals online, for example, which could be tremendous for any innovative entrepreneur who figures this out.

Developments have occurred in the past few decades. These have had proven new ways to onboard profitably, sustaining previous swaths of denizens that have been shunned by traditional financial services. One important innovation has provided three million people in Haiti access to some basic saving instruments. They also have access to locally instant fund and payment transfers through mobile banking. Digicel's mon cash has provided an original way that avoids the inconvenience, costs, and, in some cases, insecurity of visiting a physical bank. Over 3,000 partner agents allow users to deposit and/or withdraw money. Alternatively, they can pay for goods and/or services across Haiti. During 2019, at least 1.6M people of their user base performed at least one transaction per month.

Since its foundation in 2012, the industry has seen steady growth. Natcom, another major mobile carrier in Haiti, is set to introduce its own mobile banking option. That'll bring another million people or more online. Populus is open to new tools and concepts. If it's appropriately engaged and its access is wide enough, then engagement can follow.

The other big development, of course, is that of microcredit. Participants are provided small unsecured loans at low interest. Though, this is done in a group matter. Participants are held accountable by other members. Haitians already have a version of this lending in the form of "Sôl." All Sôl group members contribute a portion of their salary to a single individual, moving in a round-robin style until everyone has had a turn.

Business Concepts

Engage and bring aboard lower-income, inner-city people. These dispersed people have dominated others without conventional banking accounts. A big part of this engagement involves building trust and understanding.

It's important to understand the ways these folks currently set aside any residual income they may have. Then, they speak to the benefits of storing them alternatively within a system. People from all income levels have a mobile phone, and even more have smartphone variants. It makes utilizing a mobile banking platform much easier. (Talk about coupling with microcredit.)

Niche Ideas

- Micro-credit for rural people, street merchants (mostly women), and artisan traders.
- Hyper short-term loans, lasting only a few weeks to a few months. Offer these to street merchants, Madame Saras, and traders.
- Domestic payment systems allowing for digital payments.

Top Department & Policy Guidance

Mobile banking works anywhere in Haiti. Though it's grown, mobile banking depends heavily on the existing customer base. More specifically, this is Digicel's and Natcom's user bases. Both actors currently have near-hegemonic control in the sector because of this integration. Competing requires aggressive marketing, as well as dedication to accessible agents across Haiti. This bolsters convenience and fees, both which compete with transaction and withdrawal fees. This not only works for mobile banking. It additionally works for any traditional or micro financial institution.

The more ignored a region is, the more likely that a provided alternative financial service will succeed.

Action & Tips

Any sort of financial-based institution within Haiti requires legal procedures. Ensure you're equip with knowledgeable backed in a financial institution's legal and/or regulatory procedures. Haitian financial professionals will assist you throughout your entire startup process.

Success Story

Nupeye - Kevin Neil Thompson

Kevin Neil Thompson, a Jamaican national who has patriated Haiti, has been successful in making real progress. When it comes to making contributions to Haiti, he's achieved real market share. He's captured an idea on the tip of any tech entrepreneur's mind. Kevin owns Nupeye, a digital and cashless payment mobile application. His grassroots approach reaches out directly to retail locations, offering his Nupeye platform as a payment option. He provides a quick and effortless distribution of funds to that retailer. He leverages technologies such as SSL encryption, ensuring his customers' funds are both secure and easily accessible to his customers. Furthermore, he integrated tools into the app that help customers better understand their spending habits. These also help foster more prudent habits. He's aware the Haitian Central Bank has an extensive way to go toward a proper regulatory framework for Fintech companies like his. Still, he's confident a change will come soon. And so, his company will be well-positioned to take advantage of the larger opportunity.

69. Entrepreneurs Are Haiti's True Resource – Invest in Them

Starting a business is challenging anywhere in the world; but in Haiti, there's it's extra difficult because of a non-existence of capital. Funding gaps exacerbate the country's prospects for progress. It prevents generations of young and ambitious minds from acting upon business opportunities.

Many of Haiti's socio-economic problems are rooted within this disparity. Through supporting this morbid situation, you'll discover that banks and governments aren't fulfilling their roles. Their ultimate function is helping to facilitate necessary funds to small or mid-sized enterprises (SMEs). Unless someone is already exuberantly rich, or a company is so sufficiently large that they borrow in voluminous and collateralized amounts against large asset holdings, then acquiring lent capital is difficult.

There're available ways to reverse this situation, so now we'll go over some of those possible iterations.

1. **Venture Capital** - Financial capital is provided to early-stage and high-upside firms. There's a significant inherent risk, but early stakeholders can be rewarded for their equity position – should or if the company becomes public. These backers can cash out those initial shares, while the potential of similar schemes in Haiti is ignored. A successful model's key entails

many small to moderate payouts for ventures. All these can be sold later.

The arduous process involves corporation registration. Moreover, a lighter LLC version has been sitting with parliament since 2017 waiting for a vote. And so, part of any capital injection requires an entity's registration. These can cost upwards to $3-$4,000. Any business prospect receiving this early injection must be considerably vetted. Eventually, upside is reasonably assured.

1. **Angel Investment -** The difference between an angel investor and a venture capitalist is that angel investors use their own money. The latter uses pool funds including other people's money. As such, an angel investor is generally a wealthy individual. He or she provides capital to startups and small businesses. Because it's a single person, the risk tolerance is usually lower. Thus, a greater diversity of investment deals results from it.

This type of investment is similarly not common. In most cases, this sort of funding comes from a family member, who helps start a small merchant or trader business. However, we're still discussing more sophisticated business startups. These opportunities require much more funding. It further requires the startup's legal registration component, which may be needed as part of the investment contribution.

1. **Crowdfunding -** Crowdfunding offers entrepreneurs wide potential as a medium because it provides them access to capital

from interested investors. It's the practice of raising capital through online contributions, deriving from large numbers of interested people. As of 2018, crowdfunding's global marketplace was at $305B. Consistent growth is expected through 2030.

The power of this investment form is its feasibility. If the entity's already registered; each backer can provide a negligible amount to that person. Thus, it's more likely to be provided if the backer can be convinced of the project's viability or prospects. With an average pledge around $96, an ordinary person can participate.

Crowdfunding attempts have been brought to Haiti, but there's not been a market leader to date.

Business Concept

If you have the capital, create an entity that invests in startup opportunities. Ensure they present themselves in Haiti and are Haitian entrepreneurs. Of course, such things take considerable complexity. There's a lack of direct facility. Haitian investment law provides in this endeavor; however, the exact structure and execution derive its own book.

1. Have complete familiarity with the legal environment, as well as how to structure contractual relationships. By their nature, they can avoid the inconvenience of the Haitian legal apparatus. For example, in lieu of a return of capital, there's an

easy and systematic capture of the working capital. You can resale the latter.

2. Finding appropriate candidates requires particular care. In Haiti, limited ability to decipher caliber exists more so than in developed countries. Many of the ablest entrepreneurs don't have easily identifiable qualities. These might include education, internships, or prior formal business experience. It becomes an estimation of character more than any other attribute, both which are far from scientific.

3. Transparency and auditing business performance must be an integral part of the post-investment process. Ideally, do this with independent specialized accountants and your own in-person supervised revision.

If properly executed, a need and profits can be derived. Someone's business plan should be respectively robust to the realities. Doing so will ensure a worthwhile endeavor. Remember, you needn't provide capital. Instead, facilitate the process as either as a firm or creating a platform (crowdfunding).

Niche Idea

- Funding for small agriculture farmers and business entities.
- Women-led entrepreneurs.
- Assisting Haitian side businesses to find backers and institutional investors.

Top Department and Policy Guidance

The need for such entities exists throughout Haiti. It's critical to build successes. Early reputation and a consistent track record will be pivotal in aspiring confidence in an activity. This will have a perceived risk factor higher than other business engagement options already in existence.

Action & Tips

- Haiti isn't devoid of investment institutions or online platforms. Research and discover those that're currently a part of the ecosystem. Try to differentiate yourself.

- When it comes to attracting investors, trust is the underlying denominator. Being able to inspire yourself is trusting yourself. Who you associate with will be equally important. So, strategically seek and acquire partnerships. These will bolster those credentials both in Haiti and for your investment group, more than likely those that're abroad.

Success Story

MeNvesti.com - Lovens Gjed

MeNvesti, a recent 2019 startup with an uncertain but very promising future, aims to fill the gap of Haitian entrepreneurs. It strives to mend Haitian diaspora, who're hungry to contribute to lasting and sustainable pathways to a better future. They contribute to Haiti's future through their discretionary dollar contributions. Like other crowdfunding sites found in other countries, they allow backers to provide small amounts. Over time, these total large, impactful amounts. What's different here is that these are Haitian companies; but these Haitian companies don't charge interest on funds. The first $1,000 that's contributed has the fee waived. Further, capital raisers will receive direct consultation. Funds are disbursed and fund expenditure reports are sent to the backers. This consultant guarantees that collected funds are applied toward the stated goal. Moreover, these Haitian entities don't formally need a bank account. It's a tremendously onerous requirement for small and new businesses in Haiti, given the cumbersome legal structure.

MeNvesti has a promising future. We expect MeNvesti to be a market leader in Haitian entrepreneurship and early investment within the future.

70. Business Insurance Has Under-Realized Potential

Since the inception of humanity, human beings have lived on an uncertain planet. It's involved experiencing uncertain meteorologic events, being around less predictable human beings, and having to strategize how to avoid the worst aspects of all these things. But then, people also must learn how to deal with the negative once it arrives. Insurance is one of the world's oldest businesses. Since its humble roots of protecting for potential crop loss or inability to repay an obligation due to a natural disaster, it's an industry that's grown to preserve against countless harmful possibilities. It ensures the loss of a myriad of assets. Examples include life insurance, business insurance, auto insurance, health insurance, property insurance and liability insurance.

The insurance market is well-defined; however, Haiti's market has a long way to go. The penetration ratio is low, not even cracking 0.3% of the population. While supranational insurance pools exist, such as the Caribbean Catastrophe Risk Insurance Facility (CCRIF), individuals and businesses remain almost uniformly without protection. Areas are still prone to tropical disease, earthquakes, hurricanes, and ripple effects of civil strife.

Haiti isn't devoid of insurance companies that provide the entire gamut of recognized insurance services. Compagnie D'assurance D'Haïti (CAH) and Alternative Insurance Company (AIC) are the current big players in Haiti's business insurance industry. Still, there's much to be gained. Entrepreneurs offering insurance models are more closely attuned with ground realities of Haiti's socio-economic condition.

Business Concept

A big part of acquiring additional insurance market shares is educating the Haitian populace. Spending valuable and limited discretionary income on this expense is vitally important. Secondly, although it may time-consuming and fruitless for anyone attempting it, acquiring a public-private partnership with a national or municipal government splits the costs. It further subsidizes the operational activity and/or legally encourages patrons to carry insurance. Moreover, it offers insurance by employers. This might be fruitful for whoever can carry this activity to the finish line.

The general concept in lieu of this partnership requires significantly raised capital. It additionally focuses on approaching and dominating niches.

Niche Ideas

- Diaspora insurance / traveler insurance.
- Home insurance / business insurance / fire insurance.
- Life insurance.
- Product insurance.
- Temporary event insurance (music events, festivals).

Top Department & Policy Guidance

This is capable anywhere in the country, but to be effective, companies also need to spend resources toward educating their targeted audience. This isn't unique to Haiti, but rather to the Caribbean and Latin America. Penetration personal insurance rates average similarly around one percent. Those that take advantage of this insurance opportunity are the 'best educator." Target your niche, while then leveraging cost-effective social media to market this endeavor.

71. Money Transfer: An Important Pipeline of Fortune

A vast quantity of Haitians resides outside Haiti as Diaspora. They're responsible for a large sum of cash sent as remittances to Haitian money transfer agencies. In 2018, this totaled $3.2B. Entity fees are charged each time funds are transferred, totaling five to fifteen percent of the transfer value. It added up to millions in overall revenue.

Most transfers occur amongst a handful of market leaders. These are either Haitian-sourced transfers, or transfers based in Haiti. Despite their dominance, this market is ripe for change and transformation. Entrepreneurs have options for providing easier and inexpensive service than these entrenched players who altogether dethrone them.

Untapped catalysts leverage technology to get around traditional friction points. Xoom, for example, has pioneered convenience. Their app displays transfers within minutes. It's available from the comfort of one's home. They avoid financial regulations by partnering directly with players on the ground, who go as far as depositing the funds in local banks. Meanwhile, it's cheaper than using the money transfer partners themselves!

Business Concept

An alternative perspective to transfers is viewing them as daily matches between people who are wanting to exchange currencies. Providing a service that functions as an exchange between currencies allows customer to bank quicker and cheaper. And so, you'll attract customers. This operation reaps rewards for those who can execute new technology innovatively towards this goal.

Cryptocurrency makes a strong alternative, because it shows how transfers currently occur. It's better known as Blockchain, the decentralized distributed ledger allowing cryptocurrency to operate. Blockchain enables any transaction to be automatically registered across the entire registrar in almost real-time. There's an inherent ability to function as a currency transfer medium. Other novel industry applications include real estate, retail, and domestic security. It'll be challenging to merge this ideal into real-world usage, since the friction point remains with the entry. Likewise, any existence of currency into and out of its digital counterpart is considered. The investment would need to be spent providing substitute methods of access, specifically in Haiti. These neither attract the anti-evolutionary ire of domestic financial regulators, nor traditional financial institutions in the country.

Niche Ideas

- Blockchain
- Foreign exchange apps
- Payment APIs allowing for international payments or easy transfers to domestic banks.

Top Countries & Policy Guide

Starting in the metro areas and spreading to rural areas is advised. Leveraging independent agent sellers is advisable, since it maximizes the market's access. It further extends the likelihood of someone using your service in two different locations.

Action & Tip

- Before investing too much, engage early with Haitian banking regulators. The money market is tightly supervised. Things that may impact the central bank's ability to direct currency flows will get pushback unless previously approved.

The Internet & IT

"We are still in the very beginnings of the internet. Let's use it wisely."

— Jimmy Wales, Wikipedia Founder

One thing can be said about Haiti's internet. Despite its infrastructure limitations and restrictions, we've seen consistent growth in internet access over the past decades. For example, Haiti had an eight percent internet penetration rate in 2010. By 2018, it had risen to thirty-two percent. While that's quite the exponential growth rate, nearly seventy of the population (around 8.4 million people) aren't benefiting from daily internet usage. This represents an incredible opportunity for the right entrepreneur.

Understand that the internet's growth has been driven by mobile phones' proliferation across Haiti. It's improved fiber-optic networks, along with information and communication technology. Though it's still comparable to be developed countries' internet access, pricing has considerably been reduced over the past decade. Competition amongst the mobile carriers, as well as traditional or specialized internet carriers, make these services affordable. The quality, stability and connectivity of these services has all improved. As a result, there's more access across Haiti now than there was in years past.

The culture has ordained toward inexpensive, low capital. Still, there's stable and yielding income. The internet presents a well-suited plan for entrepreneurs wanting to further their ambitions. The path it provides is neither limited to a physical street corner nor a neighborhood. Being online means being part of a global, a regional, or a national marketplace. It operates twenty-four hours a day and seven days a week, most of which a brick-and-mortar store can't provide.

We'll explore many of the most promising opportunities existing in internet and IT. Despite its many leaps and achievements, the internet is still in its early phase. Many opportunities haven't yet been explored or fully exploited in Haiti.

72. Outsourcing Holds Incredible Potential

In the early '90s, a bit of a revolution in business philosophy occurred. A company needn't be vertical. It can purchase operational services from external vendors. Therefore, it can better spend its time, resources, and energy on that which the company produces. Customer service and certain redundant back-office operations – like data entry, the IT help desk, billing & coding, and compliance – are amongst responsibilities at which firms look to outsource to countries. It's through outsourcing that their per dollar expense goes much further. By outsourcing their business, the company pays lower wages.

Haiti has advantages in outsourcing. Being on the Eastern Standard Time, its latitude is much more compatible than Asian work hours. After all, Haiti is just a short 1.5-hour flight from Miami. Short flights mean less costly quality control checks. So, supervisors need to visit facilities. Haiti has perhaps the most diverse language competencies due to its population's migratory tendencies. Many young, energetic potential employees can speak fluent English and Spanish, along with French and Haitian creole.

This space is a big opportunity for those interested in capitalizing off Haiti's comparative low labor rates, which are made available for educated professionals. Initial startup fees can be a bit steep, so your facilities will require infrastructure that allows your operation to function twenty-four-seven. This includes an installation of solar panels, backup generators, and different active lines of fiber optic internet. Additionally, furniture and computers are included alongside the hard operational requirements. But once the money's spent, there's substantial long-term opportunity revenue and margins.

Business Concept

Start a call center or back-office outsourcing company. If you're a non-resident of Haiti but looking to enter the market, first become familiar with your home market. Use its resources and contacts to acquire company contracts, which you'll need to cheaply expand their capacity. Join a chamber of commerce, participating in conferences where you can network with decision-makers and present your firm.

Specific outsource networks allow you to list your firm, services, and pricing. Find specific ones that're used in the industry in which you're most interested. Consider registering your entity at the Center for Facilitation of Investments (CFI), a Haitian government entity created to help large employment impact ventures and outsourcing. Similarly, they'll add your company to a database that makes it easier for international firms to locate your services.

Niche Ideas

1. Startup focused customer service. The need to scale can happen quickly.
2. Freelance services (videographer, web development, graphic design, etc.).
3. Transcription.
4. Bookkeeping and basic bookkeeping.
5. Specialized app/software component development.

6. Business research.

7. Email management services.

Top Department & Policy Guidance

The viability of this opportunity depends on consistent electricity and stable and fast internet. These considerations limit such outsourcing activity to two places, and that's Port-Au-Prince and Cap-Haitien.

Action & Tips

1. Ensure you have a strong web presence by placing an easily found website on Google. Also list your website for call centers or BPO-related searches. Many of your business opportunities will arise from individuals, often from people at large firms researching leads through a common online search.

2. Invest in robust facilities that can allow employees to rest overnight. Many agreements demand certain service level agreements. These can only be fulfilled when there's a domestic disturbance or a natural crisis. They needn't risk commuting that same evening.

3. Partner with schools of higher education and language. These establishments can provide handy, qualified, and youthful candidates.

Success Story

CETEMOH Digital Center - Duquesne Fednard

Duquesne is a serial entrepreneur. He who has many successful ventures under his belt, but none are more important than the BPO center he founded in early 2012. CETEMOH Digital Center is associated with a school sitting on property he owns. The BPO functions as a very important funnel. The best and brightest students can transition and obtain employment opportunities four times the national wage. From humble beginnings to Haiti's most notorious neighborhoods of Port-Au-Prince and Cite-Soleil, it's grown to a job oasis. Now, 200 people enjoy full-time employment. Its facilities have a full cafeteria, dormitories, and onsite clinic.

The employees work an assortment of different outsource contracts from companies across the world. They work claims, data entry, data testing, IT helpdesk, AI and machine learning support, and data mining. Recently, they've begun looking at opportunities related to inbound and outbound calls. Their ability to deliver speaks for itself when you understand that their operation has grown without any marketing or visibility. Instead, their marketing has been strictly through word of mouth, satisfied customer referrals, and trade shows. The firm is a genuine testament to what can be accomplished in this industry.

73. Tap the Huge Market for Professional Websites

It may be hard to believe, but not every established business entity makes it a priority to be on the internet. Thus, not every entity's represented with a domain name. Nor is every entity a properly branded business, with an informative and fully functional website. But surprisingly, most established brick-and-mortar businesses expected to have this technology, don't. They either don't have a website at all, or they're entirely inadequate. By doing this, these businesses are missing out on incredible revenue-making potential!

Integrating the internet into every company is necessary. Build up company talent as a result. Hire web developers, programmers, designers, graphic artists, and other professionals. All can contribute to such a modern website. Likewise, they'll match the eventual demand for high-quality Haitian websites. For businesses, these websites are a potential venture. The advent of plug-and-play websites that exist, wherewith minimal technical know-how, provides people the opportunity to build fully functional websites. It's never been easier to engage in the industry.

Business Concept

Providing a service that improves the digital footprint of these companies isn't a straightforward activity. Often, these entities don't prioritize this. Under the digital realm, however, this is prioritized. A potential revenue exists by properly integrating their business into this realm. Drafting a consultancy can provide value-informed education. As an integral part of this offering, it becomes a client sales strategy.

Growth in this industry is straightforward. As one's business expands their portfolio of well-structured websites, one will gain additional business through referrals and word of mouth. Especially if one's websites has produced tangible results for a client, such as increased sales or improved customer attainment rates. Further busines venture options include offering SEO, click funnels, media integration and soft site features (like blogs or engagement campaigns). Compare a company's priorities to their customer needs. These may include such things as attaining customers or financial assistance, specific international market exposure or improved domestic market product or service recognition. Provide concrete actions their site use to improve their content.

Many of Haiti's businesses are informal. Many could benefit from initiatives that offer people and small businesses simple designed web pages, consistent of a landing page and a way to purchase the product. This strategy is a limited effort which can rapidly be duplicated with slight modifications within the business. Still, it's possible to market specific templates for industries en masse.

Don't forget Haiti's major industrial and manufacturing players. Many have archaic sites, if any, at all. Visiting industrial parks to market products and services, while attempting to attract clients, is a worthwhile endeavor. Textile manufacturers notoriously have unengaging websites. So, take advantage of this opportunity.

Niche Ideas

- Large retail, industrial, and manufacturing operators. They most notoriously have poorly designed sites if anything at all.
- Tour, travel, and tourism companies and agencies. Often, these companies have uninspiring websites.
- Small to medium ventures. Typically, they don't have a website.
- Periphery web objects, such as WordPress themes and plugins.

Top Department & Policy Guidance

These opportunities are successful anywhere throughout Haiti. Still, you'll see the most success in cities. Internet access is a bit more ubiquitous. Therefore, it's a bit easier to sell the importance of why companies should integrate with the internet.

Action & Tips

Start with analysis. Acquire Haiti's largest companies and entities that have under-inspired websites. Compare these sites with their international counterparts. Understand what's missing. Present the output of this research to prospective clients.

74. Digital Marketing Has Made People Millions, and Can Be Harnessed in Haiti

Digital marketing is new. It's still being exploited in more developed economies but already it's an indispensable aspect of business development and growth. It's a vein that has just now begun to be tapped. This avenue remains virgin terrain in Haiti. In fact, few players have yet to fully capitalize on this opportunity.

Many companies still utilize traditional media. These include radio, billboards, and newspapers. All must market themselves. Unbeknownst to them, they ultimately are at the whims of people, either driving by or are those engaging on the channel when it's played. Though, effective outside of improved sales are scant. Through digital marketing, one posts an ad on websites. Then, it's shown through people's social media feeds. In this manner, an exact number of impressions can be counted. Moreover, exact demographics and specific geographic locations can be targeted more precisely. Most importantly, per comparative impression, the cost is just a fraction of traditional media.

Since the business community is spending more on international advertising, global revenue is expected to reach half a trillion dollars. Therefore, it's notable how beneficial this opportunity can be, should it be implemented with the right business concept.

Business Concept

A business's line of products or services doesn't matter. Nor does their size, industry, or budget. What matters instead is that internet marketing can benefit every business and person. The goal is to provide for the most effective solution. Entrepreneurs entering this space must grasp they're the arbitrators between businesspeople and clients. Business owners need additional growth as well as efficiency in new digital practices. Conversely, what their clients lack will earn the business money. Ensure your offering is multi-faceted. It should include digital marketing, and a digital strategy. Likewise, it should include social media marketing services. We're going to talk about a few specific opportunities existing within digital marketing.

Social media marketing improves exposure. It impacts calls of action through social media, which are used on social media sites such as Facebook, Instagram, Twitter, and WhatsApp. All of these are popular social media sites in Haiti. Research from a 2018 Safitek study indicates that ninety-four percent of smartphones using respondents in Haiti were connected to social media. That's a lot of potential eyeballs for a properly sponsored product. Shift yourself into a position, allowing either you or your firm to be recognized as an "expert." Overall, this greatly benefits you. While you're expanding your company, it takes these inevitable and necessary steps towards marketing.

Search engine marketing utilizes paid features. These allow you to bid for instances when specific terms are searched. Therefore, the client's business or content returns as a top-ranked result. If a term is more popular or if it receives more bids, then there's a higher cost. Searches for a term can occur thousands of times a minute. It's still possible to rank your site, but only after other bidders have won. The larger the budget, the more times your campaign is displayed to potential buyers. While this structure describes how search engine bidding work, boosting or sponsoring posts on other sites function in a similar way. Facebook is an exceptionally powerful tool in Haiti, so don't neglect it.

Search engine optimization is another critical form of internet marketing. Instead of spending money to seek out a new customer or sale, money is spent so that you can be found by a new customer more easily. This occurs at the exact time the customer desires the item. This primarily involves configuring one's website, along with having an overall internet presence. Moreover, it's vital that one's business and content are properly indexed. Thus, it's easily searchable online. It can be as simple as ensuring that all points of metadata are filled out in-depth. Strategically structure your website architectural sitemap to maximize search bot flow through the site. It amounts to the same. Maximize passive visibility to potential customers, because it's is exceptionally valuable to clients and businesses.

Niche Ideas

- Mobile phone marketing.
- Fashion sellers and creators.
- Entertainers and musicians.
- Politicians.

- Private academic institutions and seminar holders.
- Conferences.

Top Department & Policy Guidance

Digital marketing works anywhere in Haiti since there's a wide penetration of smartphones. Basic 3G access also exists in many rural areas. However, the most lucrative relationships are found in city-based corporate entities. There's a budget large enough to pay for effective digital marketers.

Action & Tips

- Target the predictable bigger corporate players and Haiti's NGOs. Although, don't neglect the small and medium enterprises. Alleviate their skepticism by requesting a small upfront fee, which equates to a percentage of referrals.
- Any entity using traditional media for marketing is an entity that can be educated to take their marketing dollars online. Be the persuader!

75. Blogging, Vlogging, and Leveraging Informational Platforms to Triumph

Professional blogging came about after the recent advent of the internet. And quite the industry it's become. Top bloggers have been able to parlay their site traffic, branding themselves into million-dollar businesses. They do this by offering merchandise, online courses, e-books, audiobooks, and seminars for sale. People can get supplemental information along with endorsement displayed on their sites. The best blogs aren't one-person operations. Instead, they're fully fleshed out ventures. These blogs have writers, editors, and sponsor searchers. It's lucrative and scalable enough to flesh out as an opportunity fully.

This opportunity is ideal for those who are creative. They understand where there may be gaps in information or entertainment. Likewise, they've the endurance to stick it out over an extended period of consistent content production. The content may vary from informational how-to, self-help, and business-oriented programming. The content may also include gossip, lifestyle, or news. Some of Haiti's most popular sites are those that focused on the diaspora. They either provide current events or show cultural events and touristic sites that exist within Haiti.

Beyond the content variation, the actual medium can vary. Traditional bloggers use websites that are connected to WordPress. Bloggers can quickly write, post, and disburse their content. Vloggers utilize mediums such as YouTube and Facebook videos. These allow them to create meaningful, informative, or just fun/comedic pieces. All these can be disbursed. Others blend these mediums, podcasts, or specific social media mediums. These platforms may include Instagram, Snapchat, and TikTok. What matters is knowing your niche and your audience.

Business Concept

Design the style of content you want to create. Will your content be personal, or more of a formalized publication – such as a news site or informational aggregator? Perhaps it's based on reviews or entertainment. You must decide how to monetize this type of content. Some platforms provide content creators with direct shares of ad revenue. Place specifically affiliated brands on your site, making it easier to cater to corporate brands. When you monetize it, realize that your content and your audience are the most important assets. "If you build it, they'll come."

Additional income opportunities will be available as your asset base grows. You can earn income from your loyal following. Sell value consistent with the content being generated. These opportunities include selling online products like wearable merchandise, e-books, online courses, or webinars. These are fantastic passive income generators. Once you produce it, they'll generate income so long as the content remains relevant.

Whatever is offered to monetize the content must be consistent with the brand. Most importantly, you offer a degree of trust and credibility to your audience. When it comes time to leverage that, it must be done with respect. Understanding who you are to your audience. For some, monetization can be incompatible with that. Services like Patron or memberships exist and for those people. Your audience can directly donate to the solvency of your content creation activities.

Niche Ideas

- Fitness blog.
- Haitian business and success news aggregator.
- Niche business or lifestyle blogs.
- Parenting blogs.

Top Departments & Policy Guidance

Digital media is available as an international opportunity instead of only in Haiti. By virtue of the internet, your base can include Haitians everywhere.

Action & Tips

- Consider offering your content in creole, as well as French and English. Don't rely on Google Translate. Manually translate it to the different languages to ensure understandability.
- See what works by reading many popular blogs, publications, vlogs, and media creators. Learn why it works. By understanding what drives their success, you'll be able to take similar elements and add them to your success.
- Manually distribute your content – especially in the beginning. Use email, personal connection, and WhatsApp groups. Use whatever you can to help acquire an initial viewer base.

Success Story:

Haitian Times - Gary Pierre-Pierre

Haitian Times started publishing online after a long run of being a printed news source. It's emerged as one of the leading news outlets for the Haitian Diaspora. Garry Pierre-Pierre, a Pulitzer-prize winning multimedia journalist, founded *Haitian Times* in 1999. The site provides topical and timely Haitian news concerning economic, cultural, political, and environmental events which the diaspora consumes in more familiar English. In addition to keeping abreast of Haitian-produced English new stories, they've a team of in-country reporters responsible for producing original content. But *Haitian Times* isn't behind on multimedia. They also invested in video production equipment, producing original content published across social media platforms. This content drives engagement.

They've they attracted private capital as a result, with a 2018 capital injection by HaitiNex Media group. Moreover, they're a sought-after platform for Haitian and Haitian diaspora entities. *Haitian Times* attracts over 500,000 monthly page views, logging over 150,000 unique visitors. Therefore, they've remained an attractive marketing channel for many wanting to advertise their service offerings to the Haitian diaspora. Their model serves as an example of what's possible from a business opportunity perspective.

76. eCommerce & Online Marketplaces Offer Commerce Benefits Without the Fuss

eCommerce is still in the early stages in Haiti. No single entity or company is the dominant player within this digital space. And so, it's opportunities of which people can take advantage. Haitian culture is particularly adept at locating deals. eCommerce can provide preference, convenience and reliability at a competitive advantage and scale.

Certainly, hampering this industry's growth is the lack of universal online payment infrastructures. This includes PayPal and other online payment platforms throughout Haiti. Reducing friction through easy and secure electronic payments is an important part of a scalable and healthy industry. MonCash and LajanCash exist and show some promise; however, their robust API integration is still in its early stages. Thus, it's a way to dominate the e-commerce space.

Despite these challenges, the Facebook marketplace has proven that Haitians will utilize online marketplaces. Thousands of listings are added to the site each day. Countless transactions occur daily, allowing some early adapting entrepreneurs to earn a substantial revenue. Other players have emerged, allowing sellers and buyers to leverage the internet as they market and search for wares. The final point-of-sale usually occurs in person and involves the customer paying cash. Let's explore the possibilities existing in Haiti's current interpretation of the eCommerce space.

Business Concepts

The potential concepts are numerous. Products can be sold online. Considerations primarily include if there's a targeted theme, industry, or service type. From there, the goal is to work out methods. These should provide quality customer service, a quick delivery turnaround, and flexible payment options. All of these have adapted to the reality of the Haitian eCommerce marketplace. Better yet, if there's a new technology making waves in other countries, work on being the first to offer it. Offer the product at a competitive cost, as opposed to importing that product yourself. The possibilities are genuinely boundless.

Niche Ideas

- Classifieds and listings.
- Job listings.
- Cars and real estate listings.
- Business and travel directories.
- Transfer and remittances.
- Arts.
- Promotional vouchers and offers – eateries, retail stores, and service providers. (Think Groupon.)
- Products for brides.
- Products for babies and children.
- Furniture and interior design.

Top Departments

This opportunity's incredible power is that it can only be driven by growth. It depends on the diaspora and community outside of Haiti. Figuring out how to integrate this international customer base factors into dominating the market. Go a step further. Allow the Diaspora to purchase products. Perhaps it's products or services centered around food or clothing. These may be suitable for their connected associates, friends, or family.

Action & Tips

- Resources and how-to guides exist regarding how to start various eCommerce businesses. Build up a library of such resources. Keep a specific eye on adapting the lessons taught to Haiti's unique conditions.

- Being online as a consumer outside of Haiti is potentially research. View any site in which you're purchasing products as an opportunity. Replicate and improve these products for the Haitian market.

- Closely keep a pulse of electronic payment methods that develop domestically. Whenever a new API or ePayment process is presented, investigate how these platforms may be used. Incorporate these into your system.

- A small cohort of international companies allow PayPal and e-payment options on the web. Although, their fees are generally much more expensive. Moncash is an example. API is currently on the market, while other competitors will soon to be online.

There may have never been a better opportunity to engage in this activity.

Success Story:

Flash Haiti

Flash Haiti has built itself into something like Craigslist is in America. Gaining much its popularity after the earthquake, mission workers and expats looked to purchase and sell items. It's grown into a go-to as an e-classifieds site. Flash Haiti a virtual online posting commerce forum for buyers and sellers having any desirable Haitian-based product or service. This includes vehicles, furniture, knick-knacks, or being a general business registry. Flash Haiti has everything. Generally, it produces revenue from real estate and other proprietary listings. Upon a sale being finalized, Flash Haiti earns a commission. The revenue that's generated keeps the website free for most users, who post and purchase items.

77. Online Gaming Is an Untouched Cash Cow

Until recently, gaming is something that hasn't been in the discourse of serious business conversation. Ninja's escalation onto the cover of ESPN's magazine, as well as and his mainstream multi-million-dollar endorsements, brought him into the electronic gaming domain for quite some time. But games aren't for kids anymore. They're professional avenues, which can emerge as fully fleshed out business ventures. Like the prospects of tech industries of the 80s, the possibilities are nascent. If it's not taken seriously, the possibility of making billions of dollars will be missed!

This industry's potentiality exists as part of the global virtual market. It exists for professional players competing in many types of games. This market's profits have been estimated by top investment analysts. As it stands, it's earning $159B in 2020. It's expected to rise to around $200B by 2023. Demographically speaking, Haiti's youthful population and improved metro area internet coverage, coupled with its exposure to games through smartphones, ensures a base skillset and interest. It ensures financial relevancy in whatever avenue one decides to pursue.

Business Concepts

While access has improved, there're still real gaps that pose challenges to Haitian gamers seeking to enter into this industry. Simultaneously, it provides the first real business opportunity. A profitable endeavor might include providing hubs and centers. Gamers and developers could therefore have steady internet. Charging a reasonable rate for gamers or game developers to have space is a potentially lucrative idea. Gamers can be charged rent that's low and affordable. Still, it can be rather profitable when viewed at a per-square-foot rate.

This idea can be taken a step further. "Gamer houses" are specifically targeted towards building winning championships. These have payouts in the hundreds of thousands and even millions of dollars. Gamers are covered and all their expenses are paid. As they train, there's middle income generated from the stream. Additionally, there's merchandise and fan contribution. Alternatively, incubation spaces is specifically for developers. These are provided resources. These allow developers to collaborate and produce potentially award-winning and highly remunerative online games, general-purpose apps, and other digital property.

Creating a game studio and getting directly involved with game development is another option. There's a glut of programming talent Haiti, but all these gamers are unable to find meaningful work opportunities. If you come from an experienced software development background with familiarity in US marketable niches, then the cost of labor can provide a genuine competitive advantage.

Games like Candy Crush simply created and visually stimulating. At the same time, these can be very lucrative. Adapt simple games for Haiti's market, perhaps by imbuing them with lottery elements. These are popular culturally popular in Haiti, and so, it's one way you could go. However, ensure the games have offline functionality. This gives a variability to Haiti's internet connections.

Niche Ideas

- Education-based games in Creole for teens and children.
- Local gaming tournaments. (Fifa is very popular!)
- Virtual reality sales and experience center.
- Lotto-based games.

Top Departments & Policy Guidance

This opportunity depends on steady and fast internet. Port-Au-Prince and Cap-Haitien have the fastest internet connections. Thus, your options will primarily be limited to these areas.

Action & Tips

1. Negotiate directly with internet providers. Obtain exclusive high-speed internet lanes to ensure the most stable and speedy internet.
2. Acquire more than one internet connection subscription from a different company.

Success Story

Paryaj Pam - Patrick Noel

'Borlettes' and lotteries are well-established games in Haiti. Each day numbers are published. Participants have a chance to bet on numbers for each ticket they've purchased. Tickets have potential payments worth thousands of dollars. A small little gaming house is located on various street corners; here, the actual transactions and numbers are posted. Paryaj Pam and Patrick Noel, after sensing that this analog process was outdated, created an online platform in the early 2000s. It allowed betters to do so through their smartphone.

Leveraging Moncash, subscribers can transfer their digitally stored currency to Paryaj Pam. Users' accounts are registered with their Moncash phone number. After their funds are transferred, it's instantly available in their accounts and ready to be used. Lottery ticket purchasers are available to players, which is very popular. Moreover, sports betting, horse racing, slots, roulette, and even TV show outcomes are available as well. It's grown past traditional established players within a short time. By leveraging online and digital accounts, it's the number one gaming platform in Haiti, and Haiti's twelfth most-visited website.

78. Tap into High-Demand Data Backup and Recovery Services

Haiti is prone to natural disasters. Hurricanes, tropical storms, earthquakes, and man-made civil strife are random but relatively common occurrences. The political battle, too, adds to the risk of property damage and fire. Services that back up and secure information and data is more realistic in Haiti than in most countries. There's a risk of losing financial data, operation records, or sensitive customer information. It's not difficult to sell solutions to entities operating in Haiti, since they're very conscious of these real and ever-present risks.

Yet almost no companies or service providers assist with this risk. Therefore, the data backup and recovery market to an entrepreneur may offer real returns. Despite Haiti's perceived small economy, the market is huge. Businesses and organizations are all inherently risk averse. They're searching for cost-effective ways to store and retrieve their data. Further, consider the growing need for data privacy and fraud prevention. This market is only expected to grow even more.

Business Concept

Being a cybersecurity professional is helpful in this space, though it's not necessarily required. Being knowledgeable of digital existing products that can be installed in your own onsite facility or leverage cloud services already existing online are possible strategies. What matters most for clients is that the person hired offers their expertise. He or she has a degree of accountability and assurance, and would assist the client should something happen. In other words, credibility is pivotal. Positioning oneself as an entity provides crucial security.

Niche Idea

- Backup, data recovery, and data security services for:
- NGOs.
- Small and medium business.
- Corporate entities.

Top Department & Policy Guidance

- Partner with tech facilitating entities wherever possible. These include companies like Impact Hub in Haiti. Not only do they've a large reserve of talent, but these places have an expansive network. They're connected to entities that understand technology. Likewise, they're more willing to work with a startup offering some new.
- Look for service and products in growth mode. Attempt to work out consignment or authorized vendor status. This provides you additional direct support, while you might also be compensated for connecting a client with the product or service provider.

79. Computers Break. Structure a Business Around Fixing Them.

While it's easier to track mobile devices' growth because of their portability, desktop computers, laptops, and tablets have equally become ubiquitous in Haitian homes. Mobile phones are increasing in demand, even as electricity and the internet struggle. These devices are often purchased second-hand and toward the end of their estimated manufactured lifecycles. So, they're opt to break. When they do, unless someone has a nephew or niece who can perform a basic troubleshoot, they'll seek out competent assistance.

To fix computers can be lucrative, because it's a skill that few in the population have. Given the rapid speed of changes in technology, staying knowledgeable is prohibitively time-consuming for someone casually approaching a computer's maintenance or repair.

Business Concept

While the market to repair technology-based devices is obvious, ensuring that products and services are properly priced and affordable is an essential consideration. Consider providing many types of payment options. These include an upfront sort of insurance payment. Alternatively, a client may pay for their repair in portions. Meanwhile, the repairer holds important collateral with discounts for early prepayment. Finally, consider referral programs that directly provide rebates for future service. A clear price delineation strategy is critical.

Certainty lends credibility. This sort of service could be operated out of a retail store or a residential unit. These devices are sensitive and valuable. Therefore, you may consider more security and a discrete location. Use social media and referrals to gain new customers through indirect visibility. Upon acquiring your customers, go out of your way. Ensure the request answered quickly. Quality customer service is how you'll get them back.

Niche Idea

- Consider hiring specialists. Ensure they can fix home appliances and electronic devices, as well as personal computers.
- Despite the strong market share, Apple devices have very little places they can be fixed in Haiti. Provide a solution.
- The purchase and resale of spare parts and components.

Top Department & Policy Guidance

Being able to acquire parts will be easier in Port-Au-Prince and Cap Haitien. Spare components are more available in these cities. This is still a business that can be established anywhere.

Action & Tips

- Consider producing your aftermarket of components. Purchase inoperable personal computers and devices, to be used specifically for future repairs.

- Consider a service that picks up and drops off in-need-of-repair personal computers and devices.

Other Ideas

"No matter what people tell you, words and ideas can change the world."
– Robin Williams

Thus far, we've reviewed many genres and provided a strong cadre of ideas. Still, many more ideas exist that don't necessarily fit neatly in the previously expressed categories. An important theme of these additional ideas relates to finding opportunities that aren't often exploited despite demand. These are either current or on the horizon. In simpler terms, it all relates to finding one's niche. What product or service can be launched by fulfilling demand from a subset or a specific demographic in Haiti?

You'll find that these sorts of ideas exist similarly in any country. They could certainly be launched in the first world. But in those cases, you're dropping a buck of water into a large lake rather than a small child's swimming pool. The impact that's produced is geometrically larger than countries like the United States or Canada.

What'll ultimately separate these ideas' executors from either succeeding or failing are those who're able to quickly tailor their strategies to the Haitian market's realities and specific culture. Slight nuisances of emphasis and attention make all the difference. When it comes to timing, always ask yourself: If not now, when? Don't delay. Move forward with the idea, that, as soon as you can work out the necessary logistics, you'll.

Let's explore the options together.

80. Organize Networking Forums for Haitians and the Diaspora

Social networkers and professional event planners are successful business franchises in Haiti. Both hold events, offering conferences and seminars on specific topics. In Haiti, these events hold weight. They serve as a method in which professionals meet, connect, reconnect, and learn from each other. When looking to learn who's who in any industry or professional field, it's important to attend a conference or seminar yourself. At the very least, note who's speaking and who's attending the conference as attendees.

Attendees are always asked to pay an entry fee. However, with as much as eighty percent of revenue being sourced from sponsors instead of attendance fees, sponsor accommodation takes priority. In exchange for their sponsorship fees, sponsors hope to gain access to influential participants. Sponsors hope these participants will purchase or utilize their products. So, make this facilitation as seamless as possible. Don't stop at just mentioning their product or service. Have their logo displayed around the venue. The more professionals that're in attendance, then the more one's event line has been completed. As a result, more sponsors will attract higher rents.

To go a step further, create functional societies. These regularly provide resources, videos, literature, smaller gatherings, virtual lectures, and online group forums. Membership is often purchased for a reasonable annual fee. More sponsorship opportunities can be sold to connect companies with the group base. Alternatively, sweeten the pot for event sponsorship. You can provide members access to society for a period afterward.

81. Homes in Haiti Value Foliage. Open a Garden Center.

One thing to notice about Haitian properties are the homes, offices, and government administration facilities. You'll notice there're voluminous amounts of integration with greenery. Flowers, gardens, shrubbery, trees, and plants sprinkle the landscape's entirety. A preference for foliage presents a potentially for a lucrative business opportunity. It might be a tree nursery, a flower shop, or a landscaping service. Any of these businesses could additionally offer plant maintenance.

Also consider producing an inventory of seeds. These could be sold to interested patrons. Therefore, they might grow their own plants. Many subsistence works depend on seed sellers. Often, they sell a degraded version of the plant they desire. They might also sell the wrong plant altogether, which pays a premium for assurances against such possibilities. Many middle-class homeowners prefer to grow their plant rather than purchase mature, and so they might appreciate a larger selection from which they could choose.

Lastly, Haiti has a large deforestation problem. It presents an opportunity for the right entrepreneur wanting to execute a social business with a traditional garden center. Consider taking donations to plant trees along the countryside. Conversely, partner with organizations willing to earmark a certain percentage of sales for reforestation efforts. Eventually, Haiti's government will seriously take reforesting to task. Your entity will be in an advantageous position to win bids or proposals from the private sector.

82. Leverage the Artisan Sector to Produce Quality Functional Pieces for Resale

Artisanal craft making is a native home-grown industries which, despite government economic policies and large business interests pursuing importation, has seen local production levels stay consistent for small the craftsmen and women. Metal and aluminum are used to create fixtures, art pieces, knick-knacks and toys. These are also used to create larger items like wall gates, doors, and furniture.

The key to this business opportunity is understanding the production process. Combined with research, it closely relates to demand and gaps in retail stores their crafts could provide. One can alternatively function as a distributor, purchasing or exhibiting some of these artisan goods online. Moreover, these crafts could be sold on eCommerce platforms for local or international buyers.

Village Art Noailles is an artisan community located in the neighborhood of Croix-des-Bouquet, east of Port-Au-Prince. It's composed of artists and blacksmiths, working in rows of shops where they produce and sell their wares to the public. Active since the 1940s, artisans have held to a gilded structure. Many leverage resources to explore metalwork. Amongst many other things, you'll find candle holders, plates, mirror frames, and large focal wall pieces. Likewise, there's highly specialized productions, specifically crosses for cemetery tombs. Artisan areas like Art Noailles make opportunities in this space possible and scalable. Seek them out. Incorporate them into your business model.

Papillon Marketplace allows artisans from different creative genres to display, sell, and acquire consistent income through their crafts. It was founded by Shelly Jean and her husband after they arrived in Haiti to adopt children. But then, they realized the children had parents who'd preferred to give them up instead of raising them. This was because the children's parents hadn't the income to raise the children themselves. Rather than turn a blind eye to this travesty, they stayed in Haiti. Shelly Jean built an enterprise that leveraged the many talents they saw. Many of these parents had talent but were unable to profit from it. In addition to custom artisan pieces provided to them for resale, they also designed and produced a variety of wearable clothing and home decor pieces.

83. Grow and Produce for the Beauty and Hygiene Industry

Haitians have a long history of using natively grown products. These fulfill their beauty and wellness needs, which include anything from castor oil and moringa, to vetiver perfumes and carrot-based soaps. Local growers source all these items. An opportunity exists for those willing to grow these materials for use.

Haiti's wellness and beauty industry is one the country's largest sectors. It's supported by an improved middle and upper class. And so, getting in early will pay dividends later. Beyond planting Haitian staples, consider other plants such as: Lavender; Sarcococca Confusa; Hamamelis Mollis; Daphne Odora; or aloe vera. These are all amenable to Haiti's climate and could be grown as well.

Don't think you need a large swath of land, because you can get started in your backyard. Alternatively, lease land for a nominal amount annually as you have more demand. Many Haitians abroad have large land claims. These serve as a lucrative alternative to leaving the land vacant or producing only subsistence crops. With a little bit of land tilling and proper equipment to extract the plants' relevant components related to the downstream beauty or hygiene products, the returns can be large and consistent.

84. Own an Air B&B Business Without the Hassle of Building Ownership!

In almost every national economy, real estate investment is one of the most advantageous sources of revenue. Along with water and food, shelter is one of humanity's bases. There's a perpetual and near-endless demand for housing. Considering that Haiti remains one of the highest population growth rates in the Caribbean, accommodation at all levels is only set to grow.

Beyond real estate's traditional activities, such as building or purchasing homes for rent (or earning income as a landlord), Air B&B provides another way to enter the real estate market. One method entails acting as an Air B&B registration agent and listing management specialist. Register hotels, apartments, or homes onto the platform. Then, manage communications with guests. Organize cleaning and listing prep. Assist with guests' pick-ups and drop-offs. Also, offer services to the owner of the property owner, doing anything they don't want to handle. You can charge up to fifty of the net listing revenue for this assistance! If you're managing multiple properties, the monthly revenue can potentially be huge.

A second strategy allows you to keep a hundred percent of the listing revenue for a limited amount of capital. Haiti's rental market is affordable for those coming in from abroad. Its lease rates fall between $3-$10,000 for the year. An enterprising individual simply rents out multiple units across a city. Then, they immediately list those units on Air B&B. While there're added maintenance costs to this method, such as upkeep and security, these fall on the Air B&B entrepreneur. The potential revenue falls are tremendous since it's a flat rate. You don't have to share any of the revenue. The more property, the more lucrative the opportunity.

85. A Courier / Delivery Service Can Be Lucrative if It's Executed Right

Haiti doesn't have a government backed mail delivery system. If things need to be delivered, most firms or companies must employ a carrier. The carrier needs either a vehicle or a motor to function. That's purchased by the firm. For firms and businesses with multiple possible deliveries per hour, costs grow quickly. And so, this can get expensive for an operational function that's not a core business function. Because of this, most businesses willingly outsource this function for a monthly fee. That's, of course, as long as they can partner with an entity that provides reasonable delivery assurance. They'll protect items in transit, and guarantee consistency in their service.

Business-to-business commercial firms have this need, but restaurants and retail also are in high-demand for these services. Restaurants are looking to expand their customer base by offering eat-at-home options through delivery. Usually, there's a slight percentage mark up. A courier or delivery service makes their revenue by an additional delivery service charge. This is charged to the consumer, while a percentage of the cost is charge to the seller. Similarly, retailers would love to offer online purchase options that included home delivery. In this way, they'd be willing to share in item revenue for that extra convenience.

The nice thing about this opportunity is the minimal capital cost. A few bikes and a few employees are all that's needed. Most of a business's budget can go towards marketing and new client acquisition. Hiring a logistics professional to track schedules and routing is crucial as the company scales; though off-the-shelf software designed specifically designed for the company can help with that. Additional revenue lines always exist as opportunities arise. For example, these might include public transport or airport shuttle service for hotels.

Taxi Plus is a Petionville-based courier and delivery service. It's seen early and endures success. Beginning with a handful of motorcycles, its offerings include passenger transport and restaurant delivery. They now offer vehicle passenger service. In fact, they've expanded to a commercial courier service and a port-to-residential parcel delivery service for transport and logistic firms. They heavily leverage social media to acquire new customers. They've branded themselves around customer satisfaction, an ease of payment, and diverse service to their clients. They serve as a model of what can be done in that space.

86. Providing Alternative Cooking Fuel Options to the Market Is Lucrative When It's Done Right

There's food everywhere waiting to be cooked. Most cooking is completed using specific fuel. Often this includes using wood, crop waste, or propane cooking fuels. Cooking fuels are critical expenditure items for citizens, despite where they reside. Haiti isn't any different. The question becomes, then, which cooking fuel to use. Nevertheless, this is where an entrepreneur can potentially be successful.

Poorer households usually use firewood or charcoal, mostly known as 'charbon' in Krèyol. According to UNEP, as many as ninety percent of Haiti's households use charbon. Meanwhile, 2.5M and 7.3M full-size bags of charbon are consumed in Port-Au-Prince alone. Middle-income and high-income households either use either electricity or propane.

As you know, a major reason for Haiti's mass deforestation is mostly the result of an increased population. So, there's a demand for cooking fuels by poorer rural inhabitants. However, there hasn't been any government oversight or government assistance. The cost disparity between charbon and other cooking fuels drives natural economic actors. It goes that route when no government body steps in to find a solution.

In lieu of government interaction, entrepreneurs can provide competitive cost options to charbons. These might include repurposed recycled materials from other agricultural or industrial processes like alcohol, rice production and harvest. Converting those materials into burnable patties is necessary. On the other end, provide stoves and charbon pots using less wood. These will allow wood to burn longer. Businesses can increase volume and drive costs while providing demand stability. To do this, consider partnering with large distributors, corporate clients, or NGOs. All of these provide a critical anchor.

D&E Green Enterprises is a young, Haitian-owned company. After it sprang up in 2009, it alleviated some of Haiti's environmental issues caused by an overexploitation of charbon (charcoal). With over 115,000 units sold across Haiti, D&E Green Enterprises produces energy-efficient cookstoves. These are specifically tailored to local and lower income households. Many commercial street vendors, too, primarily consume charbon. These stoves can reduce charbon consumption as much as fifty percent. For their first run of production, they partnered with the Clinton Foundation. Since then, they've begun other product lines that include renewable energy generation for rural farmers. D&E Green Enterprises serves as a clear example of what's possible with environmental entrepreneurship.

87. Staffing and Recruiting Services Can Be Essential in a Country of High Unemployment

Haiti has more abled-bodied workers than opportunities. This will remain a part of their reality for a long time. Perhaps what's ironic in this situation is that, despite the girth of Haiti's unemployment, many potential employers struggle in finding skilled candidates. It's not that those skills don't exist. In fact, this is probably the biggest misconception of Haiti's labor market. Given the fluid transient nature of Haitians and their diaspora, Haitians of a multitude of skillsets and experiences exist in Haiti's labor pool. Many carry over international standards and best practices back home along with them. Yet the disconnect between employers finding able workers, and workers finding fulfilling career persist.

This is where these matches' facilitation becomes invaluable for both parties. Learning how to find qualified people searching for work and knowing how to persuade employers that you're able to find the needed workers are both assets. These pay personal dividends, while they also allow you to construct a staffing and recruitment firm. By doing this, it's a step toward assisting with Haiti's unemployment problem. Entrenched established entities have this issue. New companies, NGOs, and startups particularly struggle with finding talent. They're happy to engage with a firm who specialize in that endeavor, while being cognizant of their cultural and ethical expectations.

Furthermore, bringing about modern recruitment practices includes online posting portals for positions. Communicate by using social media because opportunities may return dividends. Traditional firms use expensive traditional media to get the word out. As time goes on, building a database of applicants can be tapped into anytime. Use this database to search for applicants whenever there's a relevant position. It's a great way to build a reputation of quick responses to client requests.

Haiti Pro Staffing was founded in 2017 by an ambitious Haitian American upon their return to Haiti. In fact, it was founded by the very author of this book! It's found success by providing exceptional and responsive customer service to clients needing staffing. Their job listings are strategically distributed across Facebook, Instagram, and LinkedIn. Haiti Pro Staffing leverages online evaluation tools which allow candidates to be quickly assessed. Credentials are confirmed in half the time of their competitors. Today, they've placed hundreds of candidates in firms around Haiti. Moreover, they continue to work with domestic and inbound international firms. These firms have quality employees and give candidates merit-based opportunities. Unfortunately, this is all too uncommon in Haiti.

88. Draft and Publish Travel and Business Guides

Capital isn't necessary for this opportunity. All that's required, in fact, is knowledge of the city or region. You must understand its history, people, and events. With this foundation, mastering social media and content creation go hand in hand toward creating content that increases your exposure to possible clients. By doing this, you can build an impressive tour guide business.

Training guides your knowledge base, allowing the profits to keep up with demand as you write more books and build your reputation. However, these guides can also be published online. Publish them behind a membership only portal, providing access to interested travelers wanting that information which would normally be provided in person. Combining this information into a book can be profitable. In this way, it's considered a souvenir for guests, and can easily be sold as a stand-alone book. When it's sold in this manner, it earns residual income easily. Inquire with current travel agents to discover possible partnership opportunities. Some may provide access to excursion or event deals, thereby completing your niche and experience offerings.

89. Consider Your Own Roadside Hardware & Construction "Quincaillerie"

A popular venture in Haiti is setting up a depot that stores construction material, hardware tools, and housing fixtures. This supply store is aptly named a "quincaillerie." It's closely tied to the need for housing. Practice is performed piecemeal. As people experience windows falling, there's a steady and consistent demand for building material. Given the precarious nature of transportation in Haiti, most will simply go to the nearest option if the prices are competitive.

Despite often rocky and always unpredictable economic conditions, construction has always remained steady. Per the Haitian Institute of Statistics and Informatics, it's shown the most consistent year-over-year growth as compared to other sectors. Expect to have access to roads, schools, hospitals, and/or retail locations whenever residents access your facilities. But you can go a step further than other competitors by providing delivery to construction sites. Take a more proactive approach to secure exclusive supply/distribution deals which you have with productive development contractors. What matters to managers is that you're able to meet their demand when they've it. Alternatively, you can meet the demand with limited delays.

The most in-demand include:

- **Cement:** Cement is a critical cornerstone in most countries and Haiti. Even though it produces tens of thousands of metric tons of cement each year, Cimenterie Nationale Haiti (a Haitian cement company) depends mostly on imports. The Dominican Republic estimates that half of its cement production goes to Haiti. The distributor chain is mature, and so, gaining access to the supply chain to sell these items retail isn't difficult.

- **Aggregates:** Haiti's informal economy has built supply chains around crushed stones, pebbles, granite, sand, and clay. Much of these supplies are obtained from queries coming from around the city. Companies fill the order and transport it to city centers. Your hardware store should have adequate space to store moderate amounts of in-demand aggregates. While most buyers pick the materials up themselves, they might also offer an on-demand delivery service.

- **Wood / Timber:** Because of aggressive deforestation, a large quantity of wood and timber being acquired comes from imports. For this reason, wood isn't as competitive in price as other building materials (such as cement). Economies of scale are related to its production, transportability, and partial domestic manufacturing policy. Still, it's used for small scale fixtures. This includes using it for doors, window siding, and flooring. Wood has endowed home buyers to utilize more of this material in their home's architecture. And so, customers are willing to buy it in bulk.

- **Plumbing Materials:** Pipes; drains; fittings; valves; assemblies; water distribution devices; heating materials; washing materials; and human waste removal are all more than eighty percent flexible. These are cheap, and easy to install like PVC and PEX plastic. These plastics are popular. Properties use

339

them for their durability and resilience against rust and decay. There're small PVC and PEX plastic operations that're produced in Haiti, but most are imported from abroad.

- **Roofing materials:** Prior to Haiti's 2010 earthquake, homes were almost exclusively produced with cement roofs. They were resilient to hurricane-strength winds and insulated against heat well. Also, these homes were cost-effective. After the earthquake, however, there was a better understanding of how quakes strain homes. Thus, the exertion of walls and other structural support of buildings are unable to withstand a quake's force. So, buildings began being built with lighter materials and became more prevalent. For example, aluminum sheets were popular among the lowest income sect because these sheets were super light and durable. You saw more high-end homes utilizing them in their architecture and final buildouts. Other options include tiles, plastic, and fiberglass. Each type of roofing option, even within a specific type like tile, depends on the cost, the style, the quality, and the client's industry. Residential, industrial, commercial, and/or institutional customers have different roofing requirements. Depending on your location and the request's frequency, it'll be best to understand those predispositions and stock accordingly.

- **Steel:** Steel is a widely used and critical component of Haitian construction. It's used to reinforce anything that utilizes concrete. This includes buildings, walls, roads, and bridges. Like cement, it's often purchased simultaneously. Steel has a single mass producer in Haiti: Acierie d'Haiti. Despite this domestic production, a significant portion must still be imported to keep up with Haiti's demand. Distributors exist throughout the countries to meet your local market's demand.

- **Electrical systems:** Electrical systems consist of electrical conduits, fittings, wires, cables, explosions, meters, breakers, connectors, electrical products, and wiring and devices. You also want to consider keeping stock of solar installation materials. These have increasingly gained popularity in Haiti. The accumulated energy from sunlight has been useful. It ensures people have electricity during long periods of blackout. Proper installation requires panels, regulators, and the batteries.

- **Glass:** Glass isn't a common fixture in Haitian homes; although, it's increasingly more important due to modern architecture preferences. Transportation difficulties related to Haiti's poor and mountainous roads, as well as glasses' fragility, has made it absent in construction. Except, it's still used for most high-end Haitian homes. Knowing which market your depot serves, and whether it's geared towards this high end, drives determination on whether you'll stock this product.

90. Brick Laying; a Cash Cow Hiding in Plain Sight

Driving around Haiti, you'll find a common sight throughout communities. There's a corner where a handful of young men are churning cement into concrete blocks, laying them out to cool. These concrete blocks then harden in the tropical sun. Immediately, they're sold for bulk order and construction all around the area. It's a manual process, where cement is mixed with water and gravel on the ground using shovels. Then, it's pressed into block molds that are manually pressed into shape before being dried.

All it takes to enter this industry is ownership or leasing. You need a stockpile of purchased cement, and molding devices to create the bricks. Bricks sell at rates well above the cost of input. A business owner can draw steady monthly income from sales. It's possible to differentiate within this field. Purchasing modern molding press devices and tubular cement mixers. These runs either on general or solar panels which can be installed onsite. One of the 2010 earthquake causes was poorly produced cement blocks. These were the result of a poor fabrication process. The market will reward you for providing competitive cost blocks of substantial quality. It holds an added awareness and importance.

91. Consider a Public Relations, Communications, and Social Media Management Agency

The need for companies, brands, and people to set themselves apart amongst an increasingly crowded media space is important. And it'll only increase in the years to come. Traditional media has already been dethroned. The preferred consumption channel by the current and upcoming generation navigate this new era often requiring professional assistance. An entrepreneur with PR, communication, and an understanding of SEO or virtual content creation can step in to make a difference. They can provide guidance while being paid handsomely.

Local organizations, companies, and people will compensate you for providing a concrete strategy. Overall, this improves their brand's visibility. It directs public opinion, improves reputation, increases followers, or connects them to other social media influencers. Become indispensable by fostering relationships with personalities, or media platform contributors. Connect with those already having large followings. They can be leveraged toward pushing out a press release, offering, or perspective that benefits a client.

Know how to boost and utilize social media marketing campaigns because this is critical. It provides an effective service offering. Know how to target audiences by demographic and keywords. Likewise, mastering engaging images and videos that entice viewers utilizes digital marketing techniques. These include click funnels and directed call-to-action channels. Those who understand the possibilities structure their relationships as a percentage of sales instead of flat rates. Therefore, they can more fairly tap into the large well of increased revenue they produce for their clients. This assures a handsome income for their knowledgeable efforts.

92. Business-to-Business Solution Servicing Is Profitable and Satisfying

Consider what services can be sold to consumers, retailers, and businesses. Take advantage of business-to-business (B2B). It benefits entrepreneurs entering into the Haitian domestic market.

- **Government Administrative Service** - Businesses and people need guidance regarding the many opaque government administrative practices. It might be payments consisting of different municipal or national annual fees. It may even consist of registering a business or a non-for-profit entity. It'll be required to partner with a local lawyer, but the lawyer can only handle the filing and legal compliance work. Your firm would concentrate on customer service, education, and repetitive aspects. These include monthly payroll and quarterly income tax filings.

  For example, an export-based company requires a bill of origin that must come from Haiti's commerce department. Tinting company vehicles' windows of requires special authorization from the police that's paid at the tax office. The list of offered tasks goes on. Take advantage of this demand. Offering these services at cost-competitive pricing. Provide assurance that they'll be done at the quickest speed which government bureaucracy allows.

- **Business Consultations** - Many abroad expecting to come to Haiti, either assist in an NGO charity or start their own ventures. They tend to have years or decades of experience in their professional fields. It might be accounting, business management, IT, banking, retail, or customer service. These years of experience can be parlayed into a consultancy that's offered directly to Haitian businesses. Between contracts and building local notoriety, conferences and seminars can be offered to the public. Leadership can be invited to sample some of the more in-depth training that's offered.

The potential income and consultancy fees can be lucrative if someone lands a major enterprise relationship. However, gaining considerable traction is possible by assisting small and medium-sized businesses. Structure remuneration in a manner that's either more affordable through payments over a longer period. This helps find additional clients by leaving marketing material on the premises. A consultancy's impact is amplified at this level. Essentially, your expertise can help alleviate their brand and improve earnings.

93. Things Get Dirty: Produce and Sell Cleaning Products

Cleaning products range from laundry detergent, dishwasher soap and scented disinfectant. These are used to mop floors, while window glass cleaner wipes down windows. These items are in demand and relatively easy to produce. Brand notoriety matters after ensuring your product can perform its primary function. If it reduces a residual effect, the others being produced might work better than what's on the market. These are being sold at a competitive price. And so, you'll be well-positioned to take a percentage of the market. Utilizing organic, locally found plants and materials also differentiates your brand. Moreover, it may afford you opportunities if it's done correctly.

Strategically spending money on marketing ensures your product is available. It's visible in as many locations as there're consumers. Most of your budget, for this reason, will go towards brand awareness. Once your brand supplements in consumers' mindsets, expanding into different sublines becomes more likely. Integrating your brand will provide significant dividend returns on this large and operational expenditure.

94. Reduce Your Insecurities by Establishing a Security Service

Haiti isn't unique needing security. All countries have private security that monitors gatehouses, secure construction sites, and guest activity. Common theft occurrences, armed robberies, or kidnappings may occur in any country at any time. If you're someone who comes from an armed training background – whether it's police or military – than founding a security service could be profitable.

Security is at the forefront of Haiti's middle class, particularly those involved in commercial or political activities. The Haitian government's public security apparatus leaves a lot to be determined in size, funding, and results. Acquiring additional services for oneself and one's business aren't just commonplace; it's expected. And so, the demand outstrips the supply. Your new firm will find contracts relatively quickly once it's well-marketed and staffed with well-trained employees.

Considerable security is numerous and goes beyond private security companies. The baseline security options should consist of guarding homes. Likewise, protection should be offered for corporate offices, banks, schools, hotels, and other facilities. Consider security for events, vehicle escorting, airport pick-ups and drop-offs, or bank deposits and withdrawals. Setting up and monitoring anti-theft and surveillance services can be particularly lucrative and important. This includes installing GPS trackers for vehicles and motorcycles – both for clients and for loved ones. Also, install security cameras and intrusion home/office alarms. Finally, consider raising, leasing and/or selling guard dogs. Guard dogs are an important part of home security, particularly for those with moderate to large estates. Have them in demand, but avoid incorporating them in your service offering.

95. From One Country to Another: Offer Relocation Services

Upon referring to relocation, we're not talking about a moving truck transporting items from one home to another. Though, a business idea is worth considering for different reasons. Instead, we focus on people and companies looking to move themselves or their staff into Haiti. The components involved in this are numerous. First, it means acquiring proper immigration status, either a visa or proving your ancestry to acquire full citizenship. This alone can be a value-added proposition. Other services include airport assistance, in-country transportation, concierge, network, housing facilitation, and security.

This business isn't capital intensive, however, and can be started part-time. Having the appropriate and previously proven contacts is required. In essence, this ensures the service can be provided at a reasonable rate. Customer service providing inbound transient is expect in Haiti. Your primary role, therefore, becomes being a coordinator and lead facilitator. After a few successful relocations, growth is solely facilitated by word-of-mouth marketing. And so, satisfied clients will refer others to you.

96. Research as a Venture Market & Business Research

Reliable data coming from Haiti is as uncommon as Haiti's ground oil. The last sentence is hyperbolic for effect. It underscores that Haiti's data is hard to come by. There's not a public exchange anywhere in Haiti. In fact, most firms are private with commercialized and verifiable data sources. Conversely, the government collects and distributes few sources of data. Statistical data relating to the census, which is crucial in most countries, doesn't happen in Haiti. It's easy to decree this lack of information; however, a well-versed opportunist with an expertise in statistics, data collection, and/or inquisitive thesis would see a successful market research venture.

The demand for data exists on many fronts. NGOs, non-for-profits, and sizeable international aid institutions all require various data-based write-ups before approving research. Private firms need to have specific research conducted before committing to large capital expenditures. Feasibility studies, business cases, market studies, omnibus surveys, evaluations, testing, focus groups, and opinion polls all may be requested. These can be charged at healthy margins.

As your firm builds a credible reputation for high-quality market research, expect free word-of-the-mouth advertising for research requests. Consider researching monthly or quarterly cycles. These are provided to interested parties through a subscription. Often, it's inexpensive to produce media content around a portion of this data. Meanwhile, it's shared with the public and can be used to your advantage. In any case, this venture idea has potential for exploitation.

97. Provide Unique Experiences Through Wedding and Event Services

Weddings and events, in which one often participates, are seldom considered an industry. Though, both these needs particular exposition. Many weddings cost between $10-$20,000. Haiti remains a popular destination spot for the Haitian diaspora. Though, often it's well beyond that. There're weeks of planning and stress. A significant percentage of these weddings are administered by well-compensated professionals.

Haiti's population is young, and so, marriage of those with a stable income is high. An economically improving Haiti will see domestic weddings skyrocket. As these opportunities arise, there's opportunities for wedding expenses. These include rentals, event centers, catering, decorating, makeup, photography, and others. All these will become additional branches that offer either in-house service or pursue primary business ventures.

It's important to non-wedding events as well. Culturally, programs consist of important social leisure activities for Haitians. Among these are parties, concerts, conferences, conventions, trade shows, festivals, galas, corporate events, workshops, and/or seminars. These all improve in their execution with a professional in charge. Likewise, they can be offered as part of a registered event planning business. Money that can be made is considerable.

98. Certified Auto Parts and Auto Repair Is an Appreciative Premium

Haiti neither has a lack of mechanics, nor is there a base deficiency in the aftermarket part industry. In fact, given the state of Haitian vehicles being older and more likely to break down, mechanics in Haiti get plenty of practice. They're less dependent on computer diagnostic machines than other countries. In these cases, a proper OEM part can't be found. As a result, there're many cars to repair, recraft, or repurpose.

However, what Haiti lacks are the very things making Haitian mechanics unique. These adept, modern shops have diagnostic and therapeutic equipment issues directly sourced from the manufacturer. For casual tier brands like Toyota, Nissan, Isuzu, etc., this deficiency isn't too much of a problem. But luxury brand owners struggle to repair or maintain their vehicles. There's an odd selection of locations available, mainly only in Port-Au-Prince. So, they've few places in which to bring their vehicles. Open your shop in any of the other major cities or open a chain in Port-Au-Prince. Take advantage of this demand.

Electric vehicles are perhaps only in single digits; but someday soon, theses may hold significant percentages in Haiti. Tesla vehicles are incredibly complicated vehicles. Essentially, these are effectively large laptops with wheels. The savvy equipment's that needed when these vehicles become a prominent guarantee include a garage with current technology. Be one of the first to take advantage of this.

An additional underserved market exists for upgrades and modifications. A brief drive around Haiti won't be completed until you pass countless vehicles with reinforced front defenses, or makeshift cages on trucks that allow for passenger transportation. Bodywork, too, is as noticeable as shoddy. Opening your shop can provide executive-level service. Clients will frequent it often, compensating you by matching your healthy premium pricing.

99. Importation Is Popular – Take Advantage of It

Haiti's trade balance of three-to-one imports presents clear evidence. There're financial advantages to bringing products into Haiti. Haiti produces little economically. By that reality, there's a demand for everything in the first world. This situation contributes heavily towards Haiti under its development. Therefore, an entrepreneur aligned with truly improving Haiti's net conditions would look at structuring a more export aligned entity. This book would be deficient without a formal discussion of already existing opportunities within that space.

Importation is particularly attractive at all levels, with its minimum capital requirements to participate. Online resources connect any budding entrepreneurs with manufacturer centers in Asia and India, making goods and products accessible at wholesale prices in bulk quantities. The entire universe of inbound commerce and trade is at one's disposal. All that's needed is a computer, email address, storage depot, and bank account and/or credit card.

Furthermore, drop-shipping has fundamentally changed the import business. "Drop-shipping" describes someone purchasing a product wholesale AFTER a retail customer has purchased it. By utilizing minimal capital, someone's effectively running their supply chain and delivering a product to a consumer. Even better, drop-shipping reduces the need for warehouse storage costs. In essence, there's fewer requirements to build out logistics network and personnel. Specific parts can be outsourced. Your entity functions as a coordinator and a profiter of the margin between the cost and per unit sell price.

The following resources and locations to leverage are as follows:

- Aliexpress.com
- DHgate.com
- IPMart.com
- Chinabrands.com
- Bangood.com
- Bluember.com
- Indiamart.com
- Baapstore.com

It's important to understand that, even though there're long-term successes, it depends more on products after they're brought into Haiti rather than products being brought into Haiti initially. Value-added importation intends to import and redesign. It further transforms, recomposes, enhances, processes, or constructs imports into a more marketable item. This works regardless of the product. It could be anything from sausages or wheat, to motorbikes or electronic devices. Consider ways to further delineate your product through ingenious marketing. These strategies will leverage traditional media effectively. Capitalize on social media's viralness, winning lifelong clients through word-of-mouth referrals. Ultimately, this allows your firm to justify prices above the market price. This ensures a higher price for your product and homogeneous unenhanced copies that may be imported. When customers are willing to accept higher prices, it means there's a better insulation to market events and growth!

Surtab, a technology manufacturer, is a brainchild of Maarten Boute. It's an import from Belgian. Maarten Boute now resides in Haiti and helps run Digicel Haitian operations. The goal was to model India's competitively priced Aakash electronic devices. Then, they'd produce inexpensive products (such as android tablets). In a 2,000-square-foot industrial park, dozens of employees assembled their Surtab tablet with computer components from across Asia and India. They leveraged Haiti's lower labor costs and geographic proximity to the larger North American market.

Workers can produce fifteen tablets per day. These tablets are marketed across North America and Africa, and the Caribbean. They're further marketed around the burgeoning NGO and education market. Moreover, they intend to offer the tablets across all Digicel's 116 Haitian retail locations. It's essential to keep an eye on Surtab. After all, it's a value-added importation business model.

100. Haitian Exports and Its Untapped Wealth

The long-term change of Haiti occurs when influential private actors argue not over importing goods into Haiti but finding Haitian-made products to export internationally. Exported products might include products that are harvested, created, or packaged directly in Haiti. This the right thing to do from a macroeconomic perspective, but it's also the best move from a microeconomic perspective. Selling your product in a foreign currency means your revenue is based on a strong international currency. Meanwhile, your costs and expenses are paid in a weaker local currency. Eventually, all prices balance out. The value of any item will exactly equal the exchange rate. The lag occurs between that which takes months. And so, there's always added financial margins.

The first part of exporting is finding goods that'll interest a foreign market. This is where the Haitian Diaspora may hold a particular advantage here. They've lived or grown up in a different market for years. Thus, they'd be much more attuned to the preferences of that market. But at the end of the day, anyone willing to research and perform market testing would be successful in their target market.

Even when the ideal product is found, there're other considerations. Haitian producers universally have an interest and desire for exporting. However, they lack the capacity. So, they're typically unable to consistently produce at the quantity or quality. Since neither of these is possible, it makes industrial scale exporting nearly impossible. Below are some critical strategies to assist with overcoming this deficit.

- Look to value-added export products. These have already been modified, transformed, or combined. Raw products tend to have mature and competitive markets. Focus on juices rather than oranges. Alternatively, focus on pre-packaged mangoes, oranges, or lemons. Turn your attention to flavored cassava treats rather than raw potatoes. All these are examples of exportable value-added distributive products. This value-added emphasis enhances the general economic impact. It further becomes an important and profitable differentiating marketing/branding strategy.

- Leverage treaties and economic compacts in which Haiti has already partaken. For example, the HOPE Act allows for easier and tariff-free importation of textiles into the USA. But other lesser known opportunities exist. Haiti is a part of CARICOM, for example. There're many opportunities to export across the Caribbean that remain untapped and untouched.

- Consider partnering with not just a single producer but also a network or association of producers. Doing this can help to round out order consistency. Moreover, it drives their economics of scale and drives down costs.

- Be visible. Attend any conferences, events, expos, or public venues. Get your set of products out to the public.

- As you scale, the transition to leveraging other wholesale distributors can give your products a revenue baseline to operate. While it's not as lucrative as setting your own distribution to the retail pipeline, diversifying your global supply chain is crucial toward building a robust revenue line.

Yvans Morisseau and Maly Sebastien Paul, **Horizon Vert** founders, recognized Haiti's situation. Eighty percent of food products are imported into Haiti. These are largely the result of domestic farmers' disparity since they couldn't tap into international markets. Worse, these farmers were simultaneously competing with heavily subsidized imported goods within their local market. As a result, they minimized taxable imported products within their local market. While they didn't control the latter, they still controlled the former. They designed an enterprise which did business directly with local farmers, hiring over a hundred people to purchase products. Then, they cleaned, sorted, and packaged them. Farmers benefited, receiving immediate and above-market cash.

Farmers have seen steady growth opportunities since the beginning. Despite Haiti's turbulent times, they continue looking at additional markets. Here they introduce their Haitian products: mangoes, Haitian rice, pitimi, and piment hot sauce. Horizon Vert is focused on its growth. It expects to finalize an important deal with the Bahamian government. Soon afterward, additional Caribbean and Latin American markets plan to join makes government deals as well.

101. Blockchain and Crypto Currency: Game-Changing, if Used Correctly

Blockchain and cryptocurrency are an obtuse mystery for many. How they function in today's modern technological world is different than regular money. Blockchain, a technology on which cryptocurrency is based, is a digital ledger. Transactions are recorded independently of one another in real-time. These bypass the need for a central authority. It's a democratization of data in a way only possible because of the internet and the world of high computational bandwidth of both personal and commercial computing.

Cryptocurrency has become most popular in the forms of Bitcoin, Litecoin, and Ethereum in a mainstream developed society and can be used as alternatives of accepted currency in addition to dollars and euros in a growing number of places. Cryptocurrency is particularly popular for its potential to revolutionize long-distance money transfers and simply purchase between parties no matter the familiarity level. And given the value of many cryptocurrencies have consistently risen in value over the years, they're also proving to be predictable investment vehicles in and of themselves.

While the future may indeed be crypto, in Haiti, that future's further away. It's only been within the last few years of this book's writing that Haiti's commercial entities have begun using credit card terminals in large percentages and are generally opposed to innovation. The government has a long way to go in even providing the basics, and the people, those who've daily access to electricity and Wi-Fi/internet, themselves haven't shown interest towards digital beyond WhatsApp, evident by Moncash's low penetration rate.

While the tone thus far for blockchain is pessimistic in the country as a stand-alone entity, there's optimism in how blockchain could be leveraged to improve funding for large scale ventures. Akon artfully performed this idea, utilizing his own cryptocurrency issuance to acquire funding for a large multi-billion-dollar real estate development project in Africa. Cryptocurrency can be used in many ways to raise capital for a Haiti venture, where digital currency is issued at an early dollar exchange rate that behaves like stock without a central stock market. Alternative schemes use cryptocurrency in innovative ways in different countries. These include lotteries or other games of chance that utilize cryptocurrency as their primary participation vehicle, and the residuals of revenue can go towards your Haiti activities.

The key here is a cryptocurrency, and the blockchain that underlies it should be reimagined for Haiti. Applying it copy and paste as how it's been in other countries just won't work. The entrepreneur(s) who figured out the winning formula certainly will be awarded handsomely by the market.

Concerning...

...Moving to Haiti and How to Minimize Failing

Don't come to Haiti only for emotional reasons. This will be restated again due to its importance: Don't come to Haiti only for emotional reasons. These spur-of-the-moment decisions only end in failure months later; though each story's version is different even though it results in the same underlying experience. Someone ran out of money. He or she felt taken advantage of by family, or they were pressured by expectations to assist associates and friends. In the end, however, they found it difficult to navigate a system like Haiti.

Their return to Haiti needs to be slow, methodical, and purposeful. First, secure income because this makes starting a Haitian business easier. Consider primarily a remote job. Choose a job that's either full-time and flexible or part-time with limited daily hours. Alternatively, look at residual income sources. These include social security, real estate, interest, and stock dividends payments. Understand the importance of having capital for your startup or venture is critical. But, having an income that provides a degree of comfort to think beyond your immediate needs are another. Being successful in Haiti can depend heavily on the latter in Haiti.

Getting a job in Haiti isn't recommended. When you accept a job as a repatriated Haitian, you're taking a job from a Haitian national. He or she already has drastically limited employment options, compared to you with your opportunity guaranteeing citizenship or residential status . Likewise, the wage levels are vastly different for an experienced white-collar professional in Haiti, as opposed to other countries. In fact, these are often only a quarter of someone's monthly salary. And so, over time this leads to dissatisfaction for the repatriated Haitian knowing they are making a fraction of what they could. Finally, there's cultural differences in the hours someone's expected to work. This coincides with communication norms and management styles. All these contentious points for people not accustomed to the Haitian workplace.   Come to Haiti to create jobs, instead of taking jobs away.

...Conceptualizing to Start-Up Reality in Seven Simple Steps

"It doesn't matter how many times you fail. It doesn't matter how often you almost get it right. No one is going to know or care about your failures. So, neither should you. All you must do is learn from them and those around you. All that matters in business is that you get it right once. Then, everyone can tell you how lucky you are." This is a relevant and informative quote from billionaire entrepreneur Mark Cuban.

Having a business idea is easy. It's moving it from the realm of an idea into action that's difficult. But one must take that very important next step. Only then can the idea become a reality. Often, it's not that someone lacks the will to do it. Instead, he or she lacks the knowledge. So, this next section provides that information. It'll allow you to feel confident to act.

Step 1: Fully understand the Haitian culture.

Many readers might reside outside of Haiti; still, these readers are aspiring to make an impact. Don't take the cultural differences lightly. There're variances in perspectives norms, and social philosophies. These predicate whether a business will succeed. All in all, you can't be successful with a genuine understanding of Haitians. You only acquire this through direct exposure to Haitians or their culture.

More importantly, you must have the capacity to reside within Haiti during the first few years. It's essential to live in Haiti as the business

366

begins. Alternatively, commute half the time for a given month. Managing from a distance leads to many operational problems. These can't be overcome by modern remote management techniques.

Understand the importance of navigating Haiti's bureaucracy. Getting direct service quotes directly as opposed from partners or subordinates makes a difference in the negotiation process. Negotiation is required in many business dealings; so, it's vital to know the correct service or sales price.

You can't run a long-distance business from Haiti. Being in Haiti on short notice is an inescapable requirement of any business.

Step 2: Have a clear & simplified business concept.

Spend time formally writing up your business idea. Also format it into a visual diagram. Many already existing business plan templates can help with composing it. Your business plan should fully incorporate your business, as well as what it'll create and by what means. It should further document the market analysis. Likewise, include an explanation of your business's sellable items. The business's long-term goals, too, should be considered. Meanwhile, acknowledge any difficulties you must overcome. What's your plan to differentiate from your competitors? A full business plan is required if you intend to involve anyone else with this venture. After all, you're asking him or her for their time, energy, or connections. This is especially relevant if you're seeking financing. Even if you're a self-funded sole executor, a business plan is invaluable. Its capacity thereby incorporates considerations, conceptualizing your entire business model with obvious aspects.

With that perspective, tackling crucial components that affect your business's success. By doing this, it brings forth simplicity. Entrepreneurs move between too many ideas. Often this splits critical resources, which are discouraged by the amount of effort being put forth into the business. To overcome this, consider your concept's scalability. If it requires too much attention while your customer base grows, consider restructuring your entity. This might keep it from being too complicated. Outsource different components of the operation. Hire staff who complements your responsibilities.

Understand what it is that you're doing. Document how to obtain success but do so in an uncomplicated manner.

Step 3: Do all necessary product and service prep work.

This step directly focuses on products and services. Acquire prototypes or samples, distributing them to friends and family. If your product and/or service consist of food, ensure that taste is consistent. Try to catch defects in your product's manufacturing. Make it more durable. If it's a service, however, ensure there's repetitions to a customer executed at the same level. Get the packaging, container, or bottle design just right. This is often referred to as soft launch. Genuinely test and tweak the product or service. Tweak the product or service in accordance with customers' feedback, catching any embarrassing mishaps.

Step 4: Set up an operations hub, with a sales channel and a marketing strategy.

Having a clear central operation location for your business is important. Though, it neither must be a fancy nor expensive commercialized space. Your home can easily serve that purpose. An old warehouse, a mobile vehicle can also serve as a business location. Conversely, offer delivery an in-home service. Although Haiti doesn't readily consider it, they should explore the informal market of Madame Saras. While they sell retail products, Madame Saras also transports goods throughout Haiti. Place miniature versions of your product in their hands, for this taps into Haitian's economy. No matter how your business sells products and/or services, be flexible and conscious of your capital base.

Consider how to provide access to your product or service. This might occur in-person through your base of operations, or it might depend on a sales team. Alternatively, it may be directly on your website. A combination of these is advisable.

The system's efficiency determines your efficiency. In turn, this will be an important to your brand. Notoriety for consistent and high-quality delivery differentiates brands in most industries. In fact, this may be enough to guarantee success.

Step 5: Complete the legal and administrative business set up.

First and foremost, register your business within Haiti and internationally. The startup cost and administrative hassle make this part a large investment. Before committing to that, it's important to execute the first five steps. By doing this, it ensures your product or service has a degree of viability. Haitian law has provisions allowing one businesses to function commercially for two years before they must lawfully register it. However, a registered entity's required if someone wants to access either bank accounts or contract agreements with vendors and suppliers.

Unfortunately, the process of legally registering a business is complex. Therefore, it deserves to be covered in its own section. Although it's difficult, it's wise to preserve and complete your business registration once you have your business plan. Registering your business is responsible thing to do, because acquiring legal protections is valuable. The credibility that's obtained through the process, both by businesses and those purchasing your product, is very important.

Step 6: Promote and sell.

No matter how innovative or customer-focused a product or service is, it's all for naught if nobody knows about it. Promote your product and/or service. Then, promote it some more. Although traditional are on their way out, they're still useful. Getting a spot in *Le Nouvelliste*, Haiti's largest daily newspaper, still has value. Television and radio can serve its purpose for specific campaigns. But as a startup, it's important to be versed in more cost-effective strategies.

- **Online marketing and social media strategy** – Haiti's mobile adoption and penetration rate is high. It increases in amount each year. Haitians of all socio-economic levels use WhatsApp,

Facebook, and Instagram. Even though there's limited digital infrastructure in Haiti, these applications are still useful. With improved access to electricity and cheaper internet, this penetration is expected to improve. Its dependency on Haitian users will reflect international usage rates in the coming years. Capitalize on opportunities of the present and future, mastering digital marketing techniques. Platforms like Coursera, Linkedin Learning, and Udemy have many great free courses to get started.

- **Local showcases and pop-ups** – Acquire space from events, conferences, or retail businesses. All these venues have high traffic, providing customers exposure to your products and services. The goal behind attending events is acquiring visibility for your brand. It further encourages large distribution partnerships while your brand is in stores. Going to events is a long-term strategy. Overall, it improves brand recognition and memorability alongside personal testimonial experience.

- **Social media and web directory services** - Consider promoting places where people can share experiences. Especially promote those that have a high rating. Review their establishment's focus, reading sites such as TripAdvisor or Google Maps. Manman Pemba (Haiti's Yelp) is important and should be taken seriously. Register on these sites. Engage with dissatisfied commenters, aiming to remedy their experience. Offer incentives for customers who shop, have a good experience and leave good ratings.

- **Traditional Word of Mouth** - Personal referrals are king in business and marketing. Word of mouth marketing is primarily dominant in more developed economies, but still there's other ways to gauge a business's service or product. Whether a Haitian business gains customer depends on what the customers say about the business overall. So, keep this in mind. Engage every customer as if they represent a hundred customers. They do.

Step 7: Leverage partnerships.

Wherever possible, leverage your relationships. Offer opportunities for your network to be win-win. An associate may have a complementary product or service which can be bundled with yours. Cross promotions are always appreciated. If these relationships are particularly strong, consider requesting a favor where you can associate a product or service at a free or a reduced rate. In return, your product or service may be offered at a discount. Doing things that your business and your associate appreciate will boost production. It relieves the administrative burden, turning customer exposures into win-wins. Don't be afraid to ask of friends, colleagues, or associates. Those who believe in you and your business will, in fact, be honored to provide a hand. Many will do so gleefully when you package the request kindly.

To collaborate with an associate at this level, it's important to foster such a relationship. In Haiti, relationships are fostered by physically meeting someone. Events such as conferences, seminars, and workshops are very popular. Here, speakers can share knowledge, providing a channel for highly productive and motivated professionals to meet others for future collaborative efforts. While in Haiti, always be on the lookout for conferences. These make it easy to connect and network with others.

...Starting a Haitian Business on a Shoestring Budget

Haitians suffer from an access to capital more than anything else. Realistically, Haitian businesses – even rudimentary businesses – have larger upfront capital requirements due to investments in foundational infrastructure. Often, these are taken for granted in other countries. Electricity, waste management, and security are included amongst these. Most entrepreneurs are, despite how appealing a business opportunity or model may seem, are restricted from accessing money and resources for years.

While this obstacle is real, it can be overcome. Entrepreneurs, many of whom are included in this book, were amongst those having started ventures on a shoestring budget. Now, they're running enterprises with dozens to hundreds of employees. This required flexibility on their part. How the business started isn't how they would've preferred, since they could've been well-capitalized. However, their idea's most crucial parts was an important test of objective valuation. Essentially it removed a lot of the overhead fluff that doesn't have the most direct investment.

For example, it's hard to build a company manufacturing motorcycles, if that company's using components to build units from scratch. Instead, consider assembling components at varying completion levels. Initially, complete the process as you can grow. Invest in equipment and staff. Build slowly and vertically, integrating parts of your supply chain as time goes on.

Below is some advice relating to starting a company on a limited shoestring budget:

1. **Be a middleman or facilitation company.**

Perhaps you want to start selling real estate, vehicles, or commercial equipment. However, you neither have the capital to purchase buildings, import a fleet of vehicles, nor build a warehouse to inventory appliances. To remedy this, you can function as a facilitator between buyers and sellers of these products. Upon selling each product, sellers earn a small commission. Vast riches can be made using this strategy.

Those immigrating to Haiti from another country have contacts and connections, many of which are valuable for businesses and Haitian entrepreneurs. Facilitate those contacts for a percentage of the sales price. This earns money on whatever is sold. It's a great way to enter any Haitian industry, because immediate value is provided. That would allow you to profit off your business while saving money. Meanwhile, you can deploy in the manner you truly desire.

2. **Partner with an associate who already has assets. Then, you provide the vision.**

You'll be surprised how frequently people with money actively seek investment opportunities. Although, they can't find ideas with which customers will resonate or will be returns. Be that person. Stop looking at institutions. Instead, aim for associates with whom you can partner in your company. Therefore, you can access more resources and pitch your opportunities to them.

As an example, idle land is very common in Haiti. Ideas expressed in the book's food module could be performed by or enhanced with large processes. Use these strategies to distribute your product. Present your idea. By doing this, you skip having to buy a large lot of land. Structure a contractual relationship to get a balloon lease. Moreover, secure a small percentage of annual sales or ownership in the firm.

Many people happenstance into assets and money under varying circumstances. They're cognizant of their lack of ingenuity, education, or knowledge. These individuals, though, willingly partner with someone who can bring their asset productivity. Specialize in being this person.

3. Crowdfunding!

Having $1,000 for a business is great, but it's not enough. If your business venture's minimum capital requirement is $15,000, then reach out to a personal network or extended network of associates. Connect with those having an appreciation for entrepreneurship, your idea, or those that believe in you. Write up that relationship clearly. Ensure that partners clearly understand clearly their return, as well as any required additional roles.

Equally, a possible avenue is leveraging online crowdfunding platforms like Kickstarter and IndieGoGo. Instead of depending on interpersonal relationships, depend on hundreds to thousands of small contributions. These donations will help you toward your goal. Depending on how much is contributed, people may get additional benefits and services. These are related to the venture and motivates them to provide more.

Simply don't be afraid to ask. A known Haitian proverb states: a silent starving man dies of hunger.

4. Leverage the efficiency of eCommerce and the online ecosystem.

eCommerce isn't attractive because it's the direction of all commerce. But it affords entrepreneurs potential entry points regarding their efficiencies, scale, and access. Unlike traditional retail and brick-and-mortar businesses – you neither need a lease, a geographic limited storefront location, nor expensive human capital expenses. These services can be started in your home, garage, or small workshop. While expenses are limited, the right product, dependent on whether it's digital, remote, or virtual services, could potentially see growth.

A lot of digital products only need to be created once. Once they're created, they'll continue to make income. Consider when someone makes an online course. He or she might charge a small nominal fee of $20 to participate. Multiply this by dozens of people per month. Over the years, along with additional and similarly priced courses, you'll see what's meant by scale.

Whatever your business, consider how you can integrate a component of it online. For example, even if you have a domestic grocery store, allow folks in Haiti to purchase online. Moreover, permit those from abroad to purchase items for their Haitian families. Just like that, you've tapped into an international market. You've accessed volume and purchasing power which wouldn't be fathomable a decade ago.

5. Your knowledge and skillset are valuable. Profit from them.

Commoditize your professional experience by independent contracting to Haitian individuals and firms. This similarly requires little upfront capital costs. Primarily, this requires you to build up a brand and leverage. Use different marketing media forms. This only requires as much money as you dedicate to that task. But once you've solidified yourself as an expert in that field, considerable earnings will rise.

Other innovative earning methods offer your capacity as a personal coach or business consultant. It's possible to go into more creative lanes as well. Become a style consultant or counsel parents. The is an extensive list of possibilities, since there're many professions and interests.

6. Get ingenious with null capital approaches. Break into your desired business.

"Hustling" means doing things that creatively, or sometimes duplicitously, allow you to network and earn additional income. You can essentially connect with people, getting a leg up with visibility and access. One example focuses on creating conferences or events. Network these in the industry into which you want to emerge. Then, invite individuals together that're in that industry. It can be as simple as a happy hour, where everyone covers their own bill. This costs you very little. And, conserving with people can immediately move you forward. Add a speaker, ticket sales, and a sponsor. Now, this event is paying you.

As mentioned previously in this book, many ideas can be started in your home or within your kitchen. Don't downplay this method's upside. A considerable make-or-break strategy consists of using assets you already have and converting them into vehicles for your business. Go a step further. Leverage the assets of the informal market into your business model. In Haiti, many of the things you're looking to do might already be done by the informal market. And so, they might be completed inexpensively. Simply pay for that product or service. Maybe it's an artisan craft, a food processed item that needs better branding, or a service such as transporting. Perhaps the transport service can be purchased through a tap-tap driver already on a route, who'll take them closer to their destination.

Instead of creating your own product, box your products in differing product packages. Also, box packages with many already produced products. We've mentioned becoming a salesman for products. When each item's sold, you earn a commission. Thus, you to avoid purchasing and stocking an inventory. Inversely, you can employ direct or indirect salespeople. They can either be commission-based salespeople, or help to get your product out. Give them a few samples to give to customers, rather than producing samples based on pre-orders. Use the collected funds to purchase the inputs needed for your product's production.

Consider being a sort of general contractor or coordinator. Connect and leverage a network of small businesses and specialists in a particular domain. As a job's acquired, components are pieced out across that network. This often is done cost-effectively and quickly. As a result of good marketing and exceptional social media, you can build a pipeline of opportunities. These will keep your network satisfied, while offering you the lowest possible prices due to business volume.

Always remember: countless businesses fail. Many of those businesses had more than enough startup capital to have been a success. Startup capital doesn't equal a venture's success. Success ultimately depends on the entrepreneur's creativity. Capital can give a boost, but it doesn't prevent. It neither prevents inappropriate management nor strategy execution flexibility. As the examples provided in this section have shown, the possibilities are endless. A lack of money is never ever an excuse to not pursue your entrepreneurial dreams.

...The Legal Process to Start a Business

Registering a business in Haiti is easily one of the most daunting and intimidating tasks of one's entrepreneurial journey. It may feel initially a bit contradictory, in fact, to write a book discussing opportunities within Haiti. Meanwhile, registration is something fraught with so much difficulty. Though, the level-headed reality is that the business registration process isn't any more inefficient or difficult than anything involving Haitian bureaucratic participation to achieve.

A driver's license is a hassle. Title transferring is a hassle. Acquiring an electricity connection for your property is a hassle. Paying annual taxes is a hassle. Everything is a hassle. And in that context, going through the effort of getting your firm registered isn't uniquely a grievance. Although, at least it'll provide you the benefit of having access to banking services. Likewise, you gain access to more lucrative business relationships. These include NGOs and select government contracts requiring up-to-date certification paperwork.

Legally, people can operate their business in Haiti for two years. Provisions must be in place to pay for prior years of operational revenue upon their registration. Many should use that window to evaluate if the business. Envision what you want or if another iteration of the idea is most appropriate. Once it comes time to register, understand that there're many different entities available to you.

Below is a list of companies recognized by Haitian law. All have legal personalities distinct from their individual members' personalities. Pros and cons are outlined for each structure.

- **The Corporation (Société Anonyme).** Its members are liable for their interest in the corporation. This is the most widely used form of the company used in Haiti. It protects its shareholders, who are only liable to the extent of their investment. However, this structure is the most onerous regarding time and money. Registration time may run for four or more months, depending upon the time of business how many ministries are required to sign off on their approval. Costs typically range around $4,000 and require a lawyer's participation. Go this route only after a few years in business. Therefore, you're certain that you want to continue the venture.

- **The General Partnership (Société en Nom Collectif):** is formed by two or more persons for the purpose of doing business under a firm name. The partners are and remain jointly and severally liable with all their property, inclusive of all the partnership debts. Considerably less expensive than an SA, this still requires more registration steps than other options; although, it's less costly at $1,000. This also requires a very strong and contractually defined list of responsibilities – both between yourself and your partner. By doing this, you avoid future conflicts. Options to divest and consolidate the business into single ownership or replace it with a different owner should be included in this agreement as well.

- **The Limited Partnership (Société en Commandite)** is formed by a contract between one or more associates. Everyone involved is jointly and severally liable. One or more associates now have limited or silent partners (commanditaires) who are mere contributors of funds. A limited partner is liable for the firm's losses, but only to the extent of the funds he's contributed to the firm. It's not very commonly used in Haiti. This follows a similar cost structure as a general partnership and offers similar advice toward defining responsibilities.

- **The Sole Proprietorship (L'entreprise individuelle):** It's the simplest form of business in Haiti. It hasn't any shareholders, partners, or limited partners. In fact, only the owner is in charge. While the company's assets, liabilities, and profits are merged with that of the owner, the entity can function as a separate entity. It's its own fictitious name, bank account, and capacity to enter contracts separately and appropriately. In this manner, it delegates functional responsibility. Furthermore, this is the least expensive and often only costs a few hundred dollars. It's also the least time-consuming option, taking just a few weeks. Lastly, it's the least requirements and steps to perform.

No matter what entity type you select, it's recommended that you use a lawyer. The listed prices and each entity's time estimates for registration are based on lawyers' charges to render the service. Legally, a lawyer is only required for SA. Though, despite instances where registration may be considered and prices are known, there's a government administration to further assess. They may regard those seeking registration as inconvenient, stonewalling bureaucracy, or expecting unrecorded, unregulated, or unpredictable additional service processing charges. However, a full list of resources related to each type's requirements is available to you. Find the additional resources located at <u>SeeJeanty.Ht</u> website for more info. Such conditions are effectively rendered sterile in the environment described above. Remember, countries like the United States, Canada, and the European Union all have strict foreign anti-corruption laws in place for their citizens. Even one dollar spent on those unrecorded, unregulated or unpredictable additional service processing charges could land you in prison for years. So, this can't be stressed enough: **Work. With. A. Lawyer.**

...Labor Law, Taxes, and Other Social Responsibilities

Haiti functions on a social labor employer relationship, which is heavily influenced by the French. The worker has considerable rights within the law, and complaints against employers from workers at the appropriate ministry are common. So, it's important that one fully understands the labor rights of both employers and employees. Therefore, they can act within those bounds. Haiti's labor law has over 516 articles spread across eighty-six pages. It'd be utterly impossible to provide an accurate exposition of such a text in this book, inclusive of all the possible angles of inquiry that exist. So, we'll go over a few topics. Then, we'll refer you to SeeJeanty.Ht for the full texts and summary articles.

Haiti's corporate tax is tiered dependent on revenue; roughly thirty percent. Property tax is dependent on land value. If there's no building on it yet, usually it's exempted from payment. Once there's a building completed, however, it's dependent on the value of the potential rental income of that property.

Wage minimums are subject to change in accordance with the Haitian parliament. Often, this occurs with no warning or immediate effect. It's important to factor such possibilities into your expectations and reserve a cushion to react to such events. There're seven or eight different industrial segments. Amongst these are education, hotels, restaurants, domestic workers, and manufacturing. A business may fall into a category that affects your required minimum daily wage per employee. Most up-to-date labor wage minimums will be found on SeeJeanty.Ht/bonuses.

There's an assortment of tax deductions that are required for salaried or waged employees. These deductions are listed below.

- **ONA:**
    - National Office for Pension Insurance (Office National d'Assurance Vieillesse).
    - Six percent is deducted from the employee, while six percent is likewise deducted from the employer.
- **OFATMA:**
    - (Office d'Assurances Accidents du Travail, Maladie).
    - Insurance Office for Occupational Accidents Sickness and Maternity.
    - Two to four percent is deducted from employees, dependent on their industry.
- **DGI (Haiti tax office):**
    - **IRI:**
        - Tax on an employee's income.
        - Conditional on salary, if the salary is at or above 60,000 HTG.
        - One percent is deducted from an employee's salary.
    - **FDU:**
        - One percent is deducted from an employee's salary.

- o **CFGDCT (1%):**
  - Administrative and Development Fund for the Territorial Localities.
  - Conditional on salaries that're above 5000 HTG.
  - One percent is deducted from an employee's salary
- o **CAS:**
  - Social Assistance Fund.
  - Only for government employees.
  - One percent is deducted from an employee's salary.

- **Other**
  - o Ten percent on bonuses.
    - **Pursuant on agreement:** loans; payday advances; reimbursement for losses regarding any damage(s) to the employer's products, properties, or facilities when an employee is proven to be liable.

End-of-the-year bonuses are codified within the labor customs and laws of Haiti. The thirteenth monthly salary, also referred to as the Boni disbursement, is required of any employee – regardless of how long they've been employed with you. This conditional bonus must be adhered to in all instances, since the labor language code is clear and hasn't muddled interpretation. For example, an employee could have started on December 1st. At the end of that month, they'll be entitled to their regular salary and a bonus equal to their regular salary.

Compared to America, Haiti has a lot of holidays. Whereas the United States has eight holidays, Haiti has 20 public holidays. For any reason, workers having to work on holidays must be compensated a day and a half of additional pay. This is partially offset by a six-day work week, where employees work 8 am to 4pm each day through Saturday. It's customary to let workers out after working half of a day.

It's advisable to have employees open bank accounts. Therefore, they can receive transferred payments. Transfers are done between persons of the same bank. In most cases, these happen instantly and are feeless. Companies can open bank accounts for their employees with minimal requirements. Often, it only requires a company badge as ID and doesn't cost employees any monthly maintenance fees.

...Labor and Cultural Norms

Generally, Haitians professionals won't work for a gourde less than what they perceive their market value. Those coming into Haiti would expect a country with seventy to eighty percent unemployment. They'd expect to see people fighting for any opportunity which gets them working at a reasonable wage point. Although, this will come as a bit of a surprise.

Day-to-day responsibilities must be clearly expressed during the interview process. Though it's often hard to predict all the stress points of a person's function, being upfront with what you do know is important. Then, you're able to vet out those who aren't a good fit. The issue with Haiti's systemic high unemployment rate is that many Haitians lack some professional etiquette. Often, they've attitudes which are often taken for granted in other countries. Timeliness works as a cohesive, communicative team. Adherence to escalation lines are examples of points requiring specific time during your onboard training. While you'll find many Haitians willingly go the extra mile, they're also willing to handle criticism. Likewise, they're more likely to adapt to unexpected challenges to the role, whereas some aren't. Further, Haiti's academic system doesn't emphasize not critical thinking. Instead, they focus on repetition and a regurgitation of information. Thus, a big part of your training program requires assisting Haitians with the tools which allow them to function independently without granular instruction.

It's common for Haitians to ask for and be granted their employer loans. Also, they receive advances during times of difficulty or a major expenditure. These may include annual rental fees, medical expenses, or life events. The amount's then repaid for a couple of months. Incorporating such a flexible compensation model is an important part of employee retention.

Because of Haiti's lack of infrastructure, small amounts of rain cause difficulties in movement and getting to work. Accidents increase whenever there's inclement weather. Nevertheless, there's relatable health risks to wearing wet clothing, such as catching a cold. Expect tardiness or no shows during such periods.

Infrastructure, or the lack thereof, affects hiring decisions. Often, individuals with impeccable experience aren't hired. Instead, those with less idealistic qualifications who reside closer to the company's location get the job. Though it's unfair to the qualified employee, weather or political instability may cause that employee to not work. Overall, factoring in distance has serious consequences to the company's operations and revenue.

The labor law in effect in Haiti is very clear. Haiti operates on a forty-eight-hour work week schedule. Employees work eight hours daily, whereas salaried employees are offered on-the-clock lunch and breaks. Most companies work their employees 8 am to 4 pm, with their lunches included as part of their work time. Also, most institutions close early on Saturdays. So, most employees expect Saturday to be a half-day. Though an increasing number of workplaces are cutting back on that, they're still choosing to have their employees only work five days a week rather than six.

...Import / Export Laws and Processes

Importing products into Haiti is fraught with difficulty and opaque activities, but it's doable. Officially, import rates vary for products between zero and fifteen percent, with an additional ten percent VAT and a four percent verification fee. However, the actual rate paid by those importing products differs considerably from this publish rate. Those who pay the proper rate get formal values registered at customs. This is different from the cash that's ultimately provided as payments to a customs officer or a middleman. An inconvenience and long review time await those who're unwilling to participate in less formal queues.

Therefore, those wanting to do business should be heavily dependent on supply chains. These waypoints consistently pass-through customs, at which point they do one of the following:

1. Consider not importing anything. Purchase from either distributor or resellers who've the input already in Haiti.

2. Importing through shipping services provides customs clearance services. When an upfront price is paid, customs handles the shipping and gets the product out of Haiti. However, be aware that most contracts have stipulations. Should customs choose to add additional fees onto what you're attempting to receive, you'll be liable to pay that amount. The larger your shipments, the more likely there's to be deviations in pre-paid amounts. These have post-paid prices through these services.

3. Develop your own contacts within Haitian customs. Alternatively, hire a specialist who can reasonably assure a hassle-free experience.

4. A franchises allows entities to import products into Haiti custom free so long as they are to produce products that will be exported. Contact the CFI if you believe your company would qualify for such a status and they will assist you in getting the necessary documentation.

Exporting products is a more straightforward exercise, but still, acquiring the initial approval to export is cumbersome. Custom commissioners within Haiti's customs must authorize an entity's right to export, approve, and regulate processes. These can be obtained and followed by the Ministry of Agriculture, the environment, finance, and/or others. Once an export license is obtained, each shipment requires custom clearance formalities. These involves the Ministry of Commerce and Industry. It provides a certificate of origin, and a sample laboratory/chemical analysis depending on the product. Additional licenses for regulatory approvals are required for the destination's country. Exports shouldn't be made until those documentations are known and in order. Otherwise, one's product may be seized at the destination port by that country's customs.

...Personal Tax Responsibilities

Americans' investing in Haiti will be explored here. It's important to seek a tax accountant's advice within your country of origin. Do this before doing any investments or business in Haiti. Every country's laws, rules, or procedures may be different. Americans investing in Haiti must declare all their country's activities. They must pay taxes on all his or her profits, income, and payments that's obtained while he or she's in Haiti. Haiti offers credits for those paying taxes in a foreign country, where they earned the revenue. In this way, the entrepreneur avoids double taxation. Further, expenses are still allowed to be deducted on their adjusted gross income. Although, this depending on how a company's legal status is constructed. For example, this is evident if someone's elected to be a sole owner of a limited liability corporation.

The Haitian government requires entrepreneurs to declare income they've earned in Haiti annually, and provide a "certificate de impot" as proof that they've paid. Many government services and documents require a company to have their certificate de impot in hand, which is obtained upon paying in Haitian taxes. The country functions in a self-declarative and effective honor system. Though if one works for a large enough entity, these entities will report income paid to you to the Haitian tax office (DGI). This may be checked against your Haitian tax id, or NIF, electronically as you're filing taxes. Then, you pay a percentage of taxes on that income. Haitian income taxes range on income tiers between ten to twenty-two percent. However, there're provisions allowing people who've earned their income outside of Haiti to pay only a minimum fee. People can acquire good standing with the DGI. There are also provisions to simply declare that you haven't earned any income that year to still obtain the certificate de impot (for students and those who were unable to earn income that year independently).

...Non-Haitian Entrepreneurship and Investment

Haiti allows foreigners to be a part of corporations (SA). Corporations may own land and transact as legal entities. It's not recommended that non-Haitians attempt to navigate Haiti's legal and business registration system. They should instead consult a cohort of trusted Haitian nationals, who're closely associated with the endeavor.

Non-Haitian nationals are required to get a permis sejour, also known as a resident visa, to reside within Haiti longer than three months. A permis sejour is further required to be employed by any registered Haitian commercial entity. Once this is obtained, its holders enjoy other benefits. They've the ability to own up to three acres of land, as well as rights of hereditary succession of that land.

Non-Haitian nationals can open personal bank accounts. All that's required is a state issued ID and proof of a permanent Haitian address. They don't need a permis sejour to gain this privilege. Each bank might have slightly different requirements; so, it's best to check with different banks. See which bank is the most accommodating. It's also encouraged to use Xoom services. These will facilitate easy and cheap transfers between banks, both inside and outside of Haiti. Xoom's transfer times vary, but usually take around twenty-four hours. Although, it takes as long as three weeks in some instances. It's best to factor in potentially long delays. Wire transfers are another transfer alternative. Even though these allow your funds to get there at a predictable twenty-four-hour interval, it can considerably be more expensive.

... Dual Haitian Citizenship

Many Haitians living abroad aren't aware that people of Haitian descent have their citizenship enshrined in the Constitution. They can have a Haitian passport while holding a different state passport, such as from America or Canada. A formal amendment was presented through a concerted effort of the diaspora. It was successfully approved by parliament and legalized. Then, President Martelly published it in the national monitor on June 19, 2012. The amendment specification removes language that previously prohibited dual nationality in the Constitution. It further defined conditions in which a person qualified for Haitian nationality at birth, despite where they were born.

Further, the law of August 12, 2002, clearly defined specialized privileges for those of Haitian nationality and their descendants. Even when a non-Haitian national holds a foreign passport is questionable, Haitian nationals had clear rights under the law despite where they resided. These rights didn't restrict their involvement in Haitian economic life. Details to that law can be found below.

Article 1. Every native-born Haitian who enjoys another nationality. Their descendants are:

1. Exempted from visa to enter and exit Haiti.
2. Exempted from the formalities of residence permits and payment of related taxes.
3. Exempted from the formalities of work permits, employment permits, and payments of related taxes.

4. Exempted from the formalities related to the license of foreigners and payment of related taxes.

5. Eligible both at the civil service and the employment market, unless in the cases expressly prohibited by the Constitution.

6. Exempted from the authorization of the Ministry of Justice to acquire any real estate properties.

7. Authorized to acquire any real property in urban areas, if an area doesn't exceed three HA eighty-seven, equivalent to three carreaux of land.

8. Entitled to fully enjoy the same rights of succession that all Haitians.

9. Authorized, in case of the auction by contract (voie parée). He or she is the proclaimed purchaser of the property assigned to the payment of its debt and statements of orders can be made in its favor.

The next question relates to how someone of Haitian descendants obtains a Haitian passport despite potentially never residing in Haiti. For a while, the Haitian embassy in DC offered a program allowing Haitian Americans to obtain a Haitian passport remotely. However, it's not certain if that program's still active. Direct inquiries to the Haitian embassy can be found here: amb.washington@diplomatie.ht.

At the time of the writing of this section, as a Haitian born abroad with a foreign Haitian birth certificate still hasn't any clearly defined legal process to obtain their constitutional rights which have been repatriated upon them. Haitian parliament still hasn't passed a bill clarifying a formal procedure. The Ministry of Haitians for Living

Abroad has made themselves available to guide Haitians in alternative scaffolded and complicated methods. These restore rights and the legal paperwork (NIF, Marticule Fiscal, National ID card, etc.). All these are necessary to function legally within Haiti. Ultimately, the counsel of an attorney versed in immigration issues in the country is recommended.

NOTE: At the time of this writing, this section was written with the 1987 Haitian Constitution enforced. A new constitution may be replacing this soon, per the announced goal of President Moise. In fact, this may occur soon after this book's publication. This new constitution is expected to have an easier process and clearer language. By using this process, those having Haitian descent can apply for their dual nationality.

...Finance and Credit

Simply put, Haiti is BYOC: bring your own credit. The process of getting financing is onerous. It's entirely inaccessible for those without an exact physical and socioeconomic footprint already in Haiti's footprint. Most banks require loans. Any loan type for any loan amount can be secured by some collateral. Further, loans come with income requirements. These necessitate proving income that's gained from registered entities within Haiti. It doesn't count any income that's been earned abroad, even if you are a resident. Income may be as low as a few thousand dollars. That loan will be secured by an acre or more of land. No matter the applicant's creditworthiness, car loans can go as high as fifteen to thirty percent in interest. Although, mortgage loans aren't commonly offered at most banks. Depending on the loan's amount, business loans require collateral of both the owners' business and/or personal property.

For most Haitians, banks are merely a place to store money – nothing more. Those coming from abroad must look at ways to access foreign credit lines that they can use in Haiti. Home equity lines of credit is one such way, where one puts a lien on your American property. They also take out cash for any use you may have involving low rates of interest. Another method is to get an unsecured line of credit. Even with a spotless credit history, the interest rate may run ten to fifteen basis points higher than prime. It'd still be comparable to, and somewhat better than, the interest charged by a Haitian bank – if you were able to qualify. Some credit cards provide checks, allowing you to cash out against your balance as another example. As someone comes from a country where there's more liberal credit access, consider using those options. These provide you the capital flexibility to do what you need in Haiti.

Acquiring a loan from a Haitian bank is acquired but isn't a totally baseless exercise. Given the gourdes historically one-sided decreasing valuation versus the dollar, you benefit from loan terms by getting a loan in Gourdes. Also, understand alternatives that exist. You should always be attentive to applying when your situation aligns with what's being requested. For example, ONA Diaspora Loan is a program that Haitians having had worked for a period in Haiti. They can continue to contribute to the Office of National Insurance's retirement fund. Thus, once they're qualified, they've access to those funds later. International aid agencies like USAID, Overseas Private Investment Corporation ("OPIC"), International Finance Corporation ("IFC"), and InterAmerican Development Bank ("IDB") frequently run special loan and grant initiatives. Ultimately, these target specific SMEs in various industries. It's imperative to periodically check these entities for any programs or services for which your venture qualifies.

However, you obtain that credit or financing. Understand it's still something that requires repayment. Rarely is it ever "free money." Use it only for opportunities. The connection between the expenditure of funds and an increase of revenue sufficient to repay that borrowed capital with residual earnings is clear. Under any circumstances is borrowing to have money for daily living expenses not a prudent use of borrowed funds.

...Acquiring Land and Real Estate

Land acquisition is delicate and fraught with ill consequence activities that someone unfamiliar with Haiti can do. The process is generally not understood, even by those charged to administer the process. Fees and expenses related to the transaction can add much as twenty-five percent to the purchase value. Except for those fully integrated into Haiti, it's something that should be avoided aggressively. We'll go over the many potential pitfalls existing in Haiti's land buying process.

The process is flawed at many points, but the first and most critical breakpoint involves how land ownership is claimed. The General Tax Office (DGI) is required to register any deed that's brought before it. Thus, registered, and transcribed deeds don't prove ownership. Further complicating matters are inheritance laws that grant rights to all offspring. (A family has ten children, and the parents have passed before selling the property. Guess what? You must formally find each child to sign off the land's sale. Otherwise, even those with clear registered titles may one day be drawn into land disputes.)

Performing appropriate due diligence isn't an easy duty. Institutions are tasked with the execution, enforcement, and processing of land policies. These include the Office of National Cadastre (ONACA), DGI, and Ministry of Justice. All have underfunded resources and don't have the required capacity to execute the law's requirements or their functions appropriately. Further, when instances of fraudulent land transactions occur, persecution of the wrong-doers and justice for those affected is rare – even in the most flagrant instances. It further complicates things when families have lived on land for generations. Though because of weak government institutions permitting millions of Haitians to live in Haiti without any legal identification, they're not even properly registered persons. This phenomenon is common in the provinces, where people spend their whole lives without ever interacting with the government. Without identification, someone can't have a legal title.

There're two methods of land sales in Haiti; the sale by authentic deed and the sale by a private seal. An authentic deed utilizes a notary, who ensures all legal formalities required by the law and state are followed. DGI taxes are paid, while transactional details are transcribed and annexed appropriately. This process can take as long as a year to complete, costing fifteen percent of the sales price. This doesn't including an attorney's cost, that often increases the price by another ten percent.

The second method is a simple contractual agreement between two parties. A notary's involvement details the transaction and sales price. Some formal steps are still required, such as surveying. It must be recorded and transcribed to protect third-party claims. However, even if a lawyer or a justice of the peace is used, this form of sale doesn't provide nearly the protection level compared to the first method.

For both methods, the details can be found online through this book's resource guide, specially the real estate portion. Any specific transaction should be done with the explicit assistance of an attorney.

Another common question relates to the cost of land. Rural land is generally sold in portions, equal to 500m2. (Confusingly, it's described as "Kawo," a creolization of French Carreau. It actually measures a much larger 3.18 acreage of land.) The carreaux is sold and can vary significantly. Price points often range from tens of thousands of dollars, to as much as hundreds of thousands of dollars. On the other hand, urban land is generally sold in quantities of centieme. A centieme is 129 square meters formally, or just shy of 1400 square feet. Prices of a centieme are often thousands of dollars per unit. Interestingly, a centieme lot with a building on it, even with an uncompleted husk, can cost hundreds of thousands of dollars! What accounts for this high price point?

The fact that Haiti's in the Caribbean does contribute to a higher inherent cost. But similar-sized lots often go for as much half in places such as the Bahamas, Turks and Caicos, and Martinique. So, that explanation isn't adequate. The truth lies in understanding that the price of land meets supply and demand. The supply of authentic deed land is low. Amongst many Haitians, there're very few acreages of land considering the cost, complexity, and lack of understanding of this process. Meanwhile, there's exceptional demand for land in Haiti. The domestic population and a diaspora population with quantitatively more means than the domestic population. Complicating things further, this diaspora population generally holds unimaginative aspirations for their Haiti investment. Many desire only to build a retirement home, a vacation property, and/or a hotel. This concentration of capital significantly raises the asset's price relative to other opportunities in the economy.

Improving the affordability of land in Haiti requires land reform. It should allow more clearly titled land in the market. Moreover, those looking to invest in Haiti's land should seek opportunities that don't include directly owning land. Meanwhile, the final word in investing in land is that one should know the person intimately that is selling the land. Have two-three personal references that can vouch for the honesty of that individual, and can attest to the rights of that person to the land they are trying to sell. Consider even interviewing people who live around the land for sale to inquire on who they know owns that property. And of course, take all appropriate steps as it relates to having an attorney and a notary review that paperwork that they provide even after those steps are complete.

...Competent Legal and Accounting Counsel

So much of Haiti's regulatory compliance and legal administration can't be done because of opaque processes and immoral government representatives. Therefore, electronic transactions aren't possible through any government's bureau. Most of the time, a licensed attorney acts as a middle person. A competent representative is crucial for company registration, land purchases, labor disputes, tax filings, and/or acquiring personal immigration status.

How do you find a competent lawyer? As you network with Haitian business owners, ask, "Who registered your company? How was that experience? Do you have an attorney that you'd recommend using?" Compile a list of recommendations. Note any lawyers that people mention to you several times. After you have around ten recommendations, interview the top three. Choose the three who are the most qualified were recommended most often.

During the interview:

- Look for attentiveness from the attorneys, ensuring they're addressing your concerns. Likewise, note how detailed they're with their responses.
- Take other cues, observing how soon he or she responds to email or phone calls.
- Ask them about their law experience, where they've worked in specific areas of law.

- Compare legal services for your business needs across each firm. How do they expect to receive payment? If they're unable to provide a fee structure, that's an important red flag.
- Inquire about who'll be handling the work – either the attorney themselves, their partner, or an assistant.
- How often will they update you on the assignment's progress?
- While in Haiti, a lot of important information can be discovered by visiting a law office. But beware of an unhappy and inattentive staff; another red flag.
- Listen to your intuition. Go through a handful of lawyers. Allow logic and rationality to dictate your evaluation. The final percentage is driven by how comfortable you feel, that which better matches your personality.

Don't hire a legal representative lightly. It's the most important decision you'll have to make. Take it slow, take it carefully, and take it prudently.

...The Topic of Security

Upon following advice you're told about Haiti, you could reasonably expect to be instantly mugged, scammed and/or assaulted as you leave the airport. But realistically, Haiti is consistently ranked amongst one of safest Caribbean countries. This is specifically sourced from UNODC. Haiti's security relates closely to truth. In this way, it's effective anywhere there's humanity: prudence trumps nativity. The more someone can practice safe behavior that enforces their well-being and decreases vulnerability, then the more advisable it is.

Tourists being harmed in Haiti is rare. Haiti's crime and malfeasances are concreted in pockets, occurring far from anywhere that tourists would either lodge or visit. Haiti is safe for visitors, despite what visitors hear while they're here. You would be inconvenienced, of course, if you found yourself in Haiti during the worst of Haiti's political instability. Still, nobody should never feel as if their life's in danger.

That said, there're practices to which someone must adhere upon deciding to move to Haiti and residing here full-time.

1. You may have a primary network of family, friends, and associates on which you can closely depend. Still, it's important to grow independent. Therefore, you're dependent on people.
2. Cultivate a relationship within your community. Establish connections and contacts. Consider the information they can

provide. Likewise, have added security. Extra eyes look for your best interests in addition to theirs.

3. Crime fancies opportunity. Limit these opportunities by reducing them. You may identify where you might be vulnerable.

When it comes to dealing with political insecurity and flare-ups related to protests occurring against government actions or inaction, it's always good to be connected to sources across social media. These keeping people informed of disturbances across Haiti. Ask friends and associates for access to private WhatsApp channels, such as where such status updates are regularly disseminated. Sign up for US Embassy or Canadian Embassy in-country security disturbance email lists.

During more sustained city protest periods, it's important to have resource reserves. These include having excess water, fuel, and food stocks. Most stores and gas stations will close during those periods. It's important to have emergency operating procedures and staff redundancies in place. Both can handle the inability of critical personnel who may be unable to get to work. Most importantly, understand that that this period will end. Haiti will return to normal. Consider this time a test. Evaluate how robust your company culture and business structure may be. Learn from where it's weak and exposed. Install a more appropriate structure, making necessary adjustments.

... Currency Fluctuations

From March 2020 through June 2020, the HTG to USD exchange rate fell from eighty HTG to 120 HTG for a single US dollar. Between August and September, during a period lasting only three weeks, the exchange rate fell from 120 HTG down to sixty HTG for a single USD. These massive fluctuations are extremely hard for business. The exchange value isn't particularly important in the long run (over many months and years). After all, prices will calibrate across the market. But in the short run, salaries don't quickly adjust. People obtain only half the HTG they did prior. Meanwhile, they still have prices attuned to the prior rate. This effectively means that prices are set at twice their inherent values. Salaries are generally difficult to cut outright. More likely, employees must be let go. New employees are rehired at acceptable rates for the company budget. This also means a slowdown for the economy, decreasing alternative work opportunities for those losing their jobs.

Business similarly experiences a distortive balance sheet effect, as seen with their employees. Revenues produce only half as much purchasing power. It's effectively halved at the same dollar revenue. Thus, one has half the money. At the same time, costs are effectively doubled and pegged at a higher exchange rate. This is an untenable situation and a dangerous socio-economic cocktail, not only for a company but for the entire economy. These fluctuations are an absolute disaster, especially for those collecting revenue in dollars. The inflexibility of costs is affected in the short run.

Circumvent the currency issue altogether. Pay your employees in the currency that you earn most of your revenue. Structure any long-standing commitments, financial obligations, and cost commitments in that currency. For instance, ensure the balance sheet is in dollars if your revenue is based on dollars. The same goes for businesses that primarily earn in Gourdes.

...Internet Connectivity

At the time of this writing, Haiti has three major internet providers: Access Haiti, Digicel, and Natcom. Haitel is a fourth company, but it's owned by Access Haiti's parent company. And so, Haitel shares the same infrastructure. Pricing structures are guaranteed to change over time, so exact pricing won't be described here. It's advisable that readers visit these firm's sites to get exact pricing for the different internet options. Connecting remotely with these entities in Haiti isn't easy. During a trip to Haiti, it's important to visit a branch office. Have them show you the equipment, while explaining the various pricing. Some companies will require several months of payments upfront, especially for the cheaper plans.

The internet comes in two primary varieties in Haiti: 4G Wi-Fi and fiber optics. 4G Wi-Fi usually comes in the form of small hotspot boxes that are provided with your service purchase. Digicel and Natcom allow for pay-as-you-go data plans, which attach to your mobile phone service. Your phone's hotspot allows your other devices to also have internet access. The common question is: which company is better for reliability and speed? Really, it depends on where you reside. Haiti is a mountainous country. So, the signal strength of your specific area is dependent on your distance and geospatial differences in elevation between that antenna. In some areas, Access Haiti may be the clear winner. In other locations, the better option might be Digicel or Natcom. The time of day also affects internet efficiency. The internet tends to slow down in the evening in residential areas. Students return from school, and adults return from work. Both add stress to the bandwidth, which is shared by the coverage area. It's further notable that many VOIP services such as WhatsApp have their services throttled. Digicel and Natcom offer specific uncapped internet usage plans for VOIP apps like WhatsApp. Although, this comes at a surcharge.. Many apps' usage restrictions are lifted after certain times in the evening.

The second variety is fiber internet. It's generally much more expensive. The base packaging is priced three to four times the base of 4G Wi-Fi. Further, the minimum fiber-optic speeds are either at or just marginally above 4G prices. But what you're gaining is a much more stable internet connection, because there's service. Note that qualifier at the end of the sentence. Depending on where you reside, one fiber provider will perform better than the other. It's important to query neighbors. See which service they've. Hear how they evaluate their performance to determine which you should acquire. Fiber plans neither restrict VOIP nor throttle the internet. For this reason, it's worth the higher price as compared to 4G. Further, less people will be sharing the bandwidth if someone purchases a higher plan. Likewise, you're going to have more stable internet. So, consider getting the highest plan you can afford.

Your area might not have ground fiber connections to which your home or office can connect, but that's only because some internet providers don't provide equivalent speed alternatives. Access Haiti, for example, offers "Air Fiber." It's a microwaved connection that transports high-quality data connected through a small satellite dish on your home. It connects to a central receiver that connects to a land fiber connection. They provide this service at speeds and rates nearly identical to what's available for land-based fiber plans.

Whatever you decide to purchase for your internet, ensure you have an alternative internet from a different provider. Two internet services are absolutely required. The internet doesn't matter if the carrier or the internet itself is woefully unstable. It's not uncommon to go a week without the internet as the internet provider is "reaching" the issue. Given the globally connected world in which we live, the internet is a basic human need. It's as essential as water, shelter, food, and electricity. Act accordingly. Have your primary service, while then selecting a cheaper alternative. For businesses, two fiber options are recommended. For homes, a fiber connection and 4G connection setup would be considerable.

Final Words

"There're generations yet unborn, whose very lives will be shifted and shaped by the moves you make and the actions you take."

-- Andy Andrews

This book aims to serve as a critical resource for those looking to do business in Haiti. Personal insights are provided, to ensure decisions that are made are shred and judicious. But the intent was to go beyond an idea board of what was possible. We wanted to provide a clear pathway for those desperate to see a better Haiti. The book works as a recipe guide that needn't be followed exactly. Instead, the ideas could be mixed and matched. The ideas could be modified by an individual and tailored to their appropriate fit. Haiti only changes when the diaspora, and those internally, can succeed in their efforts to establish successful ventures.

It's important that a new generation of Haitians and Haitian business leaders sincerely care for Haiti. Moreover, it's vital they care for Haitians residing within the country. Only then can these business owners gain a position of influence. Haiti is overdue a generation of leaders who value transparency, social responsibility, and the environment. It's unfair that Haitians have had to leave their homeland to foreign lands, where they've sought livelihoods for so many decades. Only, they've been mistreated, belittled, and demeaned with the worst perceptions of their characters and humanity. But we (the author and you, the reader) believe that Haiti will someday so be emboldened with a business.

It'll thrive with community and political leaders, who consciously and purposefully work toward better options for Haiti.

For this to become a reality, building a Haitian business must become, at the same time, similar to joining a team. You'll have the support emotionally, intellectually, and financially of other like-minded visioners. This book is a part of that support. Haiti can't change if its most dedicated and savvy entrepreneurs are chained behind desks, still spinning within foreign countries' corporate rat race wheels.

This dream of changing Haiti and starting a venture that employs hundreds or thousands requires two things. First, there must be an understanding of time's finiteness. Knowing what must be completed before time passes is critical to reaching your accomplishments. Make decisions based on the need to put off gratification today. Complete critical tasks that will enable you to launch your venture tomorrow. For example, clear your student loans and credit card obligations. Eliminate any debt that's chaining you to that work obligation. Resolve anything that's holding you back. Don't make excuses that push back regarding your involvement in Haiti's change. Haiti needs you to contribute as soon as possible.

Secondly, look beyond yourself. Being successful in Haiti requires the outreach and network of others. Find and reach out to many other like-minded Haitians that buy into your vision. Despite how many noes you get, they do exist, and you'll find them. It's time to unite as Haitians around the world. Impose Haiti's destiny amongst a thin layer within Haiti that has held it back for too long. It won't be done through activism, protests, or social media campaigns. The only successful way any lasting change can occur in this modern era is through the cultivation and exploitation of wealth for power. It's brought on by successful entrepreneurship. It not only requires people opening a business, but the purposeful support of others. We need others within our community to support us with their purchase dollars.

Please share your Haitian entrepreneurial story when the opportunity arises. Inspire others to pursue their dreams as you pursue yours. Together we will change Haiti.
Christherson Jeanty, MS & PMP

About the Author

Christherson Jeanty MS & PMP.

Christherson is a returned Haitian American. He's been making waves in the Haitian business ecosystem since 2016. He's redefining what it means to be a Haitian diaspora by reengaging in Haiti.

While in America, Christherson earned a bachelor's degree in traditional economics and international affairs. He acquired a master's degree in applied economics as well. Both degrees were obtained from Florida State University.

Christherson enjoyed a career in retail banking and business/data analytics in America. Then, he systematically engaged with Haiti. Currently, he has a growing portfolio of ventures in Haiti. These include a media company (HaPro Media, aka "SeeJeanty"), a staffing company, an outsourcing company, a real estate development firm, and an export-focused distribution company. Lastly, he's a principal of a Haiti-based investment group.

He hopes to continue publishing content supporting entrepreneurship, improving the economic condition of his fellow Haitians. His mission isn't his success. Instead, it's the success of another returning Haitian diaspora to Haiti. He hopes to build a great and representative country, congruent with the Haitian national motto: 'L'union Fait La Force.'

Links and Resources

Below is a list of resources that'll aid in your entrepreneurial endeavors:

1. SeeJeanty - www.SeeJeanty.HT
2. Center for the Facilitation of Investments - www.cfihaiti.com
3. Central Bank of Haiti - www.brh.ht
4. Haiti Libre, news website - www.haitilibre.com/en/
5. Le Nouvelliste, news website - www.lenouvelliste.com

Bonus Material

Please visit SeeJeanty.ht and click the "**additional resources**" menu to register for the for additional bonus material available with this book's purchase. Sign up for the email newsletter. Each month, we'll send a new code that provides access to the updated bonus material.

Business Plans

Any business needs a plan. Business plans ensure you have appropriate considerations, for when you want to attract investors and partners. You'll need to have clear documentation of that idea. Don't fret if this isn't your forte. Online platforms will guide you through the entire document, using industry expected standards and content.

LivePlan: Provides the gold standard in business plan development assistance. Even after developing your business plan, use this website to track its progress. Create financial statements, investment decks, and critical analytics on your venture's performance. Use this link to benefit from a special entry subscription rate and further support this book: https://bit.ly/2JmlnMo.

Endnotes

Entertainment

[1] Global Modie Production & Distribution Industry Market Research Report. August 2018. IBIS World.

[2] Haiti film makers struggle to keep cinema alive. January 2019. The National.

[3] Jesifra, General Valcourt. 2014 HaitianHollywood.com.

[4] Grande Réouverture de Rev'Cine le Cinema de Petion-Ville February 2019 Lenouvellste.

[5] The power of (Haitian) Cinema: FFFJ Continues to Expand August 2008 Haiti Innovation.

[6] Mikaben's Deal with Warner Music France and What It Means for the Artist and Haitian Music. August 2016 Kreyolicious.

[7] Soon 25,800 titles of Haitian musical works online on Diskob. Haiti Libre. May 2019.

[8] Haitian Music Industry's Dirty Secret: It Doesn't Exist.

[9] Streaming accounted for nearly half of music worldwide in 2018. 2019. TechCrunch.

[10] Can Haitian Konpa get its groove back? This 'golden' performer thinks so. February 2017. Miami Herald.

[11] Streaming Service Now Make Up 75 Percent of Music Industry Revenue. Highsnobiety. March 2019.

[12] Haiti Geography. March 2017. World Atlas.

[13] Haiti 2019 Annual Research: Key Highlights. 2018. World Travel & Tourism Council.

[14] Tourism Development Projects Caribbean Coast. 2014. Ministry of Tourism.

[15] A look into the number of sports betting in the U.S. and overseas. April 2018.

[16] Nevada Sports Betting Totals: 1984 - 2018. January 2019. University Libraries | University of Nevada, Las Vegas.

[17] Sports Max available for smartphone and tablet. January 2019. IciHaiti.

[18] Entertainment Industry Analysis. May 2011. California State University Sacramento.

[19] 50 Best Outdoor Business ideas to start with no money in 2019. 2019. Profitable Ventures.

[20] After the Earthquake, How One Man Rebuilt Golf in Haiti by Hand. October 2017. Golf World.

Waste

[21] Feasibility of Waste-To-Energy Options at the Trutier Waste. August 2014. USAID.

[22] You Probably Don't Want to Know About Haiti's Sewage Problems. July 2017. NPR.

[23] Ocean cleanup company expands operations with opening of second international cleanup facility in Port-au-Prince, Haiti to remove pounds of plastic and trash. August 2018. PRINewswire.

[24] Ticadaie, la voie vers L'Haiti de Demain. September 2016. Clean Cooking Alliance.

[25] Charbon Ticadaie: une recette pour l'écologie haïtienne. February 2012. Le Nouvelliste.

Apparel

[26] "JL Fine Shoes" revives Haitian industrial shoe repair. September 2019. Ayibopost.

[27] 4 Emerging Startups of Haitian Influence You Should Know. March 2015. Haitian Times.

[28] First of Its Kind, Women Owned Factory Creates Sustainable in Haiti. October 2018. Deux Mains.

[29] Learn more about Traditional Haitian Dress. November 2017. Restavekfreedom.org.

[30] Haitian Economy and the HOPE Act. June 2010. Congress Research Service.

[31] How I learned to stop pitying Haitians and Love the Pepe. July 2013. Medium.com.

[32] Inauguration of the first Haitian Industrial Shoemaking Factory. December 2015. Haiti Libre.

[33] Good for Your Soles: Check Out Kenneth Cole's Latest Collaboration. Jan 2015. Instyle.com.

[34] Small Orlando Sandal Business Attracts Big Attention. February 2015. Washington Times.

[35] Textiles and Apparel Industry. 2019. InvestHaiti.Ht.

[36] A local brand is creating opportunities for the people of Haiti. Feb 2020. KOAM News Now.

[37] People Over Profits: Carmel's Clothes A Cause Boutique donates 100% profits to charity. Jun 2020.

Telecommunications

[32] Port-Au-Prince Area Mobile Technology Survey. 2019. Safitek.

[33] How to Determine the Price of a Telecommunication License. December 2019. Le Nouvelliste.

Food

[34] Starting Seed Production Business - Profitable Business Plan. December 2017. Make in Business.

[35] Avenues for the development of cage fish farming. July 2020. Le Nouvelliste.

[36] Haiti poultry industry still feels pain from US imports. May 2016. USA Today Network.

[37] Haiti has a chicken-and-egg problem. January 2018. NPR.

[38] Haiti poultry production triples in the last five years. November 2018. USDA Foreign Agricultural Service.

[39] Organic Honey Market 2020: Industry Outlook by Size, Share, Business growth Opportunities Industry Plans Forecast by 2024. October 2020. The Daily Chronicle.

[40] Urban Bees for Hire. June 2013. Entrepreneur.

[41] Miel D'or, More than Succulent in a bottle. March 2019. Tourism Innovation Summit.

[42] Nonprofit coffee importer Singing Rooster adds chocolates from Haiti. March 2016. The Cap Times.

[43] Haiti Staple Food Market Fundamentals. March 2018. Fews Net.

[44] Aquaculture a promising solution for Haiti. March 2015. Haiti Libre

[45] Cassava Utilization in Food, Feed, and Industry. 2002. C Balagopalan.

[46] Climate Change Has Coffee Grow Growers in Haiti Seeking Higher Ground. October 2014. NPR.

[47] Edible Cooking Oil Market Chain in Haiti. April 2019. Schwartz Research Group.

[48] Farmer Willingness to pay for soil testing services in northern Haiti. 2016 Cambridge Core.

[49] Fish Farms: Fighting Poverty in Haiti's Rural Communities. September 2012. Clinton Foundation.

[50] Market Research of Haitian Food Processing Sector in West Corridor. September 2015. RTI International.

[51] Fruit, Lumber, Charcoal Ethnographic Value Chains in Haiti. April 2019. Schwartz Research Group.

[52] Haiti Agriculture Sector. August 2019. Export.Gov.

[53] What a Haitian Entrepreneur and Haitian Haitian-American Teach Us About Identity. Feb 2018. Forbes Women.

[54] Organic farming by necessity. January 2016. Visalia.

[55] What bean to bar strategies improve the lives of coca farmers? February 2017. Devex.

[56] These Haitian women were doing great in the U.S. - and then returned to aid quake hit nations. January 2018. USA Today.

[57] Street Food in Haiti. March 2019. Schwartz Research Group.

[58] The Haitian Cassava. February 2014. Ocean Trader.

[59] A Look Inside the Haitian Coffee Industry. July 2015. Partners of the Americas.

[60] Artisanal Fish Ethnographic Value Chain in Haiti. April 2019. Schwartz Research Group.

[61] Haiti's first bean-to-bar chocolate maker featured in University of Michigan documentary. February 2017. Candy Industry.

[62] Assessment of Haitian Coffee Value Chain. 2011. Catholic Relief Services.

[63] Fertilizer in Les Cayes, Haiti: Addressing Market Imperfections with Farm-based Policy Analysis. CIMMYT Economics Program Working Paper 88/01. 1988.

[64] Chocolate "Made in Haiti." September 2018. The World Bank.

[65] Contributing to Agricultural recovery in the Artibonite Valley. March 2009. IADB.

[66] Haiti's hatchet of hope. March 2019. Global Aquaculture.

[67] After the Earthquake: Haitian cocoa rep rises on high-end chocolate scene. February 2015. Confectionery.

[68] Haitian Coffee is making a comeback. November 2011. Miami Herald.

[69] A new major livestock feed production plant with 6.5 tons of daily output in Haiti. February 2018. Le Nouvelliste.

[70] Haitian Spices. LoveToKnow.

[71] Leather Goods Providing Opportunity in Haiti: Haiti Made. September 2017. The Honest Consumer.

[72] Port Au Prince Haiti Merchant Monopoly on Bad Snack Foods. May 2019. Schwartz Research Group.

[73] Could Specialty Cocoa Be Haiti's Golden Ticket to Prosperity. January 2014. The Salt.

[74] Like other sectors of the country, fishing, and aquaculture are wading in deplorable conditions preventing their development.

[75] Fish and Aquaculture Country Profiles the Republic of Haiti. July 2017. FAO Fisheries & Aquaculture.

[76] Haiti's boilers are in high demand in the Bahamas and in the DR. Ayibopost.

[77] The Rice Value Chain in Haiti Policy Proposal. 2013. Oxfam America.

[78] Consumption of Chicken Meat in Haiti from 2010 to 2019. May 2019. Statista.

[79] The importance of sorghum for the Haitian economy. April 2020. Le Nouvelliste.

[80] Haiti has a chicken-and-egg problem. January 2018. PRI.

[81] US poultry aids in sustainable food production in Haiti. July 2015. WhatAgNet.

Personal Care

[82] Three Haitian Beauty Brands to Add to Your List. April 2019. Haitian Times.

[83] From Luxury Hotels to slums, Haiti puts used soap to good use. June 2017. The National.

[84] Doing Laundry… Like a while girl in Haiti. January 2014. Fisher Missions.

[85] Inside Haiti's Rich History of Barbershop Art. September 2018. Cassius.

[86] Haiti's formal personal care product sector shattered by earthquake. Mar 2010. Cosmetics Business.

[87] She's a professor in toilet-paper making in Haiti. June 2016. Miami Herald.

Child Care

[88] Dispatch from Haiti: Trump and Breastfeeding. July 2018. Counterpunch.org.

[89] Donations of baby formula to Haiti strike controversy. January 2010. The Mommy Files.

[90] Early Childhood Education: An Investment in Haiti's Future. April 2017. HuffPost.

[91] Preschool curriculum, a first in the Haitian education system. April 2017. Haiti Libre.

[92] Queen Anne woman finds meaning in helping Haitian mothers. April 2013. Seattle Globalist.

[93] Pastor creates reusable diaper to help children in Haiti stay healthy. November 2015. Fox News.

[94] Haiti Early Childhood Care and Education (ECCE) programs. 2006. UNESCO International Bureau of Education (IBE).

Education

[95] Addressings Problems in Higher Education in Haiti. 2020. University of Massachusetts Boston.

[96] Azure University to Offer MBA In Entrepreneurship. December 2018. Haiti Telegraph.

[97] High Education in Haiti. K12 Academics.

[98] How Online Classrooms Are Helping Haiti Rebuild Its Education System. November 2010. Mashable.

[99] In Haiti, Community is Key to Transforming Education. August 2017. Emerson Collective.

Transportation

[100] Bright Investments Measuring the Impact of Transport Infrastructure. December 2018. IZA Institute of Labor Economics.

[101] Getting around Haiti on local transport. 2020. Lonely Planet.

[102] Haiti Automotive Sales Data & Trends. 2020. CarSalesBase.

[103] Haiti Used Car Market. 2017. JapaneseCarTrade.com.

[104] The High Cost of Low Wage in Haiti, A Living Wage Estimate for Garment Workers in Port-Au-Prince. April 2019. Solidarity Center.

[105] Logistics Capacity Assessment Haiti. April 2019. Logistics Cluster.

[106] The ordeal of customers who use parcel delivery service in Haiti. AyiboPost.com.

[107] A new approach to spatial analysis of motorcycle taxis activities - the case of Port-Au-Prince, Haiti. November 2017. Routledge Taylor & Francis Groups.

[108] The Taxi-Dlo project and congestion on the Carrefour road. November 2016. Le Nouvelliste.

[109] The road to Carrefour, what a pain! December 2017. Le Nouvelliste.

Electricity

[110] Re: Haiti and Natural Resources (Haiti has Gold, Oil, NG, etc.). January 2010. The Handstand.

[111] WTE Upgrade Will Carry Long Beach, Calif, Plant Through 2024. June 2019. Waste 360.

[112] Solar Startup Brings Renewable Energy to Haitian Businesses. April 2018. Forbes Media.

[113] Portable Generator Market Size Share and Market Forecast to 2024. October 2019. Markets and Markets.

[114] How much land is needed for wind turbines? May 2018. Richard Gaughan.

[115] Assessment of Haiti's Electricity Sector. March 2018. Boston University Institute for Sustainable Energy.

[116] Haiti wants to reform its energy sector. So, police showed up to arrest power providers. December 2019. Miami Herald.

[117] Renewables 2019. Global Status Report. 2019. REN21.

[118] GivePower takes aim at water scarcity with new solar desalination systems. PV Magazine USA. February 2020.

[119] G7 countries eye waste-to-energy incineration as part of plastic pollution solution. September 2018. CBC.

[120] Haiti Energy. January 2020. U.S. Agency for International Development.

[121] Valley Connections in Haiti show our helping nature. March 2018. The News Leader.

Health & Wellness

[122] Haiti Health Insurance. 2006. Pacific Prime.

[123] Traditional Medicine. 2015. Le Nouvelliste.

[124] Progress Toward Rebuilding Haiti's Health System. November 2013. CDC.

[125] Haiti Landscape Analysis. March 2016. Feed the Future.

Finance

[126] Latin America: Ratio of Life Insurance Premiums to GDP 2018, by country. January 2020. Statista.

[127] Crowdfunding Statistics (2020): Market Size and Growth. 2020. Fundera.

[128] Crowdfunding Statistics Worldwide: Market Development, Country Volumes, and Industry Trends. May 2020. P2PMarketData.

[129] Haiti Improving Financial Inclusion to Drive Small Business Growth. October 2019. The World Bank.

[130] Haiti Finance Inclusive. 2019 U.S. Agency for International Development.

[131] High risks, low insurance penetration - a dilemma in many Asian countries. August 2018. Munich RE.

[132] How Mobile Is Increasing Financial Stability. 2019. Haitian Times.

[133] Konbit: the other form of Haitian cooperative. May 2020. Le Nouvelliste.

[134] Caribbean Insurers Rebound After Two Catastrophic Hurricane Seasons. June 2019. Best's Market Segment Report.

[135] The Dangerous Life of Credit Officers in Haiti. April 2020. Ayibopost.

The Internet & IT

[136] Lessons from ICT Pilot Projects in Rural Haiti for Sustainable Economy with Four Inferred Coefficients for GNH Index. 2020. Miranda, Verella, Saiah.

[137] What's Shaping the Digital Ad Market. January 2019. eMarketer.

[138] Haiti Mobile Money Business and Merchant Survey Results. October 2015. Dagmar & Imagines LLC.

[139] Percentage of population using the Internet in Haiti from 2010 - 2018. 2019. Statista.

[140] Modern, Open, and Innovative: The Challengers of new Technologies in Haiti. September 2016. The World Bank.

[141] Paryaj Pam, between hope and suicidal practice. March 2019. Balistrad.

[142] Young "addicts" lose large sums in Paryaj Pa m. Ayibopost.

[143] Video Gaming Revenue to Top $159 Billion in 2020. May 2020. Kashmir Observer.

[144] What are the Top E-commerce Business and Websites in Haiti in 2019. November 2019. Monkata Marketplace.

Other Ideas

[145] D & E Green Enterprises Transforms Energy Industry in Resource-Constrained Haiti. September 2011. Clinton Global Initiative.

[146] Charcoal: Who are the millionaires in this business? 2017. Le Nouvelliste.

[147] Meet the metal-makers of the artistic village of Noailles. April 2019. Visit Haiti.

[148] A Strategy for Haitian prosperity. September 2017. Harvard Business School.

[149] Haiti's Android tablet maker Surtab to crank up production. February 2014. The Guardian.

[150] The Least Developed Countries Report 2012: Harnessing Remittances and Diaspora Knowledge to Build Productive Capacities. November 2012. UNCTAD.

[151] Haiti's boilers are high in demand in the Bahamas and in the DR. 2019. Ayibopost.

[152] In Haiti, Turning Human Waste to Flowers. January 2016. BRIGHT Magazine.

[153] Expats Want to Fix Haiti's Food Crisis by buying its food. It makes sense. June 2019. WLRN.

[154] Group seeks answers to Haiti's woes in its toilets. January 2010. CNN.

[155] Haitian Cities: Actions for Today with an Eye on Tomorrow. 2017. The World Bank.

[156] Doing Business in Haiti: 2018 Country Commercial Guide for U.S. Companies. 2018. US Commercial Service.

[157] Negative growth, hyperinflation, discount of the gourd the bad book of the Haitian economy in 2019. December 2019. Le Nouvelliste.

Made in the USA
Columbia, SC
20 October 2022